CLASS CONFLICT AND CULTURAL CONSENSUS

A volume in the
CLASS AND CULTURE Series

Milton Cantor and Bruce Laurie,
series editors

CLASS CONFLICT AND CULTURAL CONSENSUS

The Making of a Mass Consumer Society in Flint, Michigan

RONALD EDSFORTH

RUTGERS UNIVERSITY PRESS
New Brunswick and London

Library of Congress Cataloging-in-Publication Data

Edsforth, Ronald William, 1948–
  Class conflict and cultural consensus.

  (Class and culture)
  Bibliography: p.
  Includes index.
  1. Flint (Mich.)—Economic conditions. 2. Flint
(Mich.)—Social conditions. 3. Automobile industry and
trade—Michigan—Flint. 4. Automobile industry workers
—Michigan—Flint. I. Title. II. Series
HC108.F55E37 1987   330.9774'37   86–7955
ISBN 0–8135–1184–4
ISBN 0–8135–1105–4 (pbk.)

British Cataloguing-in-Publication Information Available

Dedicated to Jo

CONTENTS

FIGURES

PREFACE

It seemed obvious to me that the historian's prime duty
was to answer my childish question: "What happened next?"
It seems almost as obvious to me now.
—A.J.P. Taylor

This study of the transformation of industrial society in twentieth-century Flint, Michigan, is a very traditional history, not an exercise in historical social science. By reconstructing the experiences of the men and women who made Flint into a national center for the mass production of cars and trucks, I have tried to create a new perspective on the distinctive ways in which twentieth-century Americans have organized their economic activities, social relationships, and politics. Inevitably, my attention has been drawn to the old, but persistent, question: "why does the United States lack the kind of class-conscious culture that is characteristic of industrial capitalist countries in Europe?" While I suggest a new solution to this perennial historical problem, my work offers no original models or methods for doing social history. Nor is it based on the rather disturbing proposition, so distressingly popular in professional academic circles today, that "we cannot predict the future concretely, but we can predict the past."[1] Instead, since its inception, this social history has been firmly grounded in the traditional humanistic methodology that has always distinguished the best historical literature from deterministic presentations of the past.

Most importantly, the methods and reasoning employed here rest on the traditional assumption that human beings are more than mere creatures of circumstance; in fact, they are the agents of historical change, the ones who consciously make things happen in the present as well as the past. To the untutored reader of popular military, diplomatic, and political history, this statement may appear to be a truism. However, given the predilection of many professional economic and social historians for more deterministic interpretations of the past, the assumption bears repeating. People make history. Changes in economic institutions, society, culture, and politics occur when people act, and not merely as the result of some combination of abstract "pressures," "forces," and "factors."

Of course, it may be objected that human beings are not truly free agents, that their actions are shaped by the natural and social environments in which they find themselves. Undoubtedly this criticism has merit. The past is full of examples of the ways nature has defined the material possibilities of existence, either enriching or destroying human societies and lives. Likewise, the historian cannot ignore the evidence, repeated in every society in generation after generation, that inherited experience imbedded in language and culture, as well as social customs and institutions, weighs heavily on each human being, informing personal values and behavior. Nor is it possible for historians to present individuals as if they could have escaped the psychological implications of their own early experiences with life. Though modern advertisers have done their best to convince us otherwise, people cannot simply choose their personalities or their "lifestyles." Human freedom is clearly limited.

But does acknowledging these obvious environmental, social, and psychological conditions of human existence force us to rule out totally a place for human freedom in history? Given the undeniable influences of nature and the social-psychological circumstances over which each new generation has no control, must explanations of mankind's past ultimately be abandoned to sheer necessity and determinism? I think not. For history is about change, not about static conditions. And although the past reveals that men and women cannot control the situations into which they are thrust by nature and society, history provides plenty of evidence that indicates individuals and groups are capable of overcoming the constraints of nature and society by consciously choosing a new course for events. From the irrigation projects of ancient China and Mesopotamia to the recent eradication of smallpox and flights to the moon, people have demonstrated their ability to transcend natural obstacles through consciously planned activity. Moreover, throughout history, human beings have been able to shatter the social restraints and personal inhibitions that tie them to the status quo. Careful examination of the past shows that human efforts have determined the direction of events, even though individual humans cannot determine the circumstances that make their efforts possible. Or, to put it even more simply, while no one can choose his or her past, people can and do make their future, and thus, their history.

This philosophical perspective has not always been clear in histories of economic and social change. When looking back on vast changes in an economy or society, occurrences that have the impact of an "Industrial Revolution" or a "Great Depression," even the most dedicated humanists are drawn to the notion of inevitability that is inherent in hindsight. Today, when so many professional historians are using the past as a testing ground for theories drawn from other present-oriented disciplines, the influential decisions and human actions that were (and are) the real models for historical change have begun to disappear from view. Yet, if economic and social history is to remain "true" to events as they happened, historians in these fields must recognize that hindsight does not make the past "predictable." Tracing an event back to some antecedent set of conditions obscures the fact that the people who made the event happen could not foresee when, where, how, and why those conditions would converge. Therefore describing the setting and preconditions for historical activity never fully explains history, because such descriptions fail to illuminate the consciousness and motivations of the specific people who made change occur.

The methods of traditional history—its focus on power and the powerful, its use of archival research, and its presentation in narrative form—are time-honored ways to insure that scholars consider the perceptions and thinking of history's actors when they examine events that appear inevitable. For this reason alone, these methods should not be dismissed lightly by economic and social historians. Unfortunately, in recent years, the unique harmony between the traditional philosophical ground of history and the actual production of historical knowledge has been degraded and obscured. In a few extreme cases, the desire to create "scientifically verifiable" history has led to the rejection of the kinds of written and oral evidence historians have always used to preserve the identity and autonomy of individuals in the past. More generally, by stressing theoretical analysis and mathematical reasoning, economic and social historians have begun to reduce people to mere objects, pushing them into a realm of understanding where, as James Henretta has noted, "consciousness and meaning have been usurped by data and diagrams."[2]

This study, a history of what appears to be the "inevitable" development of the automotive manufacturing center at Flint, Michigan, is designed to avoid the deterministic pitfalls inherent in reasoning from hindsight. Specifically, I have tried to fuse the questions and methods of traditional political history with the so-called "new" economic and social history's emphasis on interpreting the mundane activities of those plain people who usually remain anonymous parts of the structure or background of historical analysis. In this history, economic and social changes are not assumed to have been inevitable or irresistible. Rather, to borrow the words of George Dangerfield, one of America's finest traditional historians, the events that lend economic and social changes

> the appearance of inevitability are of the first importance, if only because they compel us to ask what sort of people wished to bring them about and why they did so. Conversely, we are prompted to ask through the lack of what qualities—wisdom, compassion, foresight, and so forth—people to whose disadvantage they happened were unable to prevent them from happening.[3]

Put differently, it would be fair to describe what follows as a political history of economic and social development. Here, we focus on the people who attained and used power to create a modern industrial society in Flint in the first half of our own century. As it is used in this text, the word "power" means the ability to make and to implement decisions. As such, power may be exercised by individuals and groups in all realms of history, though it has commonly been the centerpiece of traditional studies of past politics, diplomacy, insurrections, and war.

Power remains a central organizing concept of traditional history. The ways in which it is acquired and used define both the existence and practical limits of human freedom in any given historical situation. When students of the past choose to ignore questions about power (who had it? how did they get it? how was it legitimized? how was it exercised? with what results?), the real connections between events in conscious human activity are lost, opening the way for deterministic interpretations of historical change. In the late twentieth century, an era when the individual exercise of power has become increasingly obscured by giant organizations that administer decisions, the willingness of historians to explain the past in terms of historical abstractions like "forces" and "models" is understandable. But fate, whether it is labeled the invisible hand of God, the invisible hand of the market, or an irresistible social trend, will never serve as history.

At the outset of this project, the temptation to squeeze events in twentieth-century Flint into a popular model of social development, derived either from Marxist or modernization theory, was very strong because my knowledge of the city's past was so limited. However, as I began to uncover more and more evidence from a great variety of sources, including official reports, newspapers and pamphlets, collections of private papers and diaries, contemporary economic and sociological studies, the files of businesses and unions, and the oral history record that is the twentieth-century historian's unique resource, my need to impose theory on events vanished. In a very real sense, I discovered for myself what E. P. Thompson once described as Darwin's greatest insight: "that a respect for fact is not only a technique, it can also be an intellectual force in its own right."[4] While gathering details about economic and social change in Flint, I saw that the most prominent theories of capitalist development, with their focus on change in eighteenth- and nineteenth-century Europe, were not adequate explanations of the complex, new kinds of events that have shaped American society since 1900. To put it more bluntly, as I now see it, neither Marxist nor modernization theory can predict the creation of an automobile-centered, consumer-goods-oriented economy or the enormous and varied ways in which that development changed the lives and consciousness of modern Americans. Yet history done in the traditional manner can tell us what happened.

Accordingly, I have chosen narrative exposition as the only proper way to present the history of Flint in the twentieth century. Though I suspect that Thompson's brilliant narrative analysis in *The Making of the English Working Class* undermines the conviction that theory is necessary to bridge the gaps in the historical record prior to World War I, recent theoretical analyses have done much to illuminate the early in-

dustrial revolution. Nevertheless, when discussing events of more recent times, scholars who fail to consider individual perceptions and
thinking cannot use the excuse that most people in the past were inar-
ticulate. For twentieth-century American historians, documents, photographs, statistics, as well as official and unofficial inquiries into the
condition of the people abound, and as a popular writer like Studs
Terkel has repeatedly shown, oral history interviews can make even
the most underprivileged members of society articulate about their
lives and experiences. Certainly, the weight of all this evidence places
a heavy burden on the historian of twentieth-century society, but
it should be one that is shouldered happily. Unlike students of an
earlier past who have to struggle with shreds of evidence to recon-
struct the character of everyday life, twentieth-century historians are
able to draw on a reservoir of material that makes it possible to write
reliable history from the perspective of both the celebrated and the
plain people.

Economic and social history can remain true to the traditional values of the discipline; it can create a truly humanistic perspective on
the recent past. As David F. Noble reminds us,

> it is the primary task of the historian to demystify history, to render it intel-
> ligible in human rather than in super-human or non-human terms, to show
> that history is a realm of human freedom as well as necessity. By describing
> how people have shaped history in the past, the historian reminds us that
> people continue to shape history in the present.[5]

To achieve this traditional purpose, men and women in the past must
not be treated as mere numbers. Difficult as it may be sometimes,
scholars must take into account all the evidence that conveys the
thoughts and perceptions of the makers of history. Moreover, to dis-
pel the illusion of inevitability that arises whenever we peer back into
the past, even economic and social history should be presented in the
traditional narrative form that best preserves our view of the past as a
place of consciousness and purposeful activity. At least these are the
convictions that lie at the heart of this history of the transformation of
class, culture, and society in twentieth-century Flint, Michigan.

ACKNOWLEDGMENTS

Many people assisted me with this project during the last eight years. First, I would like to thank Norman Pollack, my dissertation director, for his patience and constant understanding. Whenever I needed encouragement or enlightenment, he was there to help. I am indebted to the other members of my Ph.D. guidance committee, Professors Donald Lammers, Warren Cohen, David LoRomer, and the late Herbert Kisch, as well. Their unfailing confidence in my abilities was a tremendous source of strength during my long stay in graduate school. I would like to thank the other members of the Department of History at Michigan State University with whom I regularly exchanged ideas, especially Steve Botein, Bill Hixson, Peter Levine, Ann Meyering, and my good friend John Humins. Their intellectual companionship and constructive criticisms contributed enormously to my approach to history. Thanks also to Larry Bennett of DePaul University for his careful reading of the entire manuscript, Stuart Witt of Skidmore College for his help with the interpretation of political science data, and Nancy Gilchrist for her assistance in preparation of the final manuscript.

Initial research for this project was supported by fellowships from the Alvin M. Bentley Foundation of Owosso, Michigan. I am very grateful to them. Two Skidmore College faculty research grants enabled me to further my research and complete the revision process. Professor Neil Leighton of the University of Michigan-Flint and UAW pioneer William Genske gave much needed assistance with questions raised while I was revising the dissertation upon which this book is based. In addition, for their help over many years, I want to extend my appreciation to the staffs of the Walter P. Reuther Library of Labor and Urban Affairs, the Michigan Historical Collections (University of Michigan), the Flint Public Library, the National Archives, the National Records Center, the State of Michigan Archives, the State of Michigan Library, the Michigan State University Library, the Harlan Hatcher Graduate Library (University of Michigan), and the Catholic University Library.

Finally, I want to thank my wife, Joanne Devine. Without her loving support and her editorial assistance, I would never have completed this project.

CLASS CONFLICT AND CULTURAL CONSENSUS

A volume in the
CLASS AND CULTURE Series

Milton Cantor and Bruce Laurie,
series editors

1

INTRODUCTION

The Concept of a Second Industrial Revolution

Economic historians have long agreed that the industrial systems of the world's most advanced capitalist nations underwent a series of dramatic, closely connected changes in the period stretching roughly from 1890 to 1960. Though the pace and extent of these changes varied widely from country to country, the innovations that actually transformed the industrial economies of the United States, the United Kingdom, Germany, and Japan during this era were very similar. As early as 1939, the eminent Austrian economist, Joseph Schumpeter, identified a "New Industrial Revolution," which he claimed had formed the basis for global economic expansion in the twenty years preceding World War I.[1] In our own day, the terms "scientific-technical revolution," or even more commonly, "second industrial revolution," have been used to distinguish these modern developments from the initial emergence of industry in the eighteenth and nineteenth centuries. There is something quite arbitrary about this distinction. The second industrial revolution did not begin with a specific event on a specific date that clearly marks a break with the past. Instead, to use the words of the British economic historian, Eric Hobsbawm, "Since the [first] Industrial Revolution the transformation of industry has become continuous."[2] Nonetheless, the concept of a second industrial revolution persists because it summarizes the conclusions of a multitude of diverse observers so well.

The first, and probably the most significant aspect of this second industrial revolution involved a change in the place of science in the economy. In the late nineteenth century, new scientific discoveries and technology were appropriated by businessmen who created new, extremely influential industries around them. The electrical, chemical, and automotive industries that have done so much to shape modern society were the offspring of this marriage of science and technology to business. However, the impact of scientific-technical change went far beyond the boundaries of these new science-based industries. In older industries, like textiles and steel, existing products and processes were improved, while new ones were developed by scientists who worked directly for specific firms. Ultimately, this kind of in-house scientific-technical change affected most industries. "In the place of spontaneous innovation indirectly evoked by the social process of production," explains Harry Braverman, "came the planned progress of technology and product design." As a result, Braverman continues,

> The scientific-technical revolution . . . cannot be understood in terms of specific innovations—as in the case of the [first] Industrial Revolution, which may be adequately characterized by a handful of key inventions—but must be understood rather in its totality as a mode of production into which science and exhaustive engineering investigations have been integrated as a part of ordinary functioning. The key innovation is not to be found in chemistry, electronics, automatic machinery . . . or any of the products of these science-technologies, but rather in the transformation of science itself into capital.[3]

For most scholars, it was this unprecedented "transformation of science itself into capital" that defines the basic nature of the second industrial revolution.

A systematic expansion and rationalization of factory production was another primary characteristic of the second industrial revolution. Here, the break with previous practice seems far less striking than contemporary changes in the relationship between science and industry (to which it was closely related). Yet, in the long run, the development of machines that made other machines, and the reorganization of work according to the principles of scientific management first enumerated by the American "efficiency expert," Frederick Taylor, had far-reaching economic and social implications.

Most importantly, when early twentieth-century industrialists combined automatic machinery with Taylorized labor, they attained the kind of productivity increases and economies of scale that made the true mass production of complex durable goods possible. Though usually celebrated as unqualified progress because it led to significant improvements in material living standards, mass production also had its negative side. Mechanization and the minute subdivisions of the work process involved in mass production greatly intensified the alienation of factory labor by reducing skill requirements and the need to think on the job. This result was not unintended. Frederick Taylor himself stressed the idea that "all possible brainwork should be removed from the shop" as one of the cornerstones of scientific management.[4] Where the rationalization of factory labor along these lines could be accomplished without confronting the organized resistance of a large, well-established, relatively skilled workforce (as occurred in the creation of the American automobile industry), the potential benefits of mass production were realized very rapidly. However, wherever class-conscious, unionized workers were able to fight for traditional skills and control over production decisions (as occurred, for example, in Britain's motor industry), the transition to true mass production was more difficult.[5]

The third generally recognized attribute of the second industrial revolution was an enormous increase in the scale of economic activity. Wherever scientific-technical change and the rationalization of production took place, the size of firms increased while the number of firms in a given industry decreased markedly. This concentration of production and ownership proceeded in all the advanced industrial nations around the turn of the century, but it was most pronounced in the United States (where it became the focus of sustained political protest) and in Germany (where it facilitated the nation's swift rise as a world military power).

Big integrated firms were best equipped to meet the sustained high costs of science-based mass production. At the time, however, most economists argued differently, especially in Britain and the United States. Yet, as Professor Hobsbawm has pointed out, there is every reason to believe that "big business" was in fact *better* than little business, at least in the long run: more dynamic, more efficient, better able to undertake the increasingly complex and expensive tasks of development. The real case was not that it was big, but that it was anti-social.[6]

Consequently, oligopoly and monopoly tended to become the dominant forms of market organization in the new industries and in those older industries that were able to modernize quickly. Typically, the emergence of oligopolies and monopolies was expedited by government actions designed to promote industrial concentration, to protect giant companies from price competition, or to insulate big business from potentially hostile public regulation. The precise forms of state intervention in the industrial economy differed in each country, but its main effects were quite similar. Big business and the state became partners in national development.[7] The second industrial revolution thus changed the role of the state in the advanced capitalist nations. After 1890, the old liberal ideal of the state that deliberately refrained from direct intervention in the economy (laissez-faire) was abandoned in favor of a more active government role in economic affairs. At the same time, those big businesses that received governmental assistance were expected to assist the state in its attempts to expand national power both at home and abroad.[8]

The final major economic change that is usually considered an essential part of the second industrial revolution was the creation of mass markets for technologically complex consumer goods. The United States was far and away the world leader in this type of development. Indeed, for reasons that will be explained at length in the next chapter, America was the only nation in the world to develop a real consumer-oriented industrial economy in the years prior to World War II. It suffices to say here that the unique transformation of the American economy from a producer-goods to a consumer-goods orientation was not solely the result of America's "natural" economic advantages, such as the huge size of its potential national market. Wars, and the preparations for war, absorbed (and destroyed) much of the creative energies and productive capacities of the other advanced industrial nations, and where this happened, technologically complex consumer goods simply could not reach the "average" blue-collar worker. In this sense, the second industrial revolution remained incomplete in Western Europe and Japan until the post–World War II era when the relative demilitarization imposed by the destruction of the war and the terms of peace (including American reconstruction aid) permitted the development of truly modern, mass-consumer-oriented industrial economies.

A New Kind of Capitalism: Social and Political Implications of the Second Industrial Revolution

The second industrial revolution transformed far more than industry; it changed the fundamental character of society and politics in the advanced capitalist nations (as well as the relationship between those nations and the less-developed parts of the globe). To date, the deeper significance of the second industrial revolution has been recognized by numerous social critics and philosophers, but it has not been thoroughly examined by historians. As Geoffrey Barraclough pointed out in his *Introduction to Contemporary History* nearly twenty years ago, the historical profession's neglect of this subject is due, at least in part, "to the fact that many historians are still emotionally involved in the death-pangs of the old world, which they feel more deeply than the birth-pangs of the new." It is also due, to complete Professor Barraclough's observation, "to the fact that, until very recently, we were unable to stand outside the period of transition and look back over it as a whole."[9] Certainly, today's historians cannot use this excuse. Yet historians still have not generally recognized the second industrial revolution as an epoch-making transformation of society and culture comparable to the first industrial revolution of the late eighteenth and nineteenth centuries.

Perhaps the problem lies in the difficulty in identifying exactly what it is that distinguishes the advanced industrial capitalism of our own time from the industrial capitalism of a hundred years ago. The terms "technological," "affluent," "consumer-oriented," "leisure-oriented," and even the slightly absurd "post-industrial" come immediately to mind when searching for a description of contemporary society in the United States, Western Europe, and Japan. Each of these terms certainly has its relevance, but taken together or separately, they only reinforce a common compartmentalized view of the second industrial revolution that leaves the great change confined to the rather narrow realm of economic history.[10] This is unfortunate. The second industrial revolution was not a self-contained economic phenomenon. Rather, to quote Geoffrey Barraclough once again,

> Scientific, technological, and economic changes . . . are the starting point for the study of contemporary history. They acted both as a solvent of the old order and as a catalyst of the new.[11]

Clearly then what needs to be developed is an understanding of the second industrial revolution as a historical process that connects the rise of science-based mass production in large corporate units to obvious changes in society and politics (the subject matter of twentieth-century social and political history). How can this be accomplished?

To start, we must focus our attention on what E. P. Thompson recently described as the most "misunderstood, tormented, transfixed, and de-historicized" of all historical categories: social class.[12] Given the explosive ideological overtones of the word "class," especially in the United States, this task becomes a tricky undertaking. Nevertheless, it cannot be avoided because changes in the nature of class consciousness and class relations are at the heart of the historical process that links the second industrial revolution to twentieth-century social and political events.

In all its historical forms, capitalism has been characterized by a hierarchic social order in which special economic and political privileges accrue to those people who own and control the means of production. The basis of privilege in a capitalist society is, to use Robert Heilbroner's description,

> the continuous creation and allocation of a highly disproportionate share of income to . . . those who own substantial quantities of property and those who man the command posts within the business world.[13]

During the first industrial revolution, when this privilege-producing system was being perfected, tensions between the beneficiaries of the system (the business classes) and the relatively impoverished multitudes who were employed by the privileged minority (the working classes) rose to the point where many commentators, including the German radicals Marx and Engels, believed that revolution was inevitable. As late as the early twentieth century, when syndicalist unions and radical socialists challenged the business classes on both sides of the Atlantic, the revolutionary potential of the working classes in the advanced industrial nations seemed undiminished. As we all know, for a variety of reasons that differ substantially from nation to nation, revolutionary confrontations between the working class and the business class never happened in the way Marx and Engels had predicted. And now, three-quarters of a century later, the idea of such a revolution appears inconceivable, like something out of a dream.

Why is this so? To put it simply, in the truly advanced industrial nations, capitalism no longer generates revolutionary class tensions.

The primary social and political differences between contemporary advanced industrial capitalism and the industrial capitalism of the nineteenth century stem from a distinct lessening of tensions between the business classes and what are now organized working classes. Today it seems clear that countries that have experienced a complete second industrial revolution, including the vitally important transformation of industry from a producer-goods to a consumer-goods orientation, have also experienced a general decline in revolutionary political activity and in violent strikes. This decline is not a simple coincidence. Indeed, it is my contention that changes in the nature of "the system" brought on by the second industrial revolution are the root cause of the long-term decline in class tensions that marks advanced industrial capitalism.[14]

The second industrial revolution lessened fundamental class tensions in several ways. By creating an economic system that both produced and fulfilled the material wants of the working classes, it subtly but enormously strengthened the position of the business classes in society and politics. By permitting the working classes to enjoy unprecedented quantitative and qualitative improvements in their standard of living, the second industrial revolution greatly reduced the threat of poverty that had pervaded the everyday lives of working people during the first industrial revolution. Moreover (in America alone prior to 1960), the second industrial revolution dramatically altered the ways in which work and non-working hours were organized and experienced. In sum, the second industrial revolution transformed the content of working people's lives, establishing new patterns of everyday experience that undermined older forms of class consciousness. As a result, the real revolutionary potential of the working classes (whatever that might have been at an earlier stage of industrialization) has clearly diminished, if not dissipated altogether. As T. B. Bottomore wrote in his short, but extremely perceptive book, *Classes in Modern Society,*

It seems no longer possible in the second half of the twentieth century to regard the working class in the advanced industrial countries as being totally alienated from society, or, in Marx's phrase, as "a class *in* civil society which is not a class *of* civil society."[15]

The growth of the so-called "new middle classes," which is another offshoot of the second industrial revolution, has also reduced tensions between the business and working classes of the advanced industrial countries. These groups (defined by Bottomore as "office workers, supervisors, managers, technicians, scientists, and many of those who are employed in providing services") obscure the gulf between the two primary classes because they themselves are not class-conscious.[16] Instead of a social hierarchy of fixed classes, people in what Harry Braverman describes as the "middle layers of employment" believe society to be a finely graded meritocracy in which individuals rise and fall to their appropriate levels of income and status according to their own abilities.[17] The sustained growth of the "middle layers" and their ability to exercise a considerable degree of influence over popular social thought through the mass media and the educational system (where they are entrenched) has undoubtedly eased class tensions. Nevertheless, the "classless" perceptions of these middle groups do not define the totality of social reality. Indeed, as the recent expansion of white-collar unions and strikes by white-collar workers in all the advanced industrial countries seems to indicate, the power of the individualistic, status-based view of society may be on the wane among the very groups who have, in the past, done the most to promote it.

To assert that modern industrial capitalism inhibits the growth of revolutionary class tensions is not to say that any of the advanced industrial nations have become "classless" societies. Neither the business class nor the working class has disappeared as a result of the second industrial revolution. In fact, in organizational terms, both classes are more clearly defined now than ever before. What has changed is not the existence of these two basic classes, but the character of their relationship and of class consciousness itself. This is particularly true of the working classes, which have established a legitimate, powerful place for themselves within the system during the twentieth century. As the prominent Marxist economist Paul Sweezy asserted in his review of contemporary capitalism, contrary to Marx's predictions, modern society has "turned a potentially revolutionary proletariat into an actual reformist force."[18]

It is the purpose of this study to investigate in detail how and why this widely recognized, fundamental change in class relations, and thus in political culture, occurred in the first nation to experience a complete second industrial revolution. Such an investigation seems long overdue. In 1966, T. B. Bottomore wrote,

> The principle fault in many recent studies of social classes has been that they lack an historical sense. Like the economists of whom Marx said that they believed there had been history, because feudalism disappeared, but there was no longer any history, because capitalism was a natural and eternal social order, some sociologists [and historians] have accepted that there was an historical development of classes and of class conflicts in the early period of industrial capitalism, but that this has ceased in the fully evolved industrial societies in which the working class has escaped from poverty and has attained industrial and political citizenship.[19]

Unfortunately, for the most part, Professor Bottomore's observation remains true today. Although the second industrial revolution in the United States can hardly be called representative (because it was the first and because of the way America escaped the destruction of industry in both world wars), studying it does reveal the continuing importance of class in twentieth-century social and political history.

Class: A Historical Definition

Before proceeding any further, let the reader be clear about the definition of the word "class" that is used throughout this work. It is, above all else, a historical definition. As Arthur Marwick explains in his recent comparative study of class in three advanced capitalist nations, "Class is not fixed and unchanging . . . The nature and significance of class changes as society changes."[20] In other words, in history (as opposed to sociology), class is a process or long series of events, not a static category or structure. To repeat E. P. Thompson's now familiar definition,

> Class happens when some men as a result of common experiences (inherited or shared), feel and articulate the identity of their interests as between themselves, and as against other men whose interests are different from (and usually opposed to) theirs.[21]

In this sense, and not in the crude deterministic way that theory-bound Marxists and anti-Marxists alike use the term, class is one important expression of human freedom in history. Class consciousness, a living awareness of a shared identity and interests, is not a law of history, and this has always troubled those who would like to make it one.[22] However, class consciousness and class conflict are not radical pipe dreams either. Both have existed (and can be shown to have existed) in the past; both can and most likely will exist again in the future.

There are certain important corollaries of the historical definition of class that should also be clarified here. The first is that, in the field of history, the logic of class development arises out of the specific circumstances in which class consciousness and class conflict occur, not according to some abstract theory or model. Professor Marwick draws this very conclusion from his examination of the images and reality of class in twentieth-century Britain, France, and America. "The exact forms of class," he declares, "which differ significantly from country to country, are determined by the historical evolution of the particular country."[23] In practical terms, the fact that class is culturally specific in character means we must not approach the historical investigation of class with preconceived notions about what is and is not "true" class consciousness. "Consciousness of class arises in the same way in different times and places," E. P. Thompson reminds us, "but never in *just* the same way."[24] Thus, to expect twentieth-century American workers to think and act just like the workers Marx and Engels observed in mid-nineteenth-century Western Europe is to expect the impossible.

The second corollary of a historical definition of class is closely related to the first. It may be stated like this: as a historical phenomenon, class exists only as a relationship over time. Historical classes cannot be found in isolation from other social groups (who themselves may or may not be class-conscious). Nor can they be located in moments artificially frozen for study (in the manner of the sociologist). Describing patterns of social, ideological, and institutional change as they emerge from historical events is the historian's way of identifying class. Unless such patterns are uncovered and studied in detail, we can never hope to understand the specific historical logic of class development.

The second industrial revolution provides historians of capitalist society with an adequate period of social change in which to locate and describe the patterns through which twentieth-century men and women have defined class. Let us now turn to that great change as it unfolded in the United States, and using the historical definition of class outlined above, see how and why a specific society and political culture were transformed by the development of modern consumer-oriented capitalism.

2

THE TRANSFORMATION OF AMERICAN SOCIETY IN THE AUTOMOBILE AGE

"Why on earth do you need to study what's changing
this country?" said a lifelong resident and shrewd observer
of the Middle West. "I can tell you what's happening
in just four letters: A-U-T-O!"
—Robert S. Lynd and Helen Merrell Lynd, *Middletown*

The Automobile Boom: America's Second Industrial
Revolution

The automobile was the primary driving force behind the second industrial revolution in the United States. America became the world's first true consumer-oriented society during the early part of this century because its citizens were eager literally to reshape their land and their everyday lives to accommodate the gasoline-powered motor car. For this reason, the development of the American mass-produced automobile should be viewed as an event of primary national significance. The general proliferation of motor vehicles in the United States between 1900 and 1930 was a unique occurrence, not an inevitable stage or level of industrial development. While other major industrial nations were ravaged by wars, revolution, and the economic disruptions that attended both, Americans confidently built a new kind of consumer-oriented capitalism around the production, sale, and use of tens of millions of automobiles. Curiously, historians have rarely tried to present the creation of automobile-centered consumerism in this light. World War I remains a far more important event than the automobile boom in most American history textbooks. Yet, the implications of a comparative perspective seem clear. In the early twentieth century, America's automobile boom was a real historical alternative to the kind of international rivalries and militarism that shaped (and ultimately retarded) the second industrial revolution in Western Europe and Japan. Indeed, until the 1960s when those societies fully embraced automobile-centered consumerism—or what for want of a better term might be called the American model of advanced industrial development—they did not really move out of the producer-goods-oriented era.

In the first few years of this century, American motor cars were built exclusively for the affluent, adventurous middle and upper classes, just as they were in Britain, France, and Germany. But unlike their European counterparts, American producers found that they could not keep up with orders. Then in 1908 in Michigan, two important events opened up the possibility of automobile ownership to most American families. From his Highland Park factory, Henry Ford turned the first Model T loose on the nation. And in Flint, the self-proclaimed "Vehicle City," hometown celebrity Billy Durant began to put together the General Motors Corporation, using the same philosophy that had already made him co-owner of the world's largest wagon-making business: find or build an inexpensive, dependable vehicle and it will be a "self-seller."[1] Soon, Americans who had only dreamed of motoring would find ways to afford their own Ford or Chevrolet (even if it was only a used car).

Pinpointing the exact reasons for the immediate enthusiastic response to the car in America remains a matter of considerable speculation. The nation's vast size, its widely dispersed population, relatively high real incomes, huge oil reserves, and well-established petroleum industry provided the prerequisites for an automobile market far bigger than any in Europe or Asia. As Americans quickly discovered, motor cars were easier to control and cheaper to maintain than horses. Almost from the industry's beginnings, American automobiles were good products that promised and generally delivered inexpensive, reliable personal transportation not limited by the fixed tracks of railroads and trolleys. These attributes made the car particularly attractive in rural America. In fact, during the years of generally rising farm prices up to 1920, farmers and prosperous small town families formed the core of the first mass market for motor vehicles. In addition, automobiles were considerably smaller and cleaner than horse-drawn vehicles, two characteristics that promised to eliminate the significant traffic and sanitation problems facing the nation's biggest cities.[2] Urban demand for cars grew rapidly, once Ford and General Motors began to mass produce and distribute automobiles at prices that eventually made them available to regularly employed white- and blue-collar working people. In 1914, when the industrial powers of Europe diverted their capital and labor into the production of weapons of mass destruction, the car had already assumed its central place in America's just emerging mass consumer culture. By this time, automotive historian John B. Rae concludes,

> the automobile could no longer be regarded as a novelty or a rich man's plaything as it remained in Europe; it was already potentially what it would become in fact—an item of incredible mass consumption.[3]

The public's passion for the automobile quickly made possession of the machine a critical sign of personal success and respectability. As Sinclair Lewis wrote in 1922, the "motor car was poetry and tragedy, love and heroism" to all who owned one.[4] To get a car, families all across the country turned their back on the traditional wisdom to work hard and save for that inevitable rainy day. Instead, millions of them plunged into debt to buy an automobile, including many who mortgaged their homes to finance the purchase. In *Middletown,* the Lynds discovered that it was common for families to buy a car before they had completed the plumbing in their bathrooms. One woman even swore, "I'll go without food before I'll see us give up the car."[5] By the mid-1920s, when motor registrations topped the twenty million mark, the automobile had become an essential part of everyday life in America. Just as importantly, the desire to own a car had legitimized a new consumer spending ethic that cut across class and ethnic lines. In 1929, nearly half the nation's total outstanding consumer installment debt of 2.9 billion dollars had been incurred to buy automobiles.[6]

Obviously, the practical advantages of the motorcar over alternative means of transportation can only account for part of its immediate mass success in the United States. The automobile also had (and still has) a complex variety of psychological and symbolic appeals. It is important to understand these appeals because they are directly related to long-term changes in the political culture, especially the lessening of class tensions, brought on by America's automobile-centered second industrial revolution. In the early decades of the twentieth century, the car provided greater personal geographic mobility than anyone had ever experienced; thus, in a sense, the machine acted as a kind of compensation for the limitations placed on social mobility by the rise of the factory system. Unlike any other product of that system, the automobile offered individuals real escape from the regimen of industrialized work. It is important to recognize that the experience of motoring was just as significant as the practical benefits of the car. Out on the road, drivers felt they could control technology and their own destiny. In the years since World War II, television has provided a more passive means of escape and has helped to renew faith in consumer-oriented capitalism. However, the way that cars enable individuals actively to control the speed and direction of their physical movement through time and space remains unique.

Secondly, the car enabled Americans to maintain contact with the land and with nature at the very moment when most of them realized that the old agrarian/small town order was gone forever. It may seem a little thing today, after living so many years with the automobile, but in those days, a Sunday outing or perhaps even a weekend on the road were special pleasures that could provide welcome psychological relief to families caught up in the routine tasks of city life. As the Lynds observed in *Middletown*, automobiles greatly expanded the recreational options of both business and working people, "making leisure-time enjoyment a regularly expected part of every day and week rather than an occasional event," as it remained in Britain and Western Europe.[7] A recent history of the recreational uses of the automobile confirms the Lynds' observation and clearly reveals that Americans of all classes enjoyed auto-touring and auto-camping before the Great Depression. Among many examples in his *Americans on the Road*, Warren James Belasco reports,

A 1926 survey of Yellowstone visitors counted 380 occupations among party heads. Farmers were first, 6,360 in all, followed by 2,459 salesmen, 2,052 "professionals," 2,035 merchants, 1,817 teachers, 1,455 business proprietors and executives, 1,089 clerks, and 1,006 retired people.[8]

Figures like these demonstrate the way outdoor recreational activity rapidly became a valued consumer commodity, which, like the car that made it possible, blurred longstanding class distinctions.

The mass appeal of what has been dubbed "automobility" also reinforced the deep-rooted American confidence in private property by elevating the continuous accumulation of personal possessions into a socially acceptable substitute for the acquisition of real productive property. In the automobile age, regularly employed working people could reasonably aspire to car ownership, the new measure of personal success, and in the more prosperous industrial centers, even to home ownership, the traditional mark of full citizenship in the community of property-holders. Moreover, if (with the constant encouragement of advertisers) these same working people continued to formulate new material desires after making such basic acquisitions, they probably felt both successful and ambitious, despite very limited opportunities to upgrade their job statuses.[9] In the past, this assertion of the centrality of consumerism in working-class lives has been poorly received by those in the Old and New Left who have wanted American workers to behave more like their British and European counterparts. However, we have no right to impose present-day standards on the lives and consciousness of prior generations. In E. P. Thompson's words, "their aspirations were valid in terms of their own experience," and they must be understood in this context.[10] The purchase of a used car, a radio, or a kitchen appliance may no longer seem like a momentous achievement in a society glutted with consumer goods. Yet, for American working people of the 1920s, when so many products were really new, simple purchases could bring substantial advances in material comfort and social status. Thus, as Stephen Thernstrom has said of nineteenth-century working class homeownership, "*in their eyes*, these accomplishments must have loomed large."[11]

Finally, the automobile helped to establish a strong popular predilection for private, technological solutions to social and personal problems. In the age of automobiles and electricity, new machines and new techniques, not new politics, were what offered the immediate promise of a brighter future to most working people. Henry Ford, the leading folk hero of the automobile boom, made his reputation larger than life precisely because he so clearly recognized and articulated this inclination of the American public. Unlike William C. Durant, the relatively obscure founder of the General Motors Corporation, Henry Ford won national attention and admiration by self-consciously making himself into the chief spokesman for automobility. To millions of Americans, his Model T was much more than a cheap, reliable machine; it was the herald of a new and better life. Professor Flink reminds us,

> The Model T symbolized a victory of the people who looked upon the automobility as a major social reform, over a shortsighted group of budding monopoly capitalists who put short-term higher unit profits ahead of the mass-automobility desired by the average person.[12]

By maximizing the potential of mechanization and continuous-flow production techniques, and by raising wages to control a discontented workforce while lowering the price of his cars to reach the mass market, Henry Ford seemed to prove his own contention that everyone could share in the new material wealth of America without getting involved in collective political action.

Today, it is easy to agree with French cultural critic Henri Lefebvre's assertion that "the motor car is the epitome of 'objects,' the Leading Object of modern industrial society. . . . it stands for comfort, power, authority and speed, it is *consumed as a sign* in addition to its practical use."[13] Yet, in early twentieth-century America, few businessmen immediately grasped the potential of this incredible machine. In the older eastern cities, leading investors refused to back the industry around which a new consumer-oriented economy would be built. However, in the Midwest, and especially in Michigan, ambitious combinations of entrepreneurs and engineers took full advantage of the situation. Pooling their resources and their skills, these men created the giant industrial corporations that made Michigan's lower peninsula into one of the world's leading manufacturing regions, and themselves into multimillionaires. In 1904, Michigan's many small automobile shops turned out just over 9,000 cars, already 42 percent of the national total. A decade later, led by the Big Two, Ford and General Motors, the state's output had climbed to 437,000 automobiles, more than three-fourths of all the cars built in the United States that year.[14] Clearly, as Americans began to commit themselves to a way of life dependent on automobiles, Michigan automakers were putting their state in the vanguard of their nation's second industrial revolution.

The rapid growth of the automobile industry was not an isolated happening. It both energized and epitomized the broader transformation of America's economy that occurred between the severe depression of the 1890s and the Great Crash of 1929. In some of its essentials, this second industrial revolution resembled concurrent changes in the economies of Western Europe and Japan. However, the mass-consumer orientation of American developments had no parallel overseas.

The application of scientific methods and new technology to production and distribution problems and a dramatic restructuring of the business system lay at the heart of America's second industrial revolution. First, in older industries like steelmaking, automatic machinery and the mechanization of heavy labor were introduced to lower labor costs while dramatically increasing output. Then, as other industrial leaders adopted the principles of scientific management popularized by the efficiency expert Frederick Taylor, the production of a wide variety of commodities was streamlined according to time-motion studies and the stopwatch. Of course, the culmination of these advances came between 1908 and 1914 when, as Stephen Meyer has recently described it, "Ford engineers, factory managers, and others combined the most advanced features of existing industrial practice and developed the modern system of mass production."[15]

To complement this expansion of basic production capacities and to control the great numbers of workers and machines it required, the size, structure, and functions of industrial corporations underwent drastic renovation. Mergers were frequently used to speed up the creation of integrated companies that controlled all stages of production and distribution, and very often they controlled entry into their markets as well. At the peak of the first great merger movement from 1898 to 1901, nearly twenty-three hundred firms were absorbed into bigger corporations, but large numbers of significant mergers continued right through the automobile boom.

In the fast-growing automobile industry, high profits allowed the biggest firms to expand vertically and horizontally without outside financing and control by banking interests. While Ford used cash sales and consistently high turnover to build up fully integrated manufacturing operations in the Detroit area, William C. Durant tried to keep General Motors competitive by expanding on a national scale through mergers and outright purchases of smaller companies. In just two years, from 1908 to 1910, General Motors bought up at least thirty separate firms. Later, in 1919, during his second short-lived tenure as General Motors president, Durant set an important precedent for corporate diversification with his purchase of an electric refrigerator company he renamed Frigidaire. As a result of the successful consolidation policies of Ford and General Motors, the automobile industry soon took on an oligopolistic character. In 1908, there were 253 active automobile producers in the United States; by 1920, there were less than half that number in a market dominated by the Big Two. By 1929, only 44 companies remained, with Ford, General Motors, and the new Chrysler Corporation accounting for more than 80 percent of total output.[16]

The managerial problems presented by the sheer size and diversity of these new fully integrated corporations were increasingly solved by professionally paid staff, not by owners. During the automobile boom, management was studied, subdivided, and rationalized like the production process itself. Economic decision making became more of a bureaucratic process and less the sole priority of individual entrepreneurs. Henry Ford's longtime personal control of his giant company was an exception to this rule, and it contributed to the decline of the Ford Motor Company in the automobile market during the mid-1920s. More typically, in those same years, the nation's biggest businesses followed the lead of the DuPont Corporation and the DuPont-controlled General Motors Corporation by developing decentralized, multidivisional operating structures. In fact, the plan Alfred P. Sloan produced to reorganize General Motors in 1922 quickly became a model for modern corporate management and marketing practices.

Of course, the automobile industry did not create the national marketplace for consumer durables on its own. Prior to World War I, direct outlets, franchise arrangements, dealerships, chain stores, and department stores changed the distribution patterns of American business, flooding the country with some of the brand-name goods that have since become institutions of mass consumer culture. By the 1920s, improvements in road transport and electronic communication (telephone, radio, and movies) began to tie even the smallest towns into the national marketplace. As Thorstein Veblen had predicted in 1899, a "vicarious consumption practiced by the households of the middle and lower classes" in pursuit of the appearance of "the leisure class scheme of life" fast became a central feature of American daily life.[17]

To create and sustain this new pattern of conspicuous consumption, major corporations made advertising into an important industry in its own right. Using the traditional newspaper and catalogue, and more recent media like cheap mass-circulation magazines, radio, and movies, advertisers provided a steady diet of new material desires that shaped the emerging consumer-oriented popular culture. Once a minor cost consideration, expenditures on advertising rose dramatically during the automobile boom. Between 1900 and 1929, the total cost of advertisements in all media soared from 540 million dollars to a then staggering 3.4 billion dollars. Initial enthusiasm for the car and the tremendous amount of free publicity generated by automobile shows, auto-touring, auto-camping, and automobile racing permitted the automakers to hold down their advertising costs before World War I, but during the 1920s, they joined the national advertising blitz. In the decade between 1914 and 1924, General Motors advertising costs per car jumped from one dollar to ten dollars. The giant firm's advertising expenditures continued to climb after 1924 as part of the new marketing strategy outlined in the Sloan plan. Ultimately, General Motors became the nation's largest single advertiser.[18]

At the time, the rapid growth of advertising worried few people; yet even then, production for a mass market of conspicuous consumers was subtly undermining industrial standards. As industries matured (that is, reached the practical limits of first-time purchasers of their products), production was designed less to turn out goods of maximum quality and durability and more to meet transitory standards of appearance often set by their own marketing departments. General Motors was a trendsetter in this area, too. Under the dictates of Alfred P. Sloan's reorganization plan, the company emphasized "sculptured" body styles, bright colors, and frequent model changes. As Emma Rothschild has written, "On the basis of GM's strategy for 'upgrading' the American automobile, U.S. auto marketing became a worldwide model for the selling of expensive consumer goods."[19] In the late 1920s, Henry Ford's refusal to fall in line with the new marketing strategy cost his company the leadership of the American car market. By the post-World War II era, approximately one-fourth the total purchase price of American-made automobiles was going into annual styling modifications that made virtually no significant technological improvements in the basic machine.[20]

As the leading growth industry of the early twentieth century, automobile manufacturing also embodied most of the other characteristics of the second industrial revolution. To its advantage, the automobile industry was new. In the years before World War I, this meant automobile companies had no large fixed investments in older techniques and equipment to slow down the introduction and improvement of mass production methods. Nor was there an established automobile workforce reluctant to sacrifice valued skills and control over their work process for the simple goal of higher output. Though highly skilled workers in the early automobile industry (especially toolmakers and machinists) did experience a tightening up of work discipline, they were not forced down into the ranks of the lesser skilled workers in large numbers. Instead those job categories (which made up the vast majority of the new industry's labor force) were filled chiefly by immigrants from Eastern and Southern Europe and recent migrants from rural America and Canada. Like many other of the new mass-production industries, car making did not undermine the skills and social position of a traditional workforce. Rather, with its promise of high wages and relatively short hours, it drew an entirely new group of working people into factories, where a premium was placed on dexterity and speed, not on a personal understanding of complex production methods. "Given the authoritarian social relations of the industry and the managerial monopolization of technical skills and knowledge," Stephen Meyer explained in *The Five Dollar Day*,

> workers could do little to change the conditions of their work processes. So, they made their tradeoff. . . . They have traded degrading work for shorter hours and higher wages, or for more leisure with material comforts.[21]

In other words, the big automakers faced few internal impediments to expansion and what seemed to be a limitless demand for their product. They were able continuously to rationalize production and to enlarge capacity. American automakers raised the total annual output of vehicles from just over 65,000 in 1908 to 1.9 million in 1917, the first year of direct American participation in the Allied war effort; and still the public clamored for more cars.[22]

The wartime performance of the automobile industry provides convincing evidence that the automobile was already uniquely important in American culture and society. Even before the outbreak of hostilities in Europe, only American automakers had begun to reach a mass market. In 1913, for example, the British motor industry, the world's second biggest, turned out just thirty-five thousand vehicles, while American production topped the half million mark.[23] During the following year, European production of private automobiles ceased completely, but in the United States, tremendous increases in output and sales were registered right through 1917. Even in 1918, despite shortages of some raw materials and partial mobilization for war production, American automakers managed to build and sell nearly one million passenger cars. Most of these vehicles were produced by Ford and General Motors, not by the smaller car companies that were more fully committed to the government's munitions program. General Motors did manufacture Liberty aircraft engines at the Buick works in Flint and at the Cadillac plant in Detroit, yet its other far-flung facilities continued to produce cars for the domestic market. Henry Ford used government contracts for naval patrol boats to begin development of the River Rouge site, but wartime profits from record sales of the Model T and Fordson tractors went to buy out all minority stockholders in his company, not to aid the Allies. Overall, in the two years of the United States' involvement in the Great War, government contracts assumed by the automobile industry topped 1.1 billion dollars. However, at the same time, regular sales of domestic, private, and commercial vehicles totaled 2.4 billion dollars.[24] Significantly, during the war years from 1914 to 1919, personal expenditures on private transportation grew faster than at any other time during the automobile boom. Thus, while the Great War destroyed the bases for the second industrial revolution in Western Europe, it actually stimulated the creation of an automobile-centered, consumer-oriented economy in America.

During the 1920s, as Britain, France, and Germany struggled to rebuild war-torn economies, the automobile boom reached its peak in the United States. Recovering quickly from a sharp, but brief postwar slump, American automakers seemed to ensure indefinite expansion by gradually shifting away from technological and price competition toward a greater emphasis on styling, design, and marketing innovations. In the twenties, automaking took its place as the nation's leading manufacturing industry (based on the total value of its product), and it retained that position until the mid-1970s, when fast rising petroleum prices pushed the oil industry ahead of automobiles.[25]

The initial practical limits of the automobile boom were approached in 1927, the year Ford dropped the Model T and General Motors became the new industry leader. That year, demand for replacement vehicles outstripped demand from people buying their first car, even though nearly half the families in the nation still did not own an automobile.[26] To stimulate this weakening market, the Big Three automakers (as they are still known today) stepped up their advertising campaigns, pressed ahead with product differentiation schemes, and facilitated credit buying. These measures proved to be only temporary palliatives that could not alter the hard realities of American income distribution. In 1910, the bottom two-fifths of all income recipients in the United States received 19.8 percent of total national personal income before taxes; by 1929, their share was just 15.5 percent. For the most part, these were the people who could not afford the costs involved in owning, operating, and maintaining an automobile.[27] As a result, the automobile industry operated at less than 80 percent of practical capacity between 1926 and 1929, prompting Walter Chrysler to admit privately that he could "feel the winds of disaster blowing." Of course, Chrysler's premonition proved accurate. Although a record 5.3 million cars were built in 1929, that figure was not topped again until 1949.[28]

By most standards, the industrial economy that collapsed between 1929 and 1933 was a far different one than the one three decades earlier that had seen the first automobiles being built. In large part, though certainly not in all respects, the changes of those decades had been made possible by the dynamism of the automobile industry. Unlike other growing businesses of the era, automaking had a special kind of multiplier effect comparable to the impact of the railroads on nineteenth-century America. From its origins, the motor vehicle industry stimulated basic extractive industries, steelmaking, and urban construction; it also brought many new types of enterprises into existence. Moreover, like railroad building, the extension of motorized road transport amplified the dimensions of the national marketplace while it simultaneously quickened the rate at which goods and money circulated throughout the economy. Automotive transportation also paralleled the railroad experience in regard to government subsidies, calling forth a massive commitment of local, state, and federal funds for road-building projects that transformed the national landscape. Finally, the mass production and mass distribution of cars, a heavy, complex industrial product, set a powerful example for the development of other durable consumer goods industries. All totaled, between 1899 and 1929, incalculable amounts of private and public capital and innumerable hours of human labor were spent preparing the United States for the automobile; and though precise figures will never be available, some of the most important outlines of this great economic event are clear.

24

For example, once the mass market for cars was tapped, demand for wood, iron, steel, rubber, glass, and other raw materials grew steadily. Factories especially built to mass-produce tires, bodies, axles, electrical components and the hundreds of other parts essential for the finished automobile soon appeared all over the Middle West, shifting the industrial heart of the nation away from the North Atlantic coast.[29] All across the country, auto sales and services provided important new local business opportunities, while regional assembly plants opened up thousands of new factory jobs. In most areas, as the population of drivers increased, state and local governments responded by making road building and repair a major part of their responsibility to the public. This development provided a tremendous boost to the construction industry because the replacement of rough dirt roads with a network of paved streets and highways capable of handling the ever-increasing traffic seemed to be an endless task.

Public officials usually received wholehearted support for road projects from taxpayers, even though the net effect of local, state, and federal programs raised the average tax burden tremendously. Property tax increases provided basic funds at the local level. The states depended primarily on driving licenses and fees to pay for their road construction and maintenance efforts in the early years of the boom, but these monies proved to be inadequate to meet the demands of drivers. In 1919, Oregon imposed the first gasoline tax, and by 1930 every state had adopted this method of augmenting its highway funds. Congress voted the first national road improvement program into law in 1916, and then it strengthened its financial commitment by means of the Federal Highway Act of 1921. In 1929, the last year of the automobile boom, all levels of government spent two and a quarter billion dollars on road projects, with nearly 40 percent of that amount coming from special motor vehicle taxes. During the 1930s, these figures climbed steadily, despite the Great Depression because road work was so often incorporated into the overall relief effort.[30] Neither a world war nor a great depression, it seems, could stop the expansion of America's automobile-centered culture and society.

A Transformation of Class, Culture, and Society

The cultural and social transformation that accompanied the automobile boom was as striking as the changes it wrought in the economy. In fact, it is no exaggeration to claim that the automobile boom produced a new kind of capitalism in the United States, setting patterns

25

for interpersonal relationships, cultural values, and social institutions that still dominate American life today. Before the car, America was not a mature industrial society. Of course, by 1900 industrialization had advanced far enough to make the United States one of the world's leading industrial nations. However, in terms of its own potentials, the historical alternatives open to it, and the everyday life and culture of its citizens, America was still a relatively underdeveloped country at the turn of the century.

The rural character of American society before the advent of automobility is the strongest indicator of its relative underdevelopment. In 1900 only one-third of America's people lived in towns with more than eight thousand inhabitants, while fully three-fifths of the population were officially classified as "rural" by census-takers. (By comparison, in 1901, nearly four-fifths of Britain's population resided in urban places.)[31] Although New York, Chicago, and Philadelphia had more than a million residents by this time, and thirty-two other places topped the 100,000 population mark, most Americans still lived on farms or in small towns where older agrarian patterns of work, leisure, and family life remained strong. Even in the cities and mining towns, where the rhythms and rationalized discipline of industrial capitalism had penetrated everyday life, working people often held onto preindustrial, ethnic customs and values in order to buffer themselves from the relentless grind of long hours, low wages, dangerous working conditions, and lack of job security that was their common lot. Many families were able to include some agricultural undertaking (a vegetable garden, or raising poultry or livestock) in their total effort to maintain an acceptable standard of living. This apparently widespread practice was made possible by the relative abundance of cheap land in America, and it provided ordinary American people with one way of easing the transition from rural to urban society that was not generally available in Europe and Japan. Thus, as late as the 1890s in New York City, the nation's most cosmopolitan city, small farms dotted Brooklyn and Queens, while visitors observed goats and pigs as far south as Forty-second Street on Manhattan Island. And in smaller cities where tenement housing was less typical, a majority of families probably produced at least part of their annual food supply themselves.[32]

By 1930, the size, number, and geographic distribution of American cities had expanded enormously, dramatically intensifying the urban character of national life. Rapid industrialization and the concurrent emergence of the automobile-centered consumer culture combined to create recognizably modern American cities where cars, not animals and gardens, crowded the streets and open spaces. Before 1900 urban centers were still primarily concentrated along the traditional commercial routes on the ocean coasts, the Great Lakes shoreline, and the banks of the Mississippi River system. The automobile boom decisively broke this pattern, encouraging the growth of cities that were totally dependent on overland transportation. By the start of the Great Depression, ninety-three widely scattered cities boasted of populations exceeding one hundred thousand persons, and fully one-half of all Americans lived in towns with more than eight thousand residents. During the long automobile boom, New York, Chicago, and Philadelphia became true metropolitan centers, linked to surrounding suburban cities by a complex system of paved roads. The two places that best represented the popular triumph of the car culture, Detroit and Los Angeles, grew at phenomenal rates. Between 1900 and 1930, Detroit's population increased fivefold (from 300,000 to 1.6 million residents) while Los Angeles' population multiplied by more than a factor of ten (from 102,000 to 1.2 million persons). In the same period, Cleveland tripled in size, while Milwaukee and Toledo doubled their populations. Smaller boom towns like Flint, Michigan grew at even faster rates.

Of course, the new urban populations did more than simply reproduce the nineteenth-century city on a bigger scale. "There is no such thing as economic growth which is not, at the same time, growth or change of a culture," writes E. P. Thompson.[33] Certainly this was true of the United States during the automobile boom. By establishing a national economy truly based on the mass production and mass distribution of durable consumer goods like the car, America simultaneously created a new kind of social order. Clearly continuities with the past persisted, but in the booming cities and their surrounding suburbs, an older way of living gave way to a society more dependent on national corporations, mass consumerism, and the automobile. Some traditional communities survived virtually intact, especially in depressed rural areas and in industrial cities with tightly knit ethnic neighborhoods. Nevertheless, at the time, students of social change like the Lynds were consistently impressed by the fundamental differences between "the good old days" before the turn of the century and American society in the automobile age. "The horse culture of Middletown has almost disappeared," they discovered in 1925, "nor was the horse culture in all its years of undisputed sway ever as pervasive a part of the life of Middletown as is the cluster of habits that have grown up overnight around the automobile."[34]

Viewed from the perspective of contemporaries, through the eyes of Americans born in the late nineteenth century and maturing during the automobile boom, the totality of change experienced by local communities amounted to a virtual restructuring of the fundamental relationships and institutions that shaped everyday life. In economic terms, the establishment of big, integrated industrial corporations geared to the mass production and distribution of cars and other durable consumer items broke down all the barriers between local business activity and the influence of the national marketplace. Increasingly, the livelihood and the workday routines of urban America became dependent on big business organizations. More and more people went to work for bigger companies in both blue- and white-collar positions. Between 1900 and 1930, the number of blue-collar workers soared from 14.7 to 30.2 million persons, while the number of white-collar (professional, technical, and managerial) workers rose from less than three million to six-and-a-half million people.[35] In real automobile boom towns like Detroit and Flint in Michigan, or even Muncie, Indiana (the Lynds' Middletown), diversified local economies were quickly displaced by a single industry orientation and greater dependence on large, nationally owned firms. These firms or their subsidiaries rapidly became the largest employers and property owners in such cities. Though nominally independent, local businessmen and institutions (banks, stores, builders, secondary manufacturers, and even professionals), as well as local governments, were eventually forced to rely on the business cycle of the dominant industry for their economic well-being. In many cases, local businessmen and executives also invested heavily in the national corporations represented in their hometowns, thus tying both their professional and personal fortunes to the fate of America's business giants.

Linked by this common economic dependence, and augmented by the presence of a new group of corporate managers and technicians, local business communities emerged from the automobile boom more unified and better organized than ever before. Within the Chambers of Commerce, citywide employers' organizations, trade associations, and the exclusive businessmen's clubs that flourished during the 1920s, entrepreneurs and company officials mixed traditional anti-unionism, local pride, and patriotism with new-found corporate loyalties and admiration for technological achievements. The resulting ideology, often parodied as mindless "boosterism," actually expressed the terms of a vital reconciliation between small business and national corporate power. Although ultimately founded on the prosperity generated by the large corporations, expressions of a community of interest between big and small businessmen were more than empty rhetoric. In concrete situations like the implementation of capitalist welfare programs, the organization of sports and civic activities, the funding of charities, and political drives for municipal reform, local entrepreneurs and officials from national corporations worked together to build new community institutions and a common consciousness of business's dominant role in the industrial city. And, in prospering cities all across the United States, these goals were achieved. By the mid-1920s, confident in their ability to control economic development and its social and political consequences, businessmen looked forward to the second quarter of the twentieth century with hopes and with tremendous enthusiasm as a class. "United we stick, divided we're stuck. United we boost, divided we bust" may sound like just another bit of Babbittry today, but in its own time, the ritualistic repetition of such slogans heralded the making of a business class consciousness that left a permanent impression on American culture.[36]

In striking contrast to the growing unity and power of the business class, and partly as a result of it, genuine working-class consciousness and organizations disintegrated during the 1920s. Drastic declines in union membership, in the number of strikes, and in support for pro-union politicians, as well as the increasing conservatism of labor leaders like the A.F. of L.'s William Green were the most visible signs of the nationwide collapse of working-class consciousness; at the local level, things usually looked even worse for the labor movement. In reality, labor unions had almost no power at the peak of the automobile boom. As an Australian observer, who was astounded by the weakness of American trade unions, remarked in 1928, "Labour organization exists only by the tolerance of employers. . . . It has no real part in determining industrial conditions."[37]

Unions were particularly powerless in those industries that formed the backbone of the emerging consumer-goods economy. Almost all manufacturing firms, including those in the automobile, steel, electrical equipment, rubber, cement, textile, chemical, and food processing industries, conducted their employee relations on a strictly open shop basis in the 1920s. Non-ferrous metals, petroleum, road transport, utilities, banking, insurance, retail and wholesale trade, services, and the professions were also essentially union-free sectors of the booming economy. Only construction, railroads, printing, water transport, music and a handful of older "sick" industries, including coal, New England textiles, clothing, and boot and shoe making, retained significant union memberships. However, even in these unionized industries, organized labor's actual power was often sharply limited by local circumstances. In the years following World War I, it seemed as if, in Irving Bernstein's words, "the labor movement stood still as the main stream of American society swept by."[38]

Unfortunately, traditional historical judgments about the failure of the labor movement during the 1920s usually have been focused on labor leadership, management strategies, and government policy, not on the basic changes occurring in those swift-moving currents of everyday life. Both the radical and the more established Wisconsin schools of American labor history generally have grounded their interpretations of the fragility of working-class consciousness and organizations after World War I on assumptions derived from the nature of industrial capitalism as it existed before the automobile boom. As a result, neither group of labor scholars has systematically explored the possibility that the experiential bases for working-class consciousness might have been dramatically reshaped by the extremely rapid creation of an industrial economy truly geared to the mass production and mass distribution of durable consumer goods. In fact, even the most recent revisionists, the so-called "new" labor historians, have focused almost exclusively on events preceding the automobile boom. Twentieth-century American labor history continues to be written almost as if mass consumerism and automobility never happened, or at best, as if these things could have developed without simultaneously transforming the traditional values that informed working-class protest and organization.[39]

There are enormous difficulties inherent in making an accurate assessment of the social, cultural, and political impacts of mass consumerism and automobility on America's industrial working people, but certain vital points can be established unequivocally. First, the automobile boom created huge numbers of new industrial workers who had little or no industrial experience. As already noted, the size of America's blue-collar workforce doubled in the first three decades of this century. At the same time, immigration peaked and then was abruptly cut off by war and restrictive legislation. As a result, in the 1920s, the nation's working population was "Americanized." In part, this extremely important cultural change stemmed from the ever-increasing migration of rural Americans (both black and white) to the industrial cities, as well as the entrance of American-born sons and daughters of immigrants into the workforce. Yet, Americanization was also embodied in concrete public efforts to integrate foreign-born families into the language, beliefs, and habits of the native-born white community. These efforts ranged from wartime propaganda and the political pressures of the Ku Klux Klan to adult education classes in English and citizenship administered by local YMCAs and boards of education. Of course, when culturally distinct groups of white Americans mixed with each other and with foreign-born citizens for the first time in the 1920s, many people reacted defensively, retreating into prejudices and forms of ethnic-group solidarity that temporarily frustrated all proponents of working-class unity. Nevertheless, these barriers were not impervious to the automobile boom. As time passed, the standardization of daily work and life inherent in the mass-consumer-oriented car culture reduced the significance of ethnicity. By the 1930s, workers of diverse ethnic backgrounds would be able to work together to establish permanent industrial unions.

At the end of the automobile boom, the everyday life of American workers had been transformed. This was especially true in prosperous new mass-production industries like automobile manufacturing. Certainly, the drawbacks usually associated with mass-production jobs, like low skill requirements, incessant routine, and individual anonymity, obliterated the traditional rewards of work. Nevertheless, most workers did not feel the loss of craft status. Whether they were rural migrants or the new generations of city dwellers, they entered industry in positions where skills were already degraded. Moreover, as psychologist Robert Reiff, a former Chrysler welder, has recently pointed out, the popular academic stereotype of the alienated worker ignores the fact that workers "show a great deal of initiative in developing ways to get satisfaction out of the work *situation* rather than the product itself."[40]

Even more significantly, by the late 1920s, the material and psychological rewards of consumer-oriented capitalism had begun to compensate for the demands of work. There can be no doubt that working people's real wages and leisure time increased significantly during the automobile boom. Between 1922 and 1929, the average real wages of American factory workers rose nearly 15 percent, while the average factory work week dropped below forty-four hours (as compared with fifty-one hours in 1909).[41] In addition, during the twenties, for the first time in American history, credit was extended to industrial workers to finance major purchases of consumer durables. Here too, the automobile industry was the trendsetter. In the years after 1919, when William C. Durant established the General Motors Acceptance Corporation, installment credit became the cornerstone of the automobile marketplace. In 1925 alone, three out of every four automobile purchases were financed by loans that totaled more than 2.6 billion dollars.[42] This kind of expansion of credit resulted in qualitative improvements in workers' living standards which cannot be measured by wage increases alone. By 1929, most industrial working people lived in electrified homes or flats with central heating and indoor toilets. Many workers had also begun to own and use cars, home appliances, radios, and phonographs. Thus, unlike their nineteenth-century predecessors or their contemporary counterparts in other industrial countries, American workers no longer struggled to maintain living standards at or near the subsistence level; they labored to become part of the world's first true consumer-oriented society.

The ways that the automobile boom and mass consumerism undermined working-class consciousness and labor organization in the 1920s generally have been downplayed by labor historians because the real wages of most blue-collar workers remained relatively low (compared to wages in the post-C.I.O., post-World War II era). A more meaningful comparison can be made with workers overseas. According to an International Labour Office study conducted in July 1928, real wages (indexed at 100 in London) were just 66 in Berlin, 55 in Brussels, 48 in Vienna, and 179 in New York. These figures reveal why only American working people could become consumers in the 1920s.[43]

Yet working people did not have to buy lots of new products to become consumers. While real wages slowly improved (as they did throughout the automobile boom), mass advertising and the growing mass-media industries shaped the material expectations of American workers. There should no longer be any dispute about such a common-sense observation. As the eminent business historian Thomas Cochran has commented,

Unquestionably some of the "saturation" campaigns produced new consumer wants and in this way readjusted markets for goods bought with discretionary income. But even markets for basic necessities could be altered. Advertising could lead to a life sustained more by meat and Coca Cola than by unadvertised farm products.[44]

In brief, American working people internalized consumer values long before they could actually afford to satisfy all their new consumer wants.

The popularity of the new, commercialized mass media during the automobile boom greatly facilitated the making of America's national consumer culture. "It is impossible to overestimate the role of motion pictures, advertising, and other forms of publicity in this rise in subjective standards," the Lynds concluded in 1929,

> In the place of relatively mild, scattered, something-for-nothing, sample-free, I-tell-you-this-is-a-good article seen in Middletown a generation ago, advertising is concentrating increasingly on a type of copy aiming to make the reader uneasy, to bludgeon him with the fact that decent people don't live the way *he* does; decent people ride balloon tires, have a second bathroom, and so on.[45]

As more and more people became avid magazine readers, moviegoers, and radio listeners, they could not help but be influenced by the commercial messages and images of affluence that were designed to change their behavior. In the later 1920s, even workers began to display the peculiar self-consciousness of the mass media's ideal modern consumer. In other words, they started to "need" brand-name products to allay the self-doubts inculcated by mass advertising.[46]

By its very nature, the growth of the new consumer-oriented car culture in the 1920s blurred traditional class distinctions. Advertising and the mass media encouraged working people to mimic the affluent life-style of the business class. At the same time, workers were also encouraged to compete among themselves for the material symbols of success and respectability. Again, the Lynds' observations are invaluable. "A Rip Van Winkle who fell asleep today would marvel at the change as did the French economist Say when he revisited England at the close of the Napoleonic War," they commented in the late 1920s. And why? What was "this new trait in the city's culture that is shaping the pattern of the whole of living?" On this point, the Lynds had no doubts. In the Middletown they studied, "Both businessmen and working men seem to be running for dear life in this business of making the money they earn keep pace with the even more rapid growth of their subjective wants."[47] Here in the everyday dynamics of what was already a true consumer-oriented society, is the most important source of the apparent "classlessness" of modern America.

Once American working people had made a commitment to what Henri Lefebvre calls the "ideology of consumption," the fundamental tension between themselves and the business class dissipated.[48] This new value system led most industrial workers to see their jobs as instruments, not as ends in themselves. As they became consumers and the nineteenth-century workplace faded from living memory, these workers learned to accept the big corporation, the mechanized factory, and the alienation of their labor as inevitable. These things were dominant and oppressive facts of everyday life; their very "weight" as part of everyday experience encouraged fatalism. And there was also their seductive side. Big corporations, mechanized factories, and alienated labor provided working people with the material goods that unrelenting publicity placed at the center of everyday life and culture. They learned to dream, not of a society controlled by its farmers and working class, but of products and of a materialistic utopia populated by affluent, happy consumers of new technology. By 1930, a new, extremely attractive popular culture—a synthesis of automobility, mass consumerism, and Americanization —had driven a kind of cultural wedge between urban-industrial workers and their own pasts, cutting them off in particular from the tenuous working-class traditions of America's first producer-goods-oriented industrial revolution. As tiny groups of rank-and-file communists, socialists, and other radicals discovered during the Great Depression, such traditions were not easily revived. Nevertheless, after the automobile boom, America's industrial working people could still act as a class (as they demonstrated in building up the labor movement in the 1930s and 1940s). However, when they acted as a class, the overwhelming majority revealed an unwillingness (one is tempted to say an inability) to project an alternative to industrial capitalism. The organization of industrial unions and the New Deal reforms that legitimized organized labor were the great achievements of the working class of the 1930s and 1940s. Yet, as we can see clearly now, neither development pointed towards the radical restructuring of the industrial business system feared by so many opponents of the labor movement. The organized working class of the post-World War II era has been content with a "New Deal formula" that combined state-subsidized economic growth, a social security system, legally regulated collective bargaining, and a political alliance between labor unions and the Democratic Party.[49] This kind of a working class has not threatened property rights, the factory system, or two-party politics. Instead, this mid-twentieth-century American working class accepted a recognized, but distinctly subordinate, place for itself within a political economy still dominated by the corporate promoters of automobile-centered, mass consumerism.

Given the enormous size of the United States and the diversity possible within its continental borders, generalizations about the political culture of the automobile age must be tempered with a bit of skepticism. Capitalism developed unevenly in America, just as it has in the world as a whole; and because of this uneven development, regional distinctions have always played an important part in the nation's history. Before 1950, many Americans were not integrated into the new car-centered consumer culture, although automobiles were by then widely used in every section of the country. In the North, black workers and some ethnic minorities who generally had been excluded from higher paying industrial jobs preserved their independence from the new popular culture. In the South, outside the cities, cars slowly replaced horses without disrupting the cultural mix of bi-racial poverty and racial segregation that had its roots in the late nineteenth century. And, finally, in the Far West, vast areas remained virtually undeveloped until after World War II, despite the growth of a few widely scattered industrial cities.

Yet where the automobile-centered consumer culture was firmly established prior to the Great Depression—in the Northeast, the Middle West, and California—it set vital precedents for the kind of sprawling urban-industrial development that has encompassed all of America since 1950. During the 1920s the first four-lane highways, the first suburbs, and yes, even the first shopping malls were built to serve highly mobile consumer-citizens. Most historians have ignored these changes, or treated them essentially as prosaic developments. But is it possible to look at the United States today, with over 140 million cars on the road, and deny the fundamental significance of the automobile boom to twentieth-century American history? Between 1908 and 1930, the reorientation of national economic priorities to suit the needs of an automobile-driving public made American capitalism into a new kind of society unlike any other of the so-called "advanced" industrial nations. While the costs of colonial and military rivalries and the terrible destruction of the Great War kept Britain, France, Germany, and Japan locked into the producer-goods-oriented stage of economic or industrial development, the United States transformed its economic and social order. Neither the Great Depression of the 1930s nor World War II reversed this fundamental transformation. After 1945, a booming, powerful America literally exported its car-centered, consumer-oriented version of high-technology capitalism to war-torn Western Europe and Japan. As a result, American mass consumerism and automobility, not the patterns of turn-of-the-century industrial society, became the model for economic revival and for the reconstruction of world capitalism.

Today, the United States is more of a social and cultural unity than ever before because of its successful second industrial revolution. With its omnipresent strips of drive-in businesses, shopping centers, gas stations, and parking lots, the consumer-oriented car culture dominates the American landscape and continues to distinguish America from other nations. Even now, after the tremendous proliferation of cars around the globe, Americans still own well over half of the world's motor vehicles, while making up just 6 percent of its population.[50] Nowhere on earth have mass consumerism and automobility played such an intrinsic role in national development. The automobile-centered second industrial revolution is the central fact of twentieth-century American history. Ultimately, everything in American culture and society, including its politics, has been transformed by it. Surely, it is an event we can no longer afford to ignore.

To Flint

Few scholars have pursued the interpretation of modern American history presented in this chapter. As a result, our historical understanding of the deeper social, cultural, and political significance of the automobile boom remains quite tentative. Identifying the boom as a second industrial revolution that transformed and undoubtedly strengthened industrial capitalism in the United States is not the same thing as describing historical logic behind that transformation. To discover that logic—the how and the why of America's second industrial revolution—we must confront the experiences of early twentieth-century Americans who were swept up in the automobile

FIGURE 1.   Flint circa 1940.

SOURCE: Michigan Writers Project, *Michigan: A Guide to the Wolverine State* (Oxford, 1941).

boom more directly; we must examine in detail the complex, inter-related sequences of economic, social, and political events that actually changed the character of class and culture in a particular industrial community.

During the first half of the twentieth century, the industrial community in Flint, Michigan lived on the cutting edge of America's second industrial revolution. As the birthplace and largest production center of the General Motors Corporation, Flint experienced all the basic economic changes of the automobile boom in a compressed, dramatic way that accentuated their impact on everyday life, on class relationships, and on political culture. In Flint, the use of new science and technology by industry, the simultaneous development of mass production and consumer-oriented mass marketing, the concentration of production and ownership in huge units, and a related "managerial revolution" transformed a rather sleepy late nineteenth-century industrial town into a truly modern industrial city (complete with suburbs) in just three decades. Of course, Flint's extremely rapid growth and transformation were extraordinary, even by automobile boom standards. For this reason, one cannot claim that the city was a typical early twentieth-century industrial community. Nonetheless, precisely because the pace of fundamental economic change in Flint was revolutionary, its history does throw the effects of the automobile boom on contemporary society, culture, and politics into sharper perspective. Moreover, although Flint was an exceptional boom town, it was not separated from what have been seen traditionally as the main currents of American history. Indeed, what makes a case study of the second industrial revolution in Flint so valuable is the way in which most of the major developments of twentieth-century political and social history—such as municipal socialism and progressive reform, welfare capitalism and Americanization, the New Deal, and militant industrial unionism—were lived out there in conjunction with a local automobile boom and its aftermath. In this sense then, Flint seems remarkably representative of the making of modern America. To find out just how representative, it is now time to examine the history of this important automobile production center in detail.

3

THE EARLY AUTOMOBILE BOOM IN FLINT

The men at the head of Flint's industries . . . are the men who made Flint and who are making it. There is no question of competition, of lack of power. — John Ihlder, *The Survey* (1916)

A Village Grown Overnight into a City

The origins of the automobile boom in Flint, Michigan, are not mysterious. Like fundamental economic and social changes elsewhere in American history, Flint's great boom began in a series of investment decisions made by prominent local businessmen. In the late summer of 1903, five directors of the Flint Wagon Works, led by the firm's founder and president, James H. Whiting, borrowed ten thousand dollars so they could purchase the financially troubled Buick Motor Company of Detroit.[1] At the time, David Dunbar Buick's internal combustion engine-making enterprise was actually owned entirely by Frank and Benjamin Briscoe, a pair of automobile-minded sheet metal entrepreneurs who wanted to unload the debt-ridden company in order to back a rival car being developed by Jonathan Maxwell. Ever since opening in 1899 as the Buick Auto-Vim and Power Company, just one of Detroit's numerous, struggling automotive pioneers, Buick's firm had been plagued by his own inept management and by financial difficulties that stemmed from expensive, time-consuming experiments in automobile technology. Nevertheless, Whiting's group felt there was profit potential in Buick. The company made a respectable line of engine parts, transmissions, and other automotive components, as well as a dependable stationary internal combustion engine that could be easily marketed through the Wagon Works' own farm agencies. Buick and his chief associate, Walter Marr, also promised to improve automobile performance significantly with their powerful new "valve-in-head" engine, once it was perfected and tested. In September 1903, the purchase was completed, amidst local speculation about the possibility of Flint becoming an automotive production center, and by year's end, the first steps toward that end had been taken. On December 11, 1903, twenty-five workmen began to make the first Buick engines in a hastily constructed factory adjacent to the Wagon Works. A new era in local history was about to dawn.[2]

During the first half of 1904, while Whiting and his partners tried to create a firmer financial foundation for the Buick Motor Company in Flint, back in Detroit, David Buick and Walter Marr continued work on an experimental car utilizing the "valve-in-head" engine. In July 1904, a prototype was ready for testing.[3] After a remarkable run in which Marr averaged nearly thirty miles per hour over a rough 115 miles from Flint to Detroit and back to Flint again, Buick's powerful little Model B was put into production. Perhaps as many as twenty-eight of these cars were constructed in Flint during the next few months, with the first one going to local automobile enthusiast, Dr. Herbert Hills. By combining high performance and a relatively low-selling price of $950, the Model B soon caught the attention of the Midwest's motoring public, but even more importantly, Buick's car convinced William C. Durant, Flint's leading businessman, that the time had come to take the plunge into the automobile industry.

Until September 4, 1904, the day Dr. Hills took Billy Durant for a demonstration ride in his new Buick (at the request of James Whiting), the millionaire road-cart entrepreneur had resisted every attempt to induce him to invest in motorcar manufacturing. A salesman at heart rather than an engineer, Durant had yet to see an automobile he could market confidently. But Buick's Model B was different. After two months of test driving the car under the most difficult conditions he could find, Durant invested in Buick because the Model B "was a vehicle like the old Flint Road Cart—one that he could sell with a clear conscience and one which would, in fact, sell itself."[4]

Durant's commitment came none too soon for James Whiting and the other directors of the Flint Wagon Works. By mid-1904, before Buick had produced a single car, the company's backers had borrowed an additional twenty-five thousand dollars from each of three hometown banks, tying the fate of the Wagon Works, a major employer, and hundreds of local depositors to the still shaky automobile company. To Durant, a co-creator of the world's biggest vehicle making company, Buick's problems seemed clear. The company needed more capital, larger facilities, and a vigorous marketing campaign. It also needed strong leadership to replace the incompetent Buick and the part-time participation of Whiting and his associates. Thus, when Durant formally entered the Buick Motor Company on November 1, 1904, he asked for and got absolute managerial control over the firm.[5]

Under Durant's dynamic leadership, Buick's fortunes were quickly and dramatically reversed. Using his enormous influence within the city's business community, Flint's "El Capitan de Industria" easily raised enough capital to set Buick on a vigorous program of expansion and acquisition.[6] As soon as he took power, Durant increased the Buick Motor Company's capitalization from $75,000 to $500,000. It was then tripled only ten months later in September 1905, and raised again to $2,600,000 on June 12, 1907. Almost all of this money came from a network of prominent Flint businessmen already linked by their interests in the city's prosperous horse-drawn vehicle industry, in local banks, and in real estate speculations. This business elite was, in the words of Durant's most recent biographer, "a form of extended clan, comprising thirty or forty families laced together by shared interests, ancestry, trust, and marriage."[7] Since he dealt mainly with friends, relatives, and hometown competitors who had long admired the success of the Durant-Dort Carriage Company, Buick's new chief executive seldom resorted to the "hard sell." In fact, on one memorable occasion, Durant sold half a million dollars of Buick stock in Flint in just forty-eight hours, even though, as he recalled in his memoirs, "Few of the subscribers had ever ridden in an automobile."[8] Given this kind of trust, Durant apparently could not resist adding a little bit of water to the company's first stock issues. Yet, on the whole, he was an honest, energetic promotor who immediately put Flint's capital to work expanding Buick's capacity and sales network.[9] In addition, Durant always seemed able to design his plans for Buick in ways that would especially enrich himself and his closest hometown associates, a fact that would have tremendous impact on the patterns of economic development in Flint.

To reach volume production and generate a substantial cash flow quickly, and to cajole more capital from Flint's business community as well, Durant established Buick assembly operations in a large, conveniently vacant factory located in Jackson, Michigan. The plant had formerly housed a major wheel manufacturer, but was still actually owned by the Durant-Dort company.[10] At the same time, in Flint, Buick's expansion and Durant's other business interests intersected in an even more dramatic way. In 1905, the company began construction of a huge, fourteen-acre manufacturing complex in the city's north end, several miles from the original Buick engine factory. The site selection in the Oak Park subdivision was not accidental, for Oak Park, already the home of several Durant-Dort facilities, had been wholly owned by a group of local speculators, including Durant, J. Dallas Dort, and the banker-politician D. D. Aitken, since 1900. Soon Oak Park, a former 220-acre family farm, became the new industrial and residential heart of Flint, as the fast-growing Buick Motor Company attracted smaller supplier firms and thousands of working people to its environs. And, of course, with each new addition, the profits of the participants in the Oak Park Development Association and the local reputation and influence of Billy Durant grew apace.[11]

The strategy used to expand Buick was based directly on lessons Durant had learned from more than two decades in Flint's traditional vehicle industry. Having parlayed a two-thousand-dollar contract to assemble simple road carts into a multimillion-dollar company that produced a wide range of horse-drawn vehicles, Durant knew that only a complete range of reliable suppliers could insure truly efficient volume production. In his unpublished memoirs, the founder of General Motors recalled the experiences of building up the Durant-Dort Carriage Company, outlining, in a very real sense, the same principles he would use in the automobile industry. Recollecting his original partnership with J. Dallas Dort in the Flint Road Cart Company, circa 1886, Durant explained:

> We started out as assemblers with no advantage over our competitors. We paid about the same prices for everything we purchased. We realized that we were making no progress and would not unless and until we manufactured practically every important part that we used. We made a study of the methods employed by the concerns supplying us, the savings that could be effected by operating the plants at capacity without interruption, and with practically no selling or advertising expense. Having sat-

isfied ourselves that we had solved our problem, we proceeded to purchase plants and the control of plants, which made it possible to build up, from the standpoint of volume, the largest carriage company in the United States.[12]

Similarly, in the years 1905 to 1908, when the vast new Buick plant was under construction in Oak Park, Billy Durant sought to insure his sources of automotive parts, components, and supplies. As before, his final goal was nothing less than to create a fully integrated company, capable of dominating the market for its particular products.

Flint, a well-established carriage and wagon making center, already had a number of firms that could produce some of the parts and components Durant needed to turn Buick into a mass producer. In 1905, in addition to the major assemblers (Durant-Dort, the Flint Wagon Works, and W.A. Paterson) that had diverted capital and personnel into the new industry, several other important local firms were drawn directly into the Buick orbit when it expanded production in Oak Park. The Imperial Wheel Company, Armstrong Steel Spring, the W. F. Stewart Body Works, Flint Varnish Works, and Flint Axle Works all made the transformation from traditional vehicle suppliers to automotive manufacturers, through rapid expansion and, ultimately, absorption into Buick and General Motors. Other new independent companies, like Michigan Motor Castings and the Oak Park Power Company were also bought up quickly by General Motors after its formation in 1908, when Durant tried frantically to complete his rationalization of Flint's industrial economy while simultaneously launching similar plans for the national automobile industry.[13]

Some of Buick's needs simply could not be filled quickly by the city's traditional vehicle factories, particularly in this first decade of the new century when wagon making remained a highly profitable business.[14] Thus, for Buick to expand rapidly, Durant and his associates had to attract certain reputable automotive producers to Flint immediately. In 1905, to secure a dependable, high volume source of automobile axle assemblies, Durant and Dort put their considerable persuasive powers to work luring a major new producer, the Weston-Mott Company, away from its home town of Utica, New York. After first offering Charles Stewart Mott and his partner William Doolittle a choice site right next to Buick in Oak Park, then adding a sole supplier contract with the growing automaker, and finally sweetening the deal with a $100,000 to cover the costs of a new factory, Flint's leading businessmen convinced the New Yorkers to move, despite their misgivings that the self-proclaimed "Vehicle City" was just "a hick town."[15]

The Weston-Mott Company was duly reincorporated in Michigan in 1906. Charles Mott remained the firm's president, and William Doolittle was named treasurer. However, to safeguard Buick interests, the automobile company's lawyer, John J. Carton, became vice-president, while Durant's trusted banking associate, Arthur Bishop, took the post of secretary with sole responsibility for the building fund.[16] By February 1907, Weston-Mott's management and machinery had moved, and the company began production at rates that soon established it as an industry leader. Ten months later, William Doolittle died, leaving Charles Stewart Mott the sole owner of this booming enterprise and a rising star in Flint's business community. Yet, Mott did not seek greater independence, even though Weston-Mott's success had already made him a millionaire.[17] Instead, after Durant announced the formation of a General Motors holding company in September 1908, Mott quickly agreed to exchange 49 percent of his firm for stock in the new venture. Later, in 1913, Mott went further, surrendering all of Weston-Mott in return for more General Motors stock and a seat on the giant corporation's board of directors which he would hold for more than fifty years.[18]

In early 1908, when he had already begun to consider plans for a nationwide automobile merger, Billy Durant lured another vital automotive supplier to Flint. To establish a reliable source of ignition parts for Buick, Durant convinced a Toledo, Ohio sparkplug and magneto manufacturer, Albert Champion, to move his small operation to the Vehicle City. Like the other firms Durant linked to Buick, Champion's enterprise grew rapidly when the Oak Park plant went into full production. For most of Albert Champion's backers and associates, the loss of independence that followed the absorption of their firm into Billy Durant's sprawling automobile corporation was deeply resented. Thus, when Durant confirmed his intention to have General Motors swallow up Champion Ignition in the fall of 1908, Albert Champion's old partners took their capital and his name back to Toledo where they reestablished the company that still uses the Champion trademark. Of course, a sparkplug factory and Albert Champion himself remained in Flint, and under its new name, AC Sparkplug soon became a profitable General Motors subsidiary and an essential part of the city's automotive industry.[19]

The exodus of Albert Champion's partners proved an exception among the businessmen who had been drawn into Durant's plans for the Buick Motor Company. Most stayed on in Flint as happy participants in the dramatic boom that followed the long-awaited completion of Buick's production facilities in 1908. From less than 1,000 cars in 1905, the combined output of Buick's factories in Jackson and Flint could be pushed to only 1,400 automobiles in 1906 and just over 1,600 vehicles in 1907. Still, driven by a salesman's faith in the car market, Durant remained confident, even when sales temporarily slumped during the brief recession of 1907. Stalling on his bills and storing cars wherever space could be found, Durant pressed forward with full production of all Buick models (from the $900 Model 10 to the more luxurious Model 5) until sales picked up and cash began to flow once more into company coffers. Finally, at this point, when orders began to outstrip capacity, the new foundry, drop forge, and final assembly sections of the Oak Park plant were brought into production, and Buick output soared. To keep pace with the growing demand for cars, the company increased its labor force to twenty-one hundred workers in February 1908. It also began running two shifts in Jackson, and three round-the-clock shifts in Flint, boosting daily capacity to fifty vehicles. In May, three-hundred-and-fifty more workers were added in Flint, increasing capacity to eighty automobiles per day. Yet output still ran behind orders. In November, with virtually all car production shifted to the completed Flint facilities, works manager C.W. Nash announced he would add another thousand men to Buick's payroll in hopes of catching up with demand by mid-1909.[20] By year's end Buick had produced and sold more than 8,800 automobiles, an industry record that approximated the combined total of the next two largest companies, Ford and Cadillac. And, of course, this was just a beginning. In 1909 Buick's output topped 14,000 units, and by 1910, at least 21,000 new Buick cars were put on the road.[21] In other words, Durant had achieved his initial goal. The Buick Motor Company of Flint, Michigan, was the world's first truly integrated mass producer of automobiles.

Buick cars sold best in this early period of American automotive history because William Durant, the master salesman, recognized that advances in productive capacity had to be matched by extensions of the sales network or the whole enterprise would fail. Thus, from his first days with the company in 1905, Durant worked hard to promote Buick car sales. Given the high level of public curiosity about all automobiles, the special interest shown in Buick's Model B, and the large number of widely scattered Durant-Dort Carriage Company outlets at his disposal, this task was not extremely difficult. Nevertheless, Durant threw himself into it with notable enthusiasm.

First, he professionalized Buick's distribution by hiring the bicycle industry's Charles Van Horn as sales manager and Studebaker's W.L. Hibbard as assistant sales manager. In 1908, Canada's biggest carriage maker, J. S. McLaughlin of Oshawa, Ontario, was given the sole rights to assemble and distribute Buicks in that country.[22] Even more importantly, Durant committed Buick to production of a wide variety of automobile models (five by 1906) because he saw the car as a universally appealing product that could be tailored to different income levels. Like the Durant-Dort Carriage Company before it, and the General Motors Corporation that he created in 1908, the Buick Motor Company never tried to maximize efficiency by making a single, standardized model, such as Ford's Model T. Instead, companies founded by William C. Durant always shaped fundamental design and production decisions to conform with a vision of American society in which individuals were ranked according to fine gradations in their incomes, and products were made to symbolize those differences. The incorporation of styling considerations based on perceptions of a highly stratified marketplace into basic production design is usually credited to Alfred P. Sloan by industry historians. Yet surely the foundation of General Motors' policy of producing a variety of car styles must be traced back to Durant's own sense of the marketplace and the expansion strategies he used in the vehicle industry beginning in the 1880s.

At first Durant personally promoted Buick cars at all the major automobile shows. He also often spent time at struggling dealerships, boosting morale and selling cars himself. However, as the company's capacity increased, he adopted more spectacular methods to generate national publicity for the new product. In 1907–1908, special trains loaded with shiny Buick cars and draped with the banners "MADE IN FLINT" were routed to Minneapolis, Kansas City, and the East. These trains traveled only by day at reduced speeds, making local headlines wherever they passed. In 1908 Durant also put together the greatest automobile racing team of the era. Bob Burman, Lewis Strang, and Louis and Arthur Chevrolet won over five hundred trophies in just three years, an unprecedented feat that helped earn

Buick a national reputation as a maker of dependable high performance cars.[23]

The rapid success of the Buick Motor Company confirmed William C. Durant's faith in the market potential of the car, encouraging him immediately to propose mergers with some of America's most important automobile manufacturers. Early in 1908, even before the new Buick plant was fully operational, Durant had contacted most major Michigan automakers about the possibility of quickly grabbing a bigger share of the growing industry through financial combination. As it turned out, Henry Ford, Ramson E. Olds, and the Lelands of Cadillac each wanted millions in cash for their firms, and the Flint automaker simply could not produce them. On the other hand, the Briscoe brothers, now with Maxwell-Briscoe, were interested in a merger with Buick, but their more conservative backers from the Morgan banking group refused to take the plunge with Billy Durant in control.[24]

Despite these setbacks, Flint's leading businessman remained determined to turn Buick into the nucleus of a multinational vehicle company by using mergers, just as he and J. Dallas Dort had already done with their carriage making enterprise. In pursuing this goal, Durant knew he could count on the unwavering support of Flint's budding automotive-oriented business class, people he later described as "my personal friends who were willing to and did risk every dollar they possessed believing as I did in the future of the automobile industry."[25] Thus, by mid-1908, when fast-rising Buick sales promised to increase the company's cash flow geometrically, Durant felt the time to advance his own plans and the fortunes of his Flint associates had arrived.

On September 16, 1908, Billy Durant announced the formation of the General Motors Corporation, a holding company chartered in New Jersey with just over two thousand dollars in original capital. Almost immediately, however, the new company's capitalization and prospects soared because both the Olds Motor Works of Lansing, Michigan, and Buick were absorbed through the exchange of stock. Before the year's end, Durant had added another of the jewels of Michigan's motor industry, the Cadillac Motor Company, to General Motors, but only after paying Henry Leland $4.7 million in cash. To this core of prominent manufacturers Durant soon attached other automakers (most notably the Oakland Motor Company of Pontiac,

Michigan), truck companies, and automotive suppliers. By 1910 a total of twenty-seven separate firms scattered across Michigan, Ohio,
New York, and Ontario had been brought under General Motors'
control, boosting the holding company's capitalization to more than
$60 million.[26]

In Flint, the six companies acquired by General Motors formed a
well-integrated operation centered on Buick car and truck production, but elsewhere, Durant's expansion strategy was far more speculative.[27] Purchasing supplies on credit, Durant could finance some
mergers with cash drawn directly out of revenues (earned chiefly by
Buick and Cadillac). More commonly, companies were absorbed by
General Motors after an exchange of securities. To make such stock
transfers attractive, General Motors declared healthy dividends, even
though Durant's many questionable acquisitions placed a heavy burden on the firm's capital resources.[28] Of course, these methods left
the holding company with virtually no cash reserves, but Billy Durant
and his closest cohorts felt no fear with demand for new cars running
consistently ahead of advances in capacity throughout 1909.

In the midst of continuous growth in the local automotive industry
and a tremendous spurt in population and general business activity,
most people in Flint retained confidence in Durant's newest efforts.
When Buick needed a million dollars to replace its old engine factory
in 1909, nearly two-thirds of the sum was raised locally in three days,
with Buick workers purchasing over $120,000 in stock themselves.[29]
By 1910 the Oak Park plant employed more than sixty-five hundred
workers, making it the biggest automobile factory in the nation. All
together, in that year, Flint factories employed over ten thousand
wage earners, more than double the number employed in 1908, and
five times as many as were employed in the city at the turn of the century. By 1909 these workers were employed at more than a hundred
industrial establishments, nearly twice the number that existed
in 1899. In addition, the salaried workforce at these establishments
increased dramatically as well. At factories alone, white-collar employment grew almost 800 percent in just ten years, creating a small
but important group of professional managers for the first time in
local history.[30]

This rapid expansion of employment in the automobile industry
generated a tremendous increase in the city's size and population.
From a town of 13,000 inhabitants in 1900, Flint had grown into a bus-
tling industrial city of more than 38,000 people by 1910, and most of

FIGURE 2.　Population Change, Flint 1900–1980

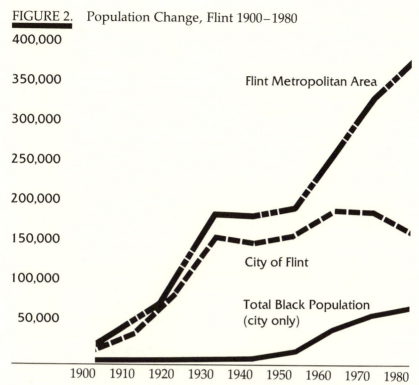

the growth occurred after the opening of Buick's Oak Park plant. Drawn together by the promise of high wages and steady employment in the automobile industry, working people literally swamped Flint's existing housing facilities, splitting shifts in rooming houses and hotels, and even setting up tent colonies that provided homes for more than a thousand families in 1910.[31] For property holders and real estate developers, this boom presented an incredibly lucrative opportunity. Property values soared, and the farm land surrounding the original town was annexed, subdivided, and sold as fast as local capitalists could work. In 1906, a group of businessmen led by Durant and longtime partner, J. Dallas Dort, founded the Flint Improvement League to encourage faster real estate development and promote the extension of necessary public services. The League established regular communications with General Motors during these early boom years, becoming, in a sense, an unofficial housing authority for the automaker. With this kind of backing, the physical expansion of Flint could be rushed to try to keep up with advances in the local automobile industry. Yet despite furious activity that saw seven square miles of farm land annexed, and thirty-two hundred sites plotted and sold in early 1910 alone, demand for new housing continued to outstrip actual construction.[32]

The boom that had begun in 1905 came to an abrupt halt in the summer of 1910 when a brief but sharp recession cut deeply into new car sales. To meet his payroll commitments, fixed costs, and the demands of creditors, while burdened with too many unprofitable operations that had drained cash reserves, Durant was forced to turn to an eastern banking syndicate to save General Motors. The price was high. In exchange for nearly $13 million in cash, the bankers received $6 million in General Motors stock, and $15 million in five-year 6 percent notes. In addition, Durant had to resign as president of the company, although he retained a seat on the five-man, five-year voting trust that was established. James R. Storrow of Lee, Higginson, and Company acted as president until 1912 when C. W. Nash, who had served as president of Buick since 1910, succeeded him.[33]

In Flint, the impact of the General Motors' cash flow crisis was especially severe. By mid-summer 1910, the Buick Motor Company had completely shut down. Construction had also ceased on a half-finished brass and aluminum foundry and another new drop forge. Elsewhere in the city, Weston-Mott and other important automotive suppliers announced big layoffs, increasing the already unprecedented mass unemployment. Of course, Flint's housing boom also stopped suddenly, as local credit dried up and some disillusioned working people simply left town.[34]

Fortunately for the unemployed, the city's economic crisis did not last long. Just three days after the loan to General Motors was approved in early September, one hundred men were recalled at Buick's drop forge, and within a week, new orders for Buick cars totaling nearly $14 million had poured into Flint from dealers all across the country.[35] The longest uninterrupted growth spurt in Flint's automobile boom was just beginning.

Economic recovery brought dramatic changes in the way the city's big automobile factories were run. During the five-year bankers trust, more sophisticated financial controls were imposed on the sprawling General Motors Corporation. The new president, fiscally conservative (some even said tight-fisted) C. W. Nash, had always been troubled by Durant's free-spending, fast-paced expansion policies. Under

Nash's direction, the corporation's top and middle management began to get lessons in the importance of accurate cost accounting and systematic cost reduction programs. In Flint, the most important of these men was Walter P. Chrysler, an extremely talented, self-made production engineer, whose previous experience lay chiefly in the railroad industry. Chrysler was a true believer in the marriage of scientific management and mechanization that would later be called Fordism. He was recruited by Storrow and Nash to rationalize Buick's operations, and he did not disappoint them. "Every minute," he later wrote of this phase of his spectacular career, "we were finding out further ways to adapt carriage-craft operations to automobile building."[36] More than anyone else, Walter P. Chrysler brought the second industrial revolution onto the shopfloors of Flint.

As soon as he took over at Buick in 1912, Chrysler began a rationalization program that raised output and drastically lowered unit and labor costs. Appalled by the lack of rigorous record-keeping and scheduling that he encountered throughout the Buick plant, Chrysler immediately set out to get control of the production process by introducing comprehensive piecework schedules and rigorous, minutely detailed cost acounting and reporting procedures. At the same time, he tirelessly scrutinized actual production operations to find ways to raise Buick's productivity. On his daily early morning tours of the plant, and during frequent shopfloor inspections, Chrysler looked for ways to redesign the work processes that still remained at least partly in the control of skilled traditional vehicle workers. His most effective early efforts were concentrated in the chassis and body shops where many of the skilled workers were located. There Chrysler initiated his rationalization program by eliminating two traditional sanding and glazing operations. A couple of months later he accelerated the painting process by raising the temperature in the drying ovens. Shortly after, Chrysler began to have parts painted before assembly. By the end of 1913, the whole operation had been redesigned so as to introduce what amounted to mass production methods. Since these changes at Buick preceded the introduction of the moving assembly line at Ford, Chrysler's description is worth quoting at length.

Instead of having the whole room filled with tables where frame members were riveted and where other operations proceeded until, one by one, each table supported a finished chassis, we had the vast room empty of all but four or five tables supported on stanchions, with benches close at hand.

Beyond these, extending clear to the far end of the room, was a trough, a pair of tracks made of two by fours. When the chassis was complete with axles, springs and wheels, a little chain hoist was used to lift it off the table to the floor, astride the track; then it was pushed along from hand to hand; two men put the fenders on, others in turn added a gas tank, and finally the chassis got its body. Once we started making cars that way we had the whole scheme of mass production going, although it was some years before people said "mass production." We were just doing it without bothering about terms.[37]

Once begun, this rationalization process seemed to have no end point. "Starting with the assembly line," Chrysler recalled,

we worked our way backward through the plant until everything was tied in. Every new thing was an invention. As soon as one problem was revealed and straightened out, twenty others had arisen. The motors began to get their shapes riding on a conveyor line; then the axles, crankshafts, camshafts; until . . . the men have machines to do their bidding.[38]

Of course, Chrysler's rapid modernization of Buick production could be seen in a very different light, for it both reduced the need for human labor, and therefore created "redundant" workers, and it degraded the skills of the traditional vehicle workers. The negative impacts of modernization on working people had surprising political implications for Flint (which are examined below). But from the perspective of Nash and Storrow and the others who sat on the bankers trust, Chrysler's achievement at Buick was a model for what had to be done throughout General Motors. In 1913–1914, Buick began to set new production records with a much reduced work force. In 1910, it had taken 6,500 employees to produce just over 20,000 cars; by 1914, Buick turned out 42,000 vehicles with only 5,000 people on the payroll.[39]

Despite the shock of mass unemployment and the subsequent reductions of Buick's workforce, as a whole, Flint's economy rebounded strongly in the years preceding the outbreak of the World War in Europe. Buoyed by the strength of the national car market and a reorganized General Motors Corporation, and impressed by the overwhelming triumph of Ford's low-priced Model T, local businessmen continued to pour their capital and energies into the automobile boom. In 1911, William C. Durant and some old associates helped William Little open the Little Motor Company in a factory vacated by the declining Flint Wagon Works. Within a year, Durant had combined Little Motor with the Chevrolet Motor Company, which he and Louis Chevrolet had founded recently in Detroit. In late 1913, while Durant began acquiring another series of automobile companies, Louis Chevrolet closed his Motor City plant to concentrate production of a new, low-priced roadster in Flint. Though just over five thousand Chevrolet 490s (the price as well as the model number) were made in 1914, production nearly tripled in 1915 without coming anywhere near satisfying demand. By September 1915 Durant was ready to use Chevrolet as a lever for regaining control of General Motors when the bankers voting trust expired. Trading five shares of Chevrolet, now a holding company capitalized at $80 million, for every share of General Motors he could lay his hands on, and forging alliances with new major stockholders, particularly Pierre S. DuPont, Durant amassed enough support to announce his control of General Motors in May 1916. Within a month, Nash resigned, and for the second time, William C. Durant took over the presidency of the national corporation that increasingly dominated life in his hometown.[40]

In these same post-recession years, other local entrepreneurs started their own automotive operations, helping to absorb the remaining slack in Flint's labor market. About the same time Durant began his gambit with Little Motor, Arthur Mason, a former Buick engineer, opened the Mason Motor Company in the original downtown Buick engine factory. For a short time, Mason's workmen built motors for Little and then Chevrolet cars, but as part of Durant's consolidation plans, Mason Motors was purchased by Chevrolet in 1915. J. Dallas Dort's quality automobile manufacturing firm, the Dort Motor Company, successfully maintained its independence from Durant and General Motors during Dort's lifetime, but ultimately, it too was swallowed up by the giant automotive corporation. Dort Motor turned out its first vehicles in 1915, two years after Dort mysteriously terminated all business connections with William C. Durant.[41] For nearly a decade, Dort workers, a group that included many highly skilled veterans of the carriage industry, specialized in finely crafted, luxury automobiles for the high-priced market. In addition, the company made trucks and cargo trailers under government contract during World War I.[42] Despite this success and the firm's solid reputation, the Dort Motor Company did not survive its founder's death in 1925. Instead, J. Dallas Dort's factory was purchased by General Motors so that AC Sparkplug could move out of its antiquated facilities and expand its productive capacity.

Beginning in 1911, new investments in the automobile industry by Durant, Dort, and other prominent Flint businessmen rapidly renewed the boom that had stopped so abruptly when General Motors collapsed. During the first two years of recovery, expansion was slow enough for local builders to catch up with the city's housing needs; however, with mass production begun at Chevrolet, the establishment of the Dort Motor Company, and finally, the further expansion at Buick all coming in quick succession between 1914 and 1916, severe labor and housing shortages developed. By the autum of 1916, Flint's industrial workforce included more than nineteen thousand production workers, almost twice the 1910 figure, without anything like a corresponding increase in the city's housing capacity. Hundreds of working people once more set up homes in tents and tarpaper shacks, while perhaps as many as 2,700 other workers commuted from Saginaw and Bay City, thirty to forty miles away.[43] Flint's automobile boom, and thus the transformation of local society, was in high gear once again.

A Challenge "From Below"

Viewed exclusively from the entrepreneurial perspective that has long dominated the history of the automobile boom in Flint, the social and political events that accompanied General Motors' financial difficulties and subsequent reorganization can be passed over as a mere interruption of long-term development trends already set in motion by the transfer of capital and labor from the traditional carriage and wagon companies to the new business of motorcar manufacturing. However, examined from a different angle, with an eye to the creation (or destruction) of class values and a sensitivity to changes in the everyday life of local residents, the recession of 1910 and its aftermath form a crucial moment in Flint's history. During those years of mass unemployment, recovery, and rationalization, doubts about the automobile boom and its social consequences troubled many citizens of the Vehicle City, and in their disillusionment, they gave the local Socialist Party a short-lived, but significant triumph at the ballot box.

Socialists actually began to organize in Flint just after the turn of the century, when local economic activities remained diversified, personalized, and clearly under local control. Although wagon and carriage making was the town's biggest industry by 1900, cigarmaking, agricultural processing, and agricultural services also held important places in the growing local economy.[44] At the time, however, the rapid expansion and the introduction of volume production techniques in the traditional vehicle industry seemed to threaten the balance and intimacy of everyday life in Flint, and as a result, the new Socialist Party of America was able to establish itself among a small contingent of disaffected workers. In 1901, the same year the national party got its start, Flint's first Socialist candidate for mayor garnered a surprisingly respectable total of over four hundred votes.[45] It is likely that most of this support came from the cigarmakers, the town's highest paid and most effectively unionized workers, and from a group of skilled vehicle workers who were fighting (unsuccessfully as it turned out) to establish a local of the Carriage and Wagon Workers Union.[46] Some members of the recently formed and struggling Typographical, Barbers, and Retail Clerks unions may also have given their votes to the first Socialist candidates, because all these organizations had just joined the cigarmakers in a Central Labor Union, which quickly became the sole local public forum for discussing socialism.[47]

In 1902, the party's second year in Flint, the Socialist vote total in the annual April municipal election dropped by more than 50 percent, and for the next four years, Socialist candidates were lucky if they drew more than a couple of hundred votes in a rapidly expanding electorate. By 1907 local organizers seemed to have lost heart. Faced with the beginnings of the automobile boom and the collapse of all union activity in the traditional vehicle industry, Flint Socialists put up no candidates for local office in 1907, 1908, 1909, and 1910. In fact, with the exception of just over two hundred Socialist votes cast in the statewide elections of November 1908, there is no evidence of any public party activity whatsoever in Flint during this boom period of accelerated expansion at Buick and the city's other automotive manufacturers.[48]

In 1910, the financial breakdown of General Motors provided a catalyst for a stunning revival of the Socialist Party in Flint. When Buick shut down completely that summer, throwing thousands of automobile workers onto the streets for the first time (but certainly not the last time) in local history, and when hometown tycoon Billy Durant simultaneously lost control of General Motors to an eastern banking syndicate, Flint's general boomtown optimism suddenly vanished. In the uncertain months that followed the reorganization of the giant automaker, Socialists sensed an opportunity to revive their party organization by capitalizing on widespread dissatisfaction with the pace and quality of recent local growth and fears that power over Flint's economy had slipped into the hands of a distant, impersonal national corporation. Spurred on by an unexpected record Socialist vote in the gubernatorial election in November, a new local organizer, James McFadden, a lawyer, revived the dormant party and began preparing it for the upcoming municipal elections.[49] Over the winter of 1910–1911, regular meetings in conjunction with the Central Labor Union were begun again. In addition, to reach a wider local audience, the party and the political committee of the Central Labor Union pooled their resources to start a weekly newspaper called *Flint Flashes: The Voice of the Exploited Worker*, which sold for three cents a copy.

During the early months of 1911, in their newspaper and at increasingly well-attended public meetings, Flint's Socialists hammered away at the city's severe housing shortage and at the poor quality of public services, placing the blame for both these pressing problems squarely on the shoulders of local businessmen and developers, and on complacent local authorities. At a time when the city was still recovering from the shock of its first major recession of the automobile age, this unprecedented attack caught both Republicans and Democrats off guard, creating political issues that only the Socialists themselves were prepared to deal with immediately. In March, the party nominated forty-five-year-old John C. Menton, a cigarmaker and longtime union member, for the office of mayor. Menton was a charter member of the local Socialist party, and he had helped to establish the Central Labor Union in 1901. In addition to serving as secretary-treasurer of the C.L.U. since its inception, Menton had been secretary of the statewide Socialist party from 1902 to 1905, as well as a Michigan member of the party's national committee. His name topped a full slate of real workingmen's candidates nominated for the April municipal elections. These Socialists ran on a platform that pledged to extend sewers, water lines, and paved roads as rapidly as possible; to regulate housing construction and food purity; and to ameliorate the plight of poorer working people by building a free public bath, a free hospital, and a central market.[50]

To a city that usually voted Republican and had always supported "reasonably conservative" businessmen and professionals, the Socialist campaign presented a truly radical departure from traditional politics, and the major parties tried to ignore it. In the past, a similar approach had seemed to be the best way to handle local socialism, but in the different circumstances of 1911, this tactic backfired. The Socialists' campaign manager, William Jackson, enlisted volunteers who waged a campaign to get out the working class vote in every ward of the city. This tactic was cheap (the *Detroit Tribune* reported the Socialists spent only ninety-seven dollars in the campaign); and it was effective. On April 4, 1911, John Menton was elected mayor by a 582-vote plurality in a three-way race that drew a record seven thousand citizens to the polls.[51] The Socialists also did well in other contests, electing three of the twelve aldermen, two members each to the Board of Supervisors and the School Board, and one justice of the peace. The latter official, a vehicle worker, Bill Adams, was immediately disqualified for his lack of legal training. This ruling returned the incumbent to office, but it did little to diminish the tremendous anti-socialist trauma that rippled through the city's establishment. "No election that the city of Flint has held within its history," editorialized the *Flint Daily Journal*, "has been a source of greater surprise."[52]

Menton and his Socialist colleagues drew votes from all parts of the city, but they ran particularly well in wards populated by both new automobile workers and traditional vehicle workmen. The Socialist vote was strongest among "the factory hands" of the central city's First Ward where an automobile worker named Louis Trafalet easily won a seat on the city council. The party also scored an impressive victory in the Fifth Ward when Orin Castle, a blacksmith for fourteen years at the Durant-Dort Carriage Company, upset that firm's treasurer, Fred Aldrich, in the clearest example of worker versus capitalist conflict of the campaign. The sudden appearance of Socialist majorities in well-established neighborhoods revealed the extent to which the automobile boom had disrupted Flint's older deferential politics. The voting patterns of 1911, the occupational backgrounds of the Socialist candidates, and their platform all suggest that this Socialist upsurge was a genuine, independent working-class response to the early stages of Flint's second industrial revolution.[53]

Once in office, local Socialists tried to create a truly ambitious reform program. To advise him on municipal problems, Mayor Menton appointed a twenty-five member commission that included representatives from all the city's crafts and professions. Some of the measures he urged, like the implementation of stiffer building and health codes and greater efforts to expand parks and boulevards, were relatively noncontroversial. His investigation of corruption at the Flint Water Works and a crackdown on "blind pigs" (unlicensed drinking estblishments) were also generally popular. Yet most of the Socialist mayor's program generated vehement opposition among what became an increasingly well-organized business class. In his first few months on the job, John Menton annunced plans to open night schools for dayshift workers, build a labor temple for union meetings, push for a citywide eight-hour day, and improve the saftey of the city's workplaces. These proposals were unabashedly pro-labor; just as Menton's plans for the municipal ownership of all utilities and the garbage plant, as well as the proposed free public hospital, baths, and market were unabashedly socialist. Opposition to these aspects of the mayor's program was equally ideological, and it formed the basis for heightened business-class consciousness and unity in the years that followed Menton's triumph at the polls.

Anti-socialism gained emotional strength when Mayor Menton attempted to change the image and role of the local police department. Basically, Menton wanted to humanize the police force. As head of the city's police commission he urged the dayshift to cease carrying their clubs because, in his own words, "a policeman with a club in his hand patrolling our streets in daytime looks disgusting and brutish." He also tried to encourage the police to take drunks home rather than jailing them so that workers would not lose their jobs. Lastly, but perhaps most importantly, Menton challenged the color line by nominating George Artis, a black carpenter (who also was a registered Republican), to be police commissoner. This nomination shocked Flint's establishment. Under a page-one headline that simply read "COLORED MAN NAMED BY MENTON," the *Flint Daily Journal* reported that a majority of the alderman "do not propose to have other than a white man holding public office in Flint." Artis' nomination was overwhelmingly rejected by the council, a fate that befell most of Menton's radical program. With just three of the twelve aldermen from his own party, the Socialist mayor spent a frustrating year at city hall. Menton found he could propose his municipal socialist program but he could not deliver it. In the end, he simply could not overcome the intense, multifaceted opposition presented by the local business class.[54]

The nine to three anti-Socialist majority on the city council was at the heart of Menton's political dilemma, but hostility towards him and his reform program took other potent forms. Most importantly, the local press sustained a propaganda campaign against municipal socialism throughout Menton's only year in office. The new owners and the management of the *Flint Daily Journal*, the city's only daily newspaper, launched their especially vigorous anti-socialist campaign in June 1911, regularly featuring red-baiting headlines, and letters-to-the-editor on the front page. There were at least four major themes featured in this political effort. Socialism was atheistic (headline: "SOCIALISM DENIES GOD"); socialism was Un-American (headline: "SOCIALISTS HAVE NO PATRIOTISM"); socialism denied individual freedom (headline: "IT WOULD MEAN MOB RULE"); and finally, socialism would destroy the family (from an editorial: "it's a ballot to give up your home"). Flint's two other regular weekly newspapers, the *Arrow* and the *Wolverine Citizen* generally followed a similar line of attack. Led by the *Flint Daily Journal*, the business class quickly seized the cultural high ground, appropriating to itself the role of defender of religion, the flag, individualism, and the family. As a result, Socialists were constantly forced to speak to emotionally charged ideological issues, even as they tried to enact practical reforms designed to deal with the city's real social and economic problems.[55]

Other more heavy-handed measures were used selectively to prevent socialism from becoming a permanent part of Flint's political culture. General Motors seems to have blacklisted prominent Socialists. For example, Alderman Trafalet was laid off shortly before the election of 1911 and was out of work for seven months. He was rehired for eight weeks, only to be fired when he announced he would stand for reelection. The beleagured Trafalet next took a job under an assumed name at the General Motors' plant in Saginaw. He held that position until his true identity was discovered, and then he was quickly fired again.[56] Apparently, John Menton also felt pressured by local businessmen in his private life. At least this is the recollection of the automotive historian Arthur Pound, who was himself very much a part of the Flint establishment at this time. As Pound boasted much later,

> He (Menton) really didn't do a bit of harm because wise old D. D. Aitken, Flint's foxy grandpa, took hold of Jack by his bank mortgage and gentled him into conservatism.[57]

It is hard to say just how much the business class' hysterical red-baiting and selective arm-twisting actually contributed to the decline of socialism in Flint. Given the weakness of the Socialist position in local government and the party's failure to make good its campaign promises, as well as the slow economic recovery that temporarily eased the housing shortage and related problems, the Socialists probably would have run into difficulty in 1912 against even a weak and divided opposition. Working-class political loyalties, just recently activated by mass unemployment and the campaign of 1911, were not so deeply rooted that blue-collar voters could ignore the combination of the *Flint Daily Journal's* fear-mongering and the appearance of a strong, "progressive" candidate drawn from the city's traditional leadership group. In early 1912, Flint's business class pushed just this sort of challenger forward in the person of Charles Stewart Mott.

The fusion of the local Republican and Democratic parties and the nomination of a full slate of "Independent Citizens," headed by the young millionaire industrialist C. S. Mott, culminated the political mobilization of Flint's business class on behalf of anti-socialism. Running as a reformer and a successful businessman with a reputation for getting things done, the president and majority stockholder of the Weston-Mott Company easily outdistanced three lesser-known contenders in the Independent Citizens' March primary election. Then, to open his showdown effort against John Menton, the millionaire Mott moved quickly to undercut the Socialist's position by presenting himself as "The Candidate of the Factory Men." To dramatize this slogan, he substantially increased wages at Weston-Mott, the city's second largest employer, amid a great deal of hoopla in the *Flint Daily Journal.*[58] Moreover, hoping to co-opt Menton's municipal socialist platform, Mott and his new Independent Citizen's Party announced their own program of public works and municipal reforms. In addition to pledges to provide new schools, paved roads, improved sewer and water services, more parks, and free public baths, Mott also promised "to assist in the passage and enforcement of additional regulations for the proper protection of life, health, and property."[59] In other words, although he acknowledged the problems created by rapid economic growth, Mott offered the voters of Flint businesslike eficiency and regulation as solutions, instead of the public ownership still advocated by the Socialists.

To counter the Independent Citizens' well-organized and well-financed campaign, Menton was forced to rely on the same combination of party and Central Labor Union resources, the *Flint Flashes*, and public meetings that had carried him to victory in 1911. However, in their new role as defenders of an incumbent without an impressive record of municipal achievements, the Socialists turned to party ideology and personal attacks on Mott to sustain their majorities in working-class wards. From the beginning of the contest, Menton and his supporters followed the lead of Ed McGurty, a national party organizer sent in from Chicago. Their platform declared that "the common people must choose between having their lives ruled by an autocracy of wealth or a democracy of industry," and that "no party can represent both classes." They branded Mott "the Flint Representative of Wall Street interests," and tried to dismiss the Independent Citizens as nothing more than the political arm of Flint's big business community.[60] They harped on Mott's close ties to the now banker-dominated General Motors Corporation, and on the fact that he was already a millionaire at the age of thirty-seven. This class-conscious style of attack sharpened in the final days of the campaign, when more specific charges were leveled against the anti-Socialist candidate. The *Flint Flashes* opened this offensive with a front-page banner headline declaring "MOTT IS A CHAMPION TAX DODGER."[61] In the same issue, the Socialists also alleged that Mott intended to squelch their water works investigation and to prepare the city police for a crackdown on potential labor organizers. Finally, Menton and his party worked to make an issue out of local unfair labor practices, especially the blacklisting of Alderman Trafalet and charges of child labor law violations brought by the State of Michigan against C.W. Nash, president of the Buick Motor Company.[62]

Despite this flurry of serious accusations, Mott defeated Menton in the April election by more than 1,500 votes. Although the Socialists still ran well in the downtown industrial neighborhoods, and they returned one of their number to the city council, Menton's tally in the all-important mayoral race fell 1,100 votes short of his winning total in 1911. Most of this shortfall can be traced to "apathy" among former supporters. While Mott appeared to have held onto the combined vote of those who had identified themselves as Republicans and Democrats in the previous election, the overall electorate shrank by more than a thousand voters, almost exactly the extent of the Socialist's decline between 1911 and 1912. Speculation about the reasons for the decline in the Socialist vote must begin by recalling the special circumstances of John Menton's victory the previous year. In 1911, the local economy was still in recession, the city was trying to cope with mass unemployment and poverty, and the business class was politically divided. Then, Socialists were able to persuade hundreds of new voters to give them a chance to correct the unprecedented problems of Flint. However, by 1912, different, but ultimately more familiar circumstances prevailed. The local economy was again expanding, mass unemployment and poverty were declining swiftly, and the traditional power elite, the business class, was fully united in opposition to socialism. Under such changed conditions—what amounts to the political-economic formula for what Warren Harding later called "normalcy"—it is not surprising that the relatively ineffective Socialists lost supporters. Nor is it surprising that the electorate as a whole shrank, because, as a rule it seems, the widening of private material horizons that accompanied the expansion of the second industrial revolution discouraged collective political action among working people.

Immediately after the 1912 election, in an article entitled "Unholy Combination Wins For a Time," the *Flint Flashes* attempted to find a silver lining among the discouraging results. "Driving the old parties together," it suggested,

> is a victory for the Socialists. The mask has been torn off. Now all workers know that these parties stand for the same thing. The Democratic party has been wiped out of existence as far as city matters are concerned.[63]

Unfortunately for John Menton, this postive interpretation of the Socialist's defeat proved to be incredibly naive. In reality, Mott's election in 1912 had actually secured the political power of the local business class, hastened the decline of the Socialist Party, and thus opened the way for the establishment of normalcy in Flint.

When C. S. Mott took office, he rapidly established his progressive credentials by pressing forward with his own version of municipal reform. First, he called in experts from the University of Michigan to evaluate the city's water and sewer systems and to make recommendations for new construction. Protests from property-holders over higher assessments slowed sewage improvements, but a new water filtration plant was begun, and ten miles of city streets were paved. Although a far cry from municipal socialism, these tangible improvements were more than the Socialists had accomplished in their year in office. And Mott was just beginning. Early in 1913, he started a stepped-up campaign against local vice, much to the delight of the city's older residents. He also mounted a successful campaign to build a new YMCA, drew up a new bond proposal, and offered a plan to revise the city charter so as to put municipal administration in the hands of an appointed professional staff.[64]

When it came time to stand for reelection in the spring of 1913, Mott and his Independent Citizens' colleagues quite naturally ran on their record, though this time they called themselves the People's Party. As the only opposition, Menton's Socialists had no alternative except to criticize Mott's record as inadequate while they simultaneously renewed their appeals to the class loyalties of Flint's vehicle workers. Hampered by continued red-baiting, financial difficulties at the *Flint Flashes*, and by the steady expansion of the local automobile industry, Menton simply could not get his socialist message across to the voters he had lost in 1912. As a result, Mott was able to increase his majority by several hundred votes in April 1913, while Menton held onto approximately the same support he had garnered in the previous election.[65] Other Socialist candidates fared just as poorly. In fact, because the People's Party picked up new votes in all parts of the city, not a single Socialist was returned to office. Moreover, Mott's bond issue passed easily in the same election, although his proposed charter revision went down to defeat.

During the rest of 1913, the same year C. S. Mott completed the merger of his Weston-Mott Company with General Motors, the pace of municipal reform quickened. Aided by business confidence in his leadership (something the Socialist Menton could never secure), Mott pushed a whole package of new regulatory laws through the city council. A rudimentary factory inspection code was initiated, and a smoke abatement law was enacted. Finally, at Mott's request, a child welfare ordinance was passed, making city-paid nurses responsible for monitoring health problems among Flint's younger population.[66]

In January 1914, Mott announced that he would run again for mayor in order to complete the task of giving the people of Flint "what they needed in the way of improvements and what I believed and still believe they want."[67] In this effort he could count on the support of many who had aided him in the past, especially leading businessmen from the automobile industry like C. W. Nash. However, by 1914, Mott's ambitious plans for the further expansion of city services in the North End, the purchase of new voting machines, and the resubmission of the city charter revision had fractured the unity of the anti-Socialist coalition. Older residents and small businessmen from downtown had begun to express outrage at the rising cost of civic improvements and municipal reforms designed to upgrade living standards in the booming North End. Led by J. R. MacDonald, a lawyer and Flint resident for thirty-five years, these conservative dissidents deserted Mott in the spring of 1914. Meeting separately as the Progressive Party, they subsequently nominated MacDonald as their candidate for mayor.

Had the Socialist Party still been perceived as a viable political challenger, the old Independent Citizens' harmony probably could have been maintained. Yet it was clear to most local observers that the election defeats of 1913 had dealt a fatal blow to socialism in Flint. After two successive failures at the polls, local Socialist stalwarts simply could not hold their movement together.

Perhaps most importantly, the Socialists had lost control of the two institutions that had given them direct access to the minds of Flint's working people. In the wake of the election debacle of 1913, the Socialists were first driven from power in the Central Labor Union by a coalition of business-oriented unionists who wanted no more involvement with radical politics. Then, to complete their triumph, these conservative union men immediately terminated the Central Labor Union's support for the *Flint Flashes*, forcing the already troubled Socialist newspaper to shut down.[68] Soon after, the newspaper's assets were purchased by George Starkweather, a former Pennsylvania Railroad worker and a member of the International Association of Machinists who had moved to Flint in 1910 and quickly established himself as the city's leading business-unionist. Under Starkweather's direction, the labor weekly resumed publication in August 1913, initially calling itself the *Flint Labor News*, but shortly after changing its masthead to the even more innocuous *Flint Weekly Review*.

In the next two decades, using the *Flint Weekly Review* as his mouthpiece, George Starkweather made himself the unchallenged spokesman for Flint's tiny band of A. F. of L. members, yet he could hardly be called a working-class hero. As the frequent president of the Flint Federation of Labor (the new name for the reorganized Central Labor Union), a vice-president of the Michigan Federation of Labor, and a local Republican activist (he ran for mayor in the 1929 primary), Starkweather consistently used his influence and his newspaper to oppose socialism, strikes, and the organization of local vehicle workers.[69] Far from continuing the *Flint Flashes'* self-appointed role as "the voice of the exploited worker," Starkweather's *Flint Weekly Review* called itself "The Official Newspaper of Flint." It typically praised the accomplishments of local businessmen and the city's many fraternal organizations, while simultaneously urging workers to cooperate with management for the good of the entire community. Like their business counterparts, George Starkweather and his supporters in the local A.F. of L. encouraged Flint's factory workers to trust sustained economic expansion and entrepreneurial leadership to meet their everyday needs. For example, in 1918, when C. S. Mott entered the Republican mayoral primary, Starkweather's labor newspaper endorsed the millionaire industrialist in headlines explaining, "'Mott For Mayor' Should Be the Slogan of Every Citizen Voter Who Desires a Just and Efficient Administration of Local Government for Progressive Flint."[70] In other words, instead of advancing class-conscious independence during World War I and its aftermath, Flint's nominal working-class leaders steered the city's principal labor-oriented institutions, the Flint Federation of Labor and the *Flint Weekly Review*, onto a course that made them paragons of patriotism and business-unionism, and pillars of the local establishment.

Undoubtedly, George Starkweather's rise to prominence and the collapse of the *Flint Flashes* were among the events that encouraged the conservative dissidents within the Independent Citizens' coalition to desert C. S. Mott and to put up their own candidate for mayor. Thus, in March 1914, Flint once again withnessed a three-way mayoral race, but unlike the election of 1911, this campaign did not lead to a surprising Socialist vistory. In fact, it sounded the death knell for socialism in the Vehicle City.

As the campaign opened, both the persistent Menton and the "Progressive" McDonald attacked Mott for his wealth and his connections with Wall Street. Yet this election would not turn on class struggle. The feebly organized Socialists still relied heavily on a party platform that had not been changed since the hard times of 1910–1911, and they were largely ignored. On the other hand, MacDonald's campaign proved formidable because it acknowledged Mott's achievements and the prospects for a continued automobile boom. These conservative "Progressives" resented Mott's riches and connections only because they felt these things blinded him to the concerns of lesser property-holders and of the small downtown businessmen who were the traditional backbone of Flint's Republican party. They wanted to slow down Mott's program for civic improvements in the booming North End, where the expansion of Buick and the other large automobile factories had created neighborhoods that now rivaled the old central city districts in size and political significance. Mott responded to MacDonald's charges of waste and extravagance with a strong defense of his businesslike administration.[71] He produced evidence to show that Flint had the lowest property assessments of any Michigan city, and a 1914 municipal budget of nearly $13,000 lower than the previous year. Still undaunted by criticism of his civic improvement plans, Mott aggressively pushed these forward during the campaign by submitting a new storm sewer extension proposal to referendum.

Ironically, in April, Flint voters approved the storm sewer funding, but turned its author out of office. MacDonald won majorities in eleven out of fourteen precincts, gaining almost 3,200 votes to just 2,445 for Mott. John Menton polled fewer than five hundred votes, a result that convinced the veteran Socialist leader to abandon his quest for a second term in the mayor's office.[72] A popular, genuinely socialist political party would never again appear in Flint as a threat to the business class' dominance of the local political culture. Politically speaking, the way was now cleared for a full-fledged second industrial revolution, including the transformation of cultural values that put an enlarged material self, not an idealized working class and community, at the center of everyday life.

Following the election, a bitter C. S. Mott eased the shock of defeat with a trip to Europe, while disheartened Socialists gave up the battle for local political power. Not surprisingly, once he took office, Mayor MacDonald abandoned all pretense of "Progressive" politics. He presided over programs already established, but staunchly refused to come up with any plans to provide basic services for the thousands of new residents who were streaming into the North End, attracted by job openings in the reinvigorated automobile industry. MacDonald's premeditated unconcern pleased older residents because it held down property taxes and preserved the visible trappings of their privileged status. However, in the outer subdivisions, living conditions deteriorated rapidly. Throughout most of this "village grown overnight into a city," there were still no sewers, no garbage pickups, and no paved roads.[73] In the worst areas, like the notoriously overcrowded section known simply as "the Jungle," hundreds of families paid one dollar down and fifty cents a week to purchase tiny lots for their tents and tarpaper shacks. Elsewhere, homeowners took in lodgers, while many rooming houses converted to double shifts, using every square foot for extra beds. Some young workers endured by cracking jokes about "the town where they sleep them so thick their feet hang out the windows."[74] Many others looked to political leadership to improve the conditions of their everyday lives.

At this point in Flint's history, when a rapid renewal of investment in the automobile industry was lifting the local economy from recovery to boom, these new working people did not embrace socialism as a political solution to their urban problems. In fact, most of the older workers, who had supported the Socialist Party for three or more years at the polls seemed to have given up on this alternative. Certainly they made no public efforts to influence local elections after 1914. Instead, Alderman William G. McKeighan, a politically ambitious twenty-nine-year-old entrepreneur (he ran a drugstore, hardware store, theater, pool hall, and babershop), seized the opportunity to make himself the political champion of the new automobile workers. Building a base of support with an organization that was particularly strong among Irish Catholics, and among recently arrived Poles, Hungarians, and other new arrivals in the North End, McKeighan felt bold enough to challenge Alderman John G. Windiate, the choice of conservative "old Flint," for the now reformed Republican Party's mayoral nomination in early 1915. McKeighan's opposition to local prohibition (including a court appearance for violation of the law) increased his support among the swelling numbers of newcomers. When Windiate proclaimed "the main issue in this campaign is the enforcement of law and order," to please older residents shocked by the "blind pigs" and prostitutes in the North End, McKeighan shrewdly posed as the candidate "for all the people" and won a narrow victory in the March primary.[75]

During the following campaign for the mayor's office, McKeighan's opponent was not a Democrat—that party had not yet reformed. But, a somewhat reluctant Charles Stewart Mott was persuaded by his friends in the automobile industry to run again, although he insisted on maintaining his nonpartisan status. Since both candidates were committed to improving conditions in the recently settled districts, this election turned on personalities and related matters, especially McKeighan's opposition to local prohibition, and Mott's continued demand for a city charter revision creating a city manager. Facing an overwhelmingly Republican electorate and a Republican opponent already considered "the young, handsome hero of the 'North-end new people,'" Mott hoped to rekindle the spirit of independent citizenship that had carried him to earlier successes as an anti-Socialist candidate.[76] However, the time for Mott's kind of liberal-progressive, nonpartisan politics had passed. In 1915, McKeighan won the first of his four widely scattered terms in city hall by a comfortable 1,200-vote margin. Auto workers in the First Ward formed the backbone of McKeighan's majority, but he ran respectably in two of the other three wards. Having successfully promoted himself as the champion of the "little guy," McKeighan would remain a force in local politics for nearly twenty years.

The Failure of Socialism in Flint

In Flint, the demise of the Socialist Party, the reformation of the local Republican Party, and the subsequent election of William McKeighan as mayor inaugurated the period of prosperity Warren G. Harding would soon label "normalcy." For the remainder of the automobile boom, the political boundaries of the anti-Socialist consensus forged by C. S. Mott's Independent Citizens held fast, keeping working-class consciousness from becoming a significant part of the political culture of the new era. This consensus, certainly Mott's most significant achievement as mayor, rested on the political assumption that businessmen alone had the responsibility for directing economic and social development, and on the need to exclude independent-minded working people from public decisions affecting these matters. In 1911–1912, Mott reminded businessmen that they had to offer political leadership and reform solutions to problems created by private economic decisions or they would face a threat to their privileges and power. Aided by the swift recovery from the recession of 1910 and by the class unity among businessmen he helped to inspire, Mott seized the reform initiative from the Socialists in 1912. And they never recovered. Confronted by a united business class ready to act on the problems they had defined, and wed to a platform that did not anticipate such political innovation, the Socialists found themselves abandoned by an electorate made up increasingly of large numbers of newly arrived automotive working people who were anxious to get on with the automobile boom.

Viewed from a distance, the rise and fall of the Socialist Party in Flint might appear to be little more than an isolated moment that expressed nothing more than short-lived emotions; it certainly did not establish any lasting working-class consciousness. Yet this brief political revolt succumbed to more than red-baiting and a loss of enthusiasm. In the very same years during which the Socialist Party and The Central Labor Union emerged, the older industries from which the Party drew most of its strength were rapidly declining. In addition, thousands of new automobile workers, most of those whom had no previous contact with ninteenth-century working-class traditions, poured into the city. Flint's second industrial revolution undercut the economic and demographic foundations of local socialism. At the same time, C. S. Mott's brand of progressive reform undercut the political appeal of municipal socialism. Having lost all support for its alternative vision of social development by 1914, the Socialist Party in Flint completely disintegrated, leaving the city without an institution capable of transmitting ninteenth-century traditions of working-class independence and socialist politics to new generations of industrial working people. Businessmen could once again dominate the economic and political decisions that shaped everyday life in Flint. In short, the failure of socialism made it possible to create an industrial community in which there was simply no place for any expression of working-class consciousness and independence.

4

THE ECONOMIC AND SOCIAL FOUNDATIONS OF NORMALCY IN FLINT

As long as possessions continue to pile up, the worker
can feel that he is moving forward; as long as his wants
do not give out, he can feel that he is ambitious.
—Eli Chinoy, *Automobile Workers and the American Dream*

Normalcy: An Overview

The renewal of heavy investment in Flint's automobile industry,
begun by William C. Durant and his associates in 1913, created a
boom that would quadruple Flint's population in just fifteen years.
Throughout World War I, a relatively brief postwar slump, and two
more reorganizations of General Motors, Flint continued to grow at a
remarkable pace because investors confident in the future of the automobile and automobility continued to pour vast amounts of capital
into the expansion of automotive production in the Vehicle City. At
the same time, these entrepreneurs and a second generation of high
company officials remained politically and socially active. Having
learned from their encounter with socialism that the shape of local society and politics could not be left to chance, Flint's progressive industrial business class tried to create a community free from institutionalized threats to their authority over development decisions. It
was not always easy, but they nearly succeeded. By the late 1920s,
normalcy, the domination of political-economic decision making

by Republican businessmen, appeared to be a permanent condition in Flint.

Prosperity was the key. It enabled businessmen to control civic affairs, establishing a social hiearchy in which every new resident (regardless of cultural background or economic status) deferred to the wisdom and power of the automotive elite. Throughout the 1920s, Flint's leading businessmen made the decisions that had the greatest impact on social relationships and attitudes in the growing city. They directed the fraternal organizations, wartime partiotism, and postwar "Americanization" programs. They also sponsored citywide welfare plans, educational and recreational reforms, and political campaigns. In this heyday of welfare capitalism, their high wage policy helped them to assemble a massive factory labor force that accepted the rigors of scientifically managed piecework without serious industrial protest. Thus, despite some ethnic diversity and very clear economic stratification, a rather homogeneous industrial society, which encouraged individual materialism and deference to business-class leadership, emerged in Flint. Although temporarily disrupted by the appearance of the Ku Klux Klan in the mid-1920s, this business-dominated political culture continued to grow in strength throughout the decade.

Ironically, just as the boom ended, in December 1929, Flint's progressive business class celebrated what should have been one of their greatest political triumphs when voters approved a new city charter establishing nonpartisan elections and a city manager form of government. The product of sustained effort by all segments of the corporate business community, the new charter was supposed to insure the permanence of business-like thinking in municipal affairs. In particular, it was designed to insulate public policy from the uncertainties inherent in the enduring competition generated by William Mc-Keighan's political machine. But the victory was short-lived. In 1930, the collapse of the national automobile market began to force businessmen to strip Flint's working people of the high wages and steady work that had formed the day-to-day underpinnings of normalcy. As a result, the city's business class soon faced challenges to its authority that could not be deflected by the subtleties of progressive politics and welfare capitalism. During the Great Depression, events beyond the control of local businessmen brought normalcy to an end.

Economic Growth and a Local Managerial Revolution

Even before the United States entered the Great War in Europe, Flint's older diversified economy and the intimate social order it supported had been replaced by an economy and society that depended entirely on the booming car and truck market. By September 1916, as one observer noted, "In Flint, there are two great industries, the manufacture of automobiles and the selling of land."[1] And, for the most part, these industries were controlled by the same people. Relentless expansion of the city's automotive capacity throughout the 1920s created a nearly constant demand for new homes and industrial construction that principally enriched those small groups of vehicle-makers and their associates who had bought land cheap before 1908.

During Billy Durant's second reign at General Motors (1916–1921), Flint's place as the corporation's leading production center was assured by steady investments in expansion at Buick, Chevrolet, AC Sparkplug, and smaller local subsidiaries.[2] New automotive capacity and jobs were also created by other members of the city's traditional vehicle making establishment in this prosperous era. While Ford's Model T still dominated the low-priced, first-car market, there was plenty of incentive for Flint's leading carriage and wagon makers to enter the competition in the higher-priced automobile and truck markets. The Durant-Dort Company turned out its last horse-drawn vehicle in 1917, but using its rural sales network, wartime government contracts, and its established name to great advantage, Dort Motors successfully sold two kinds of trucks and the finely crafted Dort automobile until the founder's death in 1925. W. A. Paterson, the city's major carriage producer, also equipped his factory for the new market, and up until his death in 1923, his skilled workers made the highly regarded Paterson car for the Midwest's more affluent driving public. Though neither of these firms survived the 1920s, in their day they created a comfortable way for some of "old" Flint's business elite and craftsmen to make the transition to the automobile age without completely sacrificing their traditional social relationships and status.

In 1917–1918, the addition of war contracts at Buick, AC Sparkplug, and Dort Motors increased the pace of social change in Flint, for rather than abandoning the car for the duration, Flint's industrialists continued to make automobiles and trucks, while borrowing against guaranteed Federal revenues in order to expand capacity to meet War Department demands. For example, under Walter P. Chrysler's reluctant but forceful leadership, the Buick Motor Company actually doubled its passenger car output when it contracted to produce Liberty aircraft engines, tank motors, and truck parts for the war effort. Despite the drafting of thousands of its workers, Buick's total labor force also doubled in just two years.[3] Increases in capacity and employment at other plants were not as dramatic, but overall, local growth was phenomenal. In 1919 Flint factories employed almost 25,000 wage-earners, up from 8,700 in 1914. And by 1920, the Vehicle City's population topped 92,000 persons, nearly two-and-a-half times its size ten years earlier.[4]

The city's well-organized employers were able to attract new workers and their families by advertising high wages, steady work, and homeowning opportunities all over Michigan, the Middle West, and nearby Canada. Flint's Manufacturer's Association had handled general recruitment and operated a free labor exchange since 1900. The following advertisement brought to Flint from Minneapolis by a young worker in the early 1920s seems typical: "Plenty of work in Flint, Michigan, good wages, steady work, and only men interested in helping build up and make a city."[5] Despite the competition from Detroit, Pontiac, Lansing, and other Great Lakes-area automobile production centers, between 1914 and 1920 no serious labor shortages developed in Flint, in part because the region's pool of surplus rural workers and single young men returning from war was so great. In these years, when the number of factory workers in the city nearly tripled, tent colonies and shanty towns were once again thrown up as fast as local speculators could buy and subdivide surounding farm lands. Within the old town, the early automotive-era arrivals and older skilled workers rented out spare rooms, and in a few cases, they actually began to buy up and rent extra houses themselves.[6]

In 1919, at Billy Durant's direction, General Motors established the Modern Development Corporation to build substantial single-family houses for its workers in Flint. Plans were also drawn up for a giant seven-story dormitory, but these were dropped during the recession of 1920–1921, when Durant was driven from the company's highest office. The operations of the Modern Development Corporation were also curtailed in 1920–1921, but over the years it eventually sold 3,200 well-built homes in the Civic Park and Chevrolet Park subdivisions (land that General Motors purchased from the Civic Building Association, a consortium of local speculators).[7] Despite this record, Flint's housing shortage remained critical. As late as 1921, *Polk's City Directory* still listed 651 families living in tarpaper shacks and another 96 in tents. And the urban homesteaders kept on coming throughout the 1920s, providing a healthy market for the services of local developers, real estate agents, banks and construction crews.

Although wartime prosperity accelerated Flint's already soaring growth rate, it also laid the foundations for the end of direct hometown control over the General Motors Corporation, the city's largest employer. In simple terms, the tremendous demand for cars, war-related revenues, and Durant's loose control over corporate finances encouraged almost everyone in the General Motors' hierarchy to make their expansion plans too grandly. Of course, by his example, William C. Durant was a principal offender, but his enthusiasm was not unreasonable. As Alfred P. Sloan, who sold the Hyatt Roller Bearing Company to General Motors in this period, recalled in his fascinating autobiography, "It was easy to be optimistic if you had been in a position to observe the booming growth of Detroit, Flint, and other places where cars were being made; and Durant had seen it all."[8] Moreover, in his defense, it should be added that many of Durant's acquisitions in his tenure as General Motors' president, of firms like Fisher Body and Frigidaire, proved to be very profitable long-term investments.[9]

Durant's worst blunder, the purchase of the Sampson Tractor Company, had cost the giant automaker $42,000,000 by 1920, the same year that the bill for the new General Motors' headquarters in Detroit skyrocketed to $20,000,000 and the firm's division managers exceeded their limits for expansion and inventories by $60,000,000. These problems were not all Durant's fault. In fact, a recent biographer has laid much of the blame for General Motors' financial difficulties in 1920 on the shoulders of John J. Raskob, the finance committee chairman and the DuPonts' highest-ranking representative in Detroit. Nevertheless, as the nation slid into its delayed postwar recession, orders for new automobiles began to drop rapidly, forcing Billy Durant to face another General Motors cash flow crisis. When Durant went to the eastern banks for loans, Pierre S. DuPont (whose company and associates had been buying into General Motors since 1916 with some of their wartime profits) led a stockholders' revolt against Durant's alleged mismanagement. Durant tried to support the price of General Motors stock out of his own funds, while drastically curtailing automobile production, but investor confidence could only be restored by a surrender to DuPont and his allies at the Morgan bank. After absorbing an estimated $90,000,000 in paper losses, Durant finally resigned from General Motors on November 30, 1920.[10]

As compensation, Billy Durant received $3,000,000 in stock and a $500,000 cash loan, but he had finally been driven from power in his own company. DuPont gained some 2.5 million shares of General Motors in the settlement, giving this family commanding control of what soon would become the world's largest, most profitable manufacturing enterprise.[11] To correct the company's immediate financial problems, the Morgan bank extended an $80,000,000 loan to General Motors. Pierre DuPont himself served as president during the initial year of the company's reorganization; he then retired, leaving the company in the extremely capable hands of his energetic assistant, Alfred P. Sloan. Sloan moved quickly to rationalize General Motors. In the early 1920s he eliminated competing models, adopted the Dupont management model based on a multidivisional structure, and urged production designers to emphasize styling and design changes to satisfy the growing market of second car buyers. These decisions, coupled with Ford's reluctance to abandon the Model T, vaulted General Motors into industry leadership in the later 1920s. Since then, General Motors has never been seriously challenged for first place in the American domestic marketplace.

In Flint, the combination of widespread automotive layoffs and General Motors' reorganization left the local economy in disarray for most of 1921–1922. In his efforts to economize, Durant had cut General Motors' total workforce from a postwar peak of 86,000 in late 1919 to just 25,000 workers a year later. In Flint, layoffs were not as severe as those in other General Motors production centers, but more than 10,000 local automobile workers were without jobs in the winter of 1920–1921. Under these conditions, the local housing boom ground to a halt and it was not fully revived until General Motors opened the first of its two Fisher Body plants in the city in 1923.[12]

Recongizing the significance of Flint to the company's operations, the new management of General Motors quickly moved to reassure local investors that the corporation would sustain its commitment to the Vehicle City. Both DuPont and Sloan visited Flint, and pledged $300,000 of General Motors' financing to help erect a Durant Hotel in the downtown business district. General Motors' new professional leaders did cease construction of the company's modern development homes. However, they also expanded the functions of the General Motors Institute, making it into a kind of corporate university where both white-collar managers and engineers were trained for well-defined places in the national organization, and the training of skilled blue-collar workers was regularized under corporate control.[13] Most importantly, General Motors continued to invest in new and upgraded production facilities for Flint.

The cutbacks of 1921–1922 were temporary, and unlike the unemployment crisis of 1910–1911, this time the local recession and the shake-up at General Motors did not create political conflict.[14] Once the national car market recovered in the second half of 1922, old employees were quickly called back. By 1924, total factory employment had topped 31,000 workers, 4,000 more jobs than the previous peak. Buick remained the city's principle employer. Between 1919 and 1928 the Buick factory's maximum capacity was increased from 350 to 2,000 cars per day, while total employment reached 22,000 workers. With William Knudsen, one of C. S. Mott's protégés, directing the division, Flint's Chevrolet production facilities were upgraded. By the late 1920s, 18,000 workers in several Chevrolet plants were turning out 400 motors per day and 11,000 completely assembled cars each month. AC Sparkplug division's output was diversified in 1925 when it moved into a second Flint location; and finally General Motors created the world's biggest body plant in Flint in 1926 when it purchased the underutilized factory put up by Durant Motors and turned it into Fisher Body 1, Buick's sole body-builder. By 1929, the Fisher Body division employed more than 7,500 Flint automobile workers. In that final year of the boom as many as 60,000 men and women found jobs in Flint factories during the peak production periods. Average factory employment would not surpass 1929 levels again until the middle of the Second World War.[15]

Since General Motors' vigorous expansion sustained the automobile boom throughout the 1920s, local businessmen adjusted rather easily to the loss of direct hometown control over the automobile industry. Reaction to Durant's second fall from corporate power illustrates this phenomenon. At the end of World War I, the automotive elite of Flint regarded Durant as "our hero, actual at the start, mythical towards the end—almost a god." Consequently, when General Motors changed hands, there was considerable trepidation among those in "old" Flint who had sunk their savings into Billy Durant's company. A few of these people, small businessmen and some older workmen, grumbled about "them Jews from Wall Street" who had taken over the town's principal industry.[16] But this extreme anti-Semitic reaction appears to have been both isolated and short-lived. As one local historian observed, once the automobile market recovered and General Motors began pouring new capital into the local economy, "Flint's first families, though having little influence in the corporation, equated the city's interests with the corporation's."[17]

The continued presence of Arthur Bishop and Charles Stewart Mott on General Motors' Board of Directors kept Flint's voice alive in company councils, further cushioning the effects of the managerial revolution in the Vehicle City. As men whose careers epitomized the way in which vast fortunes had been made by local entrepreneurs who had tied their investments in the automobile industry to other interests in real estate and banking, Charles Mott and Arthur Bishop remained living links between General Motors' old hometown and the corporation's new professional management. Mott was extremely important in this respect. In his official role as head of the corporation's advisory staff, and as a close friend of Alfred Sloan, Mott could translate his concern for Flint into action. More than anyone else, C. S. Mott shaped the decisions that made Flint the world's second-biggest automotive production center.[18]

The actual timing and the pattern of General Motors' expansion in the city also helped to diminish the impact of the passing of Flint's vehicle-making pioneers. Just as the Flint Wagon Works had formed the foundation for Buick's entry into the city, one after another the automotive companies owned by the original wagon and carriage makers were absorbed by General Motors. W. F. Sewart's body-building plant and workforce had disappeared into Buick as early as 1912. In 1923, Armstrong Steel Spring was bought up, and it was operated as a separate division of General Motors until 1933, when it was taken over by Buick. Also in 1923, most of W. A. Paterson's works and workforce were incorporated into Fisher Body 2, and just two years later, J. Dallas Dort's factory was purchased by the expanding AC Sparkplug division. Finally, as William C. Durant's last automotive holding company, Durant Motors, slid towards bankruptcy in 1926, he sold the giant new Flint Motors factory to General Motors for its Fisher Body 1 plant.[19] Thus, in terms of sustaining growth and employment and fully utilizing existing production facilities, General Motors' continued investments in Flint made the local managerial revolution a relatively painless affair. Between 1915 and 1930, real control over the city's principal industry passed easily from the hands of hometown entrepreneurs to the offices of a distant, professionally managed, DuPont-controlled corporation. Many people mourned the passing of leading citizens like J. Dallas Dort and W. A. Paterson, but with both local stockholders and workers enjoying unprecedented prosperity throughout the 1920s, few voices were raised to protest General Motors' ascendancy.

The Working People of Flint

The growth and prosperity created by General Motors' steady expansion formed the economic basis for normalcy in Flint. Yet the connections between general economic conditions and the specific content of the prevailing political culture were not made simply. To explain how businessmen could dominate local politics and industrial relations and even define the character of citizenship, and to discover why working people accepted this unequal distribution of power virtually without protest, a closer examination of the ways in which the automobile boom changed the everyday lives and expectations of Flint's industrial workers is necessary.

By early 1930, nearly 156,000 people (twelve times the town's population at the turn of the century) had settled in the Vehicle City, while as many as 24,000 others were assembled in four surrounding suburban townships.[20] Though certainly not as diverse as a metropolis like Detroit, during the automobile boom, Flint's population was far from homogeneous. Moreover, in contrast to the first generation of motorcar workers in contemporary Britain, France, and Germany, the new automobile workers of Flint were not recruited from an established industrial labor force that had inherited and institutionalized the class consciousness of an earlier era. Though some who came to Flint had had previous industrial experience prior to the Great Depression, the majority of the new arrivals were entering the factory environment and urban society for the first time in their lives.

Initially migrants from rural Michigan predominated, but soon the widely publicized opportunity to work in Flint's high-paying new industry was drawing people from neighboring states and from Canada.[21] Before 1920, when the local Manufacturers' Association advertised heavily all over the region in competition with similar employers' groups from Detroit and the other Great Lakes automotive production centers, foreign-born workers arrived in large numbers. These immigrant workers were about equally drawn from Canadian (mostly English-speaking), Western European (principally British), and Southern and Eastern European origins (particularly Poles, Hungarians, and Russians).[22] During the 1920s, white and black migrants from the rural upper South, especially Missouri, comprised the biggest blocs of people responding to ads that typically proclaimed "Come to Flint and earn $10 a day."[23] Like the older wagon workers and non-English-speaking newcomers before them, black migrants settled in previously segregated neighborhoods, but the white southerners dispersed themselves throughout the city and surrounding townships, even though their jobs were highly concentrated at Chevrolet and Fisher Body.[24]

Some native-born industrial workers (principally skilled machine tool and die makers, and miners from the copper fields of upper Michigan and the coalfields of the lower Midwest and West Virginia) also came and settled in Flint during the boom, often at the urging of a friend or relative who had already made the trip. Within these small kinship and friendship groups there were a few class-conscious veterans of union activity and strikes, but until the Great Depression, they remained silent, dwarfed in both numbers and influence by the great flood of rural migrants and foreign immigrants. Finally, in the late 1920s and early 1930s many children of the Vehicle City's first generation of industrial workers began to enter the factories, adding a new, potentially militant group to the workforce.[25] In other words, as long as the automobile boom endured, Flint's population of working people remained in flux, a collection of disparate groups and younger individuals at various stages of adaptation to permanent life in this true mass production center.[26]

Throughout the boom years, the heterogeneous nature of Flint's population certainly created what social historians sometimes call "structural barriers" to the development of a unified automotive working class. In the city's most important ethnic districts, fragments of traditional cultures were preserved by family practices, shopfloor friendships, and other neighborhood institutions.[27] The largest groups of non-native English speakers—the Poles, Hungarians, and other Eastern Europeans—settled in the old North End around the Buick factory where most of the men worked. In the 1920s, a much smaller group of Italians established themselves on the south side of Flint, close to the expanding Chevrolet plant. Flint's black population tripled in the same decade, but it remained very small and tightly packed into the traditionally segregated neighborhoods near Thread Lake and Buick.[28] Though a handful of black males obtained jobs at the Buick foundry or as sweepers and janitors in a few of the General Motors plants, for the most part, Flint's black workers had to accept low-paying, menial positions outside the booming automobile industry. As a result, more than any other group, Flint's black population was excluded from the improvements in everyday life felt by most local working people during the 1920s.[29]

Within the Vehicle City's principal ethnic neighborhoods, the church usually provided the most important center for cultural activities which sustained traditional ethnic identities, and consequently, numbed potential working-class consciousness. This was particularly true in the large Polish community, where priests at All Saints Catholic Church (established in 1910) earned a citywide reputation for their regular condemnations of socialism, communism, and radical unions like the I.W.W.[30] Of course, a strong religion-based identity was not the possession only of Flint's Polish Catholics. Organized religion grew with the whole city. By 1920, forty-five churches had been established in Flint, including All Saints, A Hungarian Reformed, two Eastern Orthodox, and three all-black congregations. Ten years later, the total number of churches had more than doubled, with the greatest increase coming among southern Protestant denominations, both black and white. Throughout the automobile boom, religion was invoked to oppose socialism, bolshevism, and other perceived threats to the social order dominated by business and industry. Though there were a few exceptions, as a rule, Flint's clergy did not sympathize with either reform or the labor movement. Generally, in Flint, political normalcy was accompanied and encouraged by the growth of conservative churches and by the use of religious ideas for conservative purposes, including the maintenance of ethnic identity.[31]

In addition to churches, minority groups created other institutions that reinforced traditional identities and social relationships. Four parochial schools contributed to the isolated education of some of the city's Catholic youngsters, away from the influence of the public schools attended by the Protestant majority. More importantly, as communities matured, people within them confirmed their ethnic identities by forming social clubs and service organiztions that exteded traditional group consciousness to new generations. In the North End, where ethnicity was strongest, a Polish National Alliance

Lodge received its charter in 1910. A Hungarian-American Culture Club got started a decade later. In the 1920s, the two organizations carried virtually the entire local population of these ethnic groups on their membership rolls. Other groups organized similarly. By the late 1920s, Flint's Italian community had formed an active Italian-American Club and a branch of the Sons of Italy. Leaders in the city's few black neighborhoods finally banded together to set up a Flint Negro Recreational Council to serve their neglected constituents in 1933.[32]

Everyday economic activities in the ethnic neighborhoods preserved a feeling for the traditional cultures, but their impact was not as clear-cut as those of religion and organized social life. Ethnic grocery stores, butcher shops, bakeries, and other small businesses dotted all of these communities, adding to the insular quality of their lives. However, these small business economies also fostered social hierarchies that mimicked the shape of the wider society. Successful ethnic businessmen tried to make themselves into neighborhood political and social leaders. To achieve this end, some of these ethnic leaders courted the favor of their far more powerful counterparts in Flint's industrial economy. For example, Edward Niedzielski, a Weston-Mott machinist and Polish National Alliance official who had left the factory to set up a prosperous grocery, regularly endorsed C. S. Mott in Polish during that industrialist's many campaigns for public office.[33] Thus, while they worked to maintain aspects of their traditional culture, ethnic community leaders could likewise reinforce the dominant political and social position of the native-born business class. By the early 1920s, this kind of two-sided posture was extremely difficult to maintain because most of Flint's industrial elite fully supported an extensive array of programs designed to "Americanize" the immigrants.

Flint's ethnic and black communities were not extraordinary. Their appearance in this era of rapid industrial expansion conformed to patterns of social development that had been observed in most American cities since the late nineteenth century. Hence, for the minority groups most affected in Flint, a leading social historian's conclusion that "ethnicity provided the major *organizational framework* for workers' adjustment to the pressures of factory labor and city life" seems a fair summary of the facts.[34] Yet, even admitting this much, ethnicity alone cannot explain the lack of working-class activity during Flint's long automobile boom. First of all, ethnic organization was limited to just a small fraction of Flint's total population of working people. On their own the mere existence of these few ethnic communities would not have prevented the great majority of Flint's auto workers from organizing a union. Moreover, ethnic workers themselves were not isolated from the other facets of the automobile boom (including the material prosperity, welfare capitalism, and 100 percent American- ism) that generally blunted the development of working-class con- sciousness. In the later 1930s, Flint's ethnic workers would be eager supporters of the U.A.W.-C.I.O. Thus, viewed in retrospect, in Flint, ethnicity appears to be just one of a variety of ways in which the working people of the 1920s, who did not feel compelled to organize themselves as a class, reconciled themselves to the transformation of everyday life in the industrial city.

It is important to remember that Flint, a genuine twentieth century boom town, was primarily populated by native-born Americans who had migrated from rural areas to find a better life in the city. By 1930, two-thirds of Flint's inhabitants were the descendents of two Amer- ican-born parents; and of the remaining immigrants and children of at least one foreign-born parent, more than half were of Canadian and British lineage.[35] Within this vast white, English-speaking majority, Irish-American Catholics retained something of their original ethnic identity.[36] However, among most of Flint's working-class people, the foremost barrier to working-class consciousness was not ethnicity, but a combination of income differences and status distinctions rooted in the possession of skills and long residence that separated the most prosperous vehicle workers from the majority of more re- cently arrived semiskilled workers, operatives, and laborers in the au- tomobile industry.

Throughout the boom years, skilled workers like toolmakers, die sinkers, and maintenance men earned considerably more than the less-skilled workers who made up the bulk of Flint's industrial work- force. Income differences were greatest before World War I. In 1916, highly skilled automobile workers reportedly averaged up to fourteen dollars per day, while newly hired semiskilled workers received between $2.30 and $3.00 each shift.[37] During the 1920s, as the corpo- ration regularized the process of advancement to both the skilled and lower supervisory ranks, tying individual progress to the passing of courses of study at the General Motors Institute, income differences between skilled and semi-skilled workers were diminished. By the latter part of the decade, the thousands of skilled workers, who still made up at least ten percent of each auto factory's labor force, earned from $2,500 to $3,000 annually. In the same period, some semiskilled workers like metal finishers, painters, and upholsterers took home over $2,000 in good years, but most less-skilled workers earned from $1,200 to $2,000.[38]

Skilled auto workers could count on longer, more regular hours than their less skilled counterparts, and they suffered less from annual layoffs for model changeovers. As a result, their generally higher incomes were more secure, allowing them to pursue material advantages that were closed to most working people. In this materialistic sense, Flint's experience confirms Andrew Dawson's general observation that labor's "skilled aristocrat remained, often meeting mechanization head on, emerging triumphant in the end."[39] But skilled workers in the automobile industry were not able to maintain full control over the work process. Management-established work rules and production schedules gradually eroded much of the craft-based independence that had once distinguisted skilled vehicle-makers from production workers on the more intimate shopfloors of old Flint's carriage industry. Most skilled workers of the later 1920s were really just higher paid wage-earners laboring in a work environment shaped by a distant, generally unseen, rule-making management.

Nevertheless, their craft positions and higher incomes brought real status and material advantages to the skilled auto workers of Flint. Most owned their own homes, usually comfortable old houses in the residential districts near downtown, or newer structures built on the city's northwest side (by the Modern Development Corporation and other developers) after World War I.[40] Since the relatively high earnings of Flint's skilled auto workers were not as susceptible to the fluctuations of the industry's business cycle as the earnings of the less skilled, over time these working people were able to accumulate considerable savings. In Flint, older skilled workers commonly made investments in real estate and in the companies that employed them. By the 1920s a few of these veteran workers had left the factories to establish small businesses; others leased one or more houses to newer arrivals.[41] In addition, many skilled workers held an interest in General Motors that they had either purchased during one of Durant's early promotions or through the companywide savings and investment plan, instituted in 1923 as part of Alfred Sloan's welfare-capitalist reforms.[42]

Extraordinary as these material achievements probably seemed by the turn-of-the-century standards that prevailed when most auto workers of the 1920s were children, they were not unusual in booming Flint. During the 1920s a great number of semiskilled automobile workers were able to build or buy their own homes.[43] Despite erratic annual earnings, some less-skilled workers also achieved a fragile kind of financial security by putting money in the bank or in the company's savings plan. For example, Emmet Gardner, a Buick sheet metal finisher whose annual earnings averaged $2,089 from 1923 to 1929 (from a high of $2,590 in 1923 to a low of $1,735 in 1925), was able to pay for an $8,000 home, put money into the savings and investment plan, and make other stock purchases before the Great Depression undermined his financial situation.[44] Yet, neither this kind of worker nor the later-arriving skilled workers could enter Flint's real laboring elite because they lacked the social status that stemmed from a long residency in the city and close association with the city's automotive elite. In other words, in Flint, although objective material standards did broadly define a local "aristocracy of labor," those standards were not the only souce of their status and influence in the political economy. Long local experience and even limited social connections with the business class still mattered greatly in the determination of a certain kind of blue-collar status during the 1920s.

The sustained political influence of Flint's labor aristocracy stemmed from the limited social relationships certain skilled workers maintained with the city's business elite. The most prominent members of Flint's aristocracy of labor consisted of some of the original carriage and wagon workers who had made the transition to automotive production, many of the exceptionally mobile skilled workers who had arrived before World War I, and the older (building) tradesmen associated with George Starkweather's Flint Federation of Labor. Most members of this influential group earned high wages at Buick or one of the smaller independent firms that eventually were absorbed by General Motors. For them, allegiance to the automobile companies was rooted in personal loyalties and friendships. In the factories, older skilled workers were frequently on a first-name basis with supervisors and managers who had been recruited from their own ranks. As Arthur Pound recalled, "a good many steady old hands from the carriage factories went over to automobiles, found better jobs, and kept on rising."[45] The quarter-century-long automobile boom in Flint created a long-term need for managers and lower-level supervisors, which (given the underdeveloped state of the management profession at the time) could only be filled from the shopfloor. Charles W. Nash's ascent from a dollar-a-day trimmer at the Flint Road Cart Company in 1890 to general manager at Buick in 1910 and to president of General Motors in 1912 was certainly the most dramatic example of this kind of mobility, but many other more humble success stories abounded, and not surprisingly, these were often used by business leaders to proclaim the virtues of life and work in Flint.[46]

As the city grew, leading businessmen and company officials gradually segregated their residences from those of even the most prosperous blue-collar workers, but they still shared memberships in a variety of men's social clubs and this prolonged some of the intimacy of the carriage and wagon making era. The Board of Commerce, Manufacturers' Association, and Rotary club provided places where the city's older industrial entrepreneurs, professionals, and small businessmen could meet on a regular basis with the newer corporate managers; fraternal groups like the Elks, the Oddfellows, and several Masonic lodges sustained social ties among veteran workers and some members of the business class. The Masons were particularly important in this respect. The Masonic conections were first made in the 1890s, when many vehicle workers shared lodge duties with leading businessmen, such as William C. Durant, J. Dallas Dort, D. D. Aitken, and Arthur Bishop.[47] By the 1920s, even though Billy Durant had departed, the fraternal links between the automotive establishment and Flint's aristocracy of labor remained significant. For example, in 1923 Buick furnished fifty cars and Chevrolet supplied its fifty-member company band to the local Knights Templar when they hosted that organization's statewide meeting. And throughout the decade, the *Flint Weekly Review*, skilled labor's "official" voice in the Vehicle City, energetically boosted both the Masons and the Oddfellows in regular news features on lodge activities.[48]

Considering their economic situation and special social status, and their own history, it is not surprising that the leading members of Flint's aristocracy of labor were ideologically wedded to the local business class. They had after all joined the coalition against John Menton's socialism before the war, and throughout the automobile boom they continued to oppose any movement that might be considered socialistic. Because workers generally abstained from direct competition for public office and thus did not often make "news," it is difficult to gather firsthand testimony about the local labor elite of this period.

Nonetheless, a comprehensive reading of the *Flint Weekly Review* covering the years from the outbreak of World War I to the Great Depression leaves no doubt that the leaders of the tiny Flint Federation of Labor closely followed the political opinions of leading Flint businessmen, especially progressives like C. S. Mott. During the war, George Starkweather's labor weekly and the local labor federation strongly supported war bond campaigns organized by J. Dallas Dort and the Board of Commerce. In these campaigns, business-class progressivism was easily fused with the superpatriotism required to sustain the nation's intervention in the world conflict. In fact, with the help of its prospering auto workers, Flint achieved the highest per capita subscription rate of any city in the United States.[49]

The experience of sharing in the creation of a wartime patriotic consensus prepared the way for Flint's labor leaders wholeheartedly to endorse the combination of welfare capitalism and "Americanization" that the business elite pressed upon automobile workers after the war. Both as a sociologically distinct group and as an active political force, Flint's "aristocracy of labor" impeded the development of a unified working-class consciousness for the duration of the automobile boom. In this sense, the political impact of organized labor's elitism was similar to that of ethnicity. However, in contrast to the ethnic groups who organized (at least partly) to protect their native cultures from the 100 percent Americanism of the business class, Flint's politically conservative skilled workers assisted Americanization efforts. Indirectly, the visible material achievements of the established skilled workers served as a model of success for other workers who were just entering the new consumer-oriented industrial economy. More directly, through their political activity, the labor spokesmen of Flint reinforced the welfare-capitalist programs, the nativism and the progressive political reforms by means of which business leaders tried to shape local society and culture.[50] As a result, the thousands of new industrial workers who had moved to Flint were denied contact with traditions of nineteenth century working-class independence. Their class traditions, if they were to have any, would arise primarily out of twentieth-century experiences.

A Consumer-Oriented Society Takes Shape

Though certain groups of Flint's working people preserved fragments of their traditional cultures throughout the automobile boom, as the city grew, the city's population became a more and more homogeneous society. To a large extent, the specific cultural content of the 1920s was the result of deliberate public programs formulated by the city's industrial leaders in order to maintain their control over all aspects of Flint's development. For this reason, normalcy cannot be viewed simply as either an evolutionary "stage" in, or a "spontaneous" response to, the automobile boom. However, the sucess of welfare capitalism and "Americanization" in promoting cultural homogeneity in Flint was built upon mundane foundations. Both the migration experiences most working people shared and the increasingly similar circumstances of everyday life and work encouraged the growth of similar material values and aspirations. By the 1920s, the nation's economic and social life reflected widespread dedication to the materialistic, pleasure-oriented livestyle popularized by mass advertising and the new mass media, especially illustrated magazines and the movies. In prosperous Flint, the new consumer-oriented culture developed quickly. There, most working people learned to see themselves as genuine participants in a new consumer-oriented society. In this matter, it is most important to note that the individual's perceptions and desires, not actual material possesions he or she had or had not accumulated, were critical. As Warren Susman wrote shortly before his death, "It is not a question of whether such abundance was a real possibility. The significant issue is the belief that it was."[51] In fact, in Flint, this belief in consumer-oriented abundance amounted to a new American Dream, which served as the primary ideological cornerstone of the political economy of normalcy.

Regardless of their backgrounds, most workers migrated to Flint because they believed the move would improve the material conditions of their lives. For the many who had found rural life hard and unrewarding, the widely advertised promise of high wages and home ownership in Flint was extremely attractive. Early twentieth-century rural America was not the bucolic utopia conjured up by some romantic reformers today. The unelectrified farms and small towns of that era were often a frustrating place for common working people. Opportunity seemed to lie in the bright lights of the city and the new technology of the factory, not on the land or in the mines and forests they knew all too well. In 1934, when a Buick assembler was asked by investigators from the National Recovery Administration to explain why he had left Michigan's Upper Peninsula nearly twenty years earlier, his answer reflected the kind of experience that had brought many auto workers to Flint. "I used to work on a farm there," Rhein-hold Draheim remembered, "and they called for men here. I was working on shares. I had no farm, and I just rented it, and I could not make a living."[52] In Flint, a working person like Draheim could (and in his case did) "make a living," which eventually included owner-ship of a house and a car. Of course, not all of Flint's auto work-ers came straight from the farm. With industry booming throughout the Great Lakes region, many working people took an indirect route to their eventual destinations. Indeed, young workers commonly moved from job to job before finally settling down at a company where conditions were tolerable.[53] But throughout the boom years, it was usually the vision of material plenty that initially led working people to the automobile production centers of the Midwest. In this sense, the auto workers of Flint (and elsewhere) were part of a self-selected group. Whether the immediate catalyst for their migration was a manufacturer's notice, the glowing report of a relative or friend who had preceded them, or even problems with a previous em-ployer, most working people who moved to Flint shared a similar set of material expectations and a similar instrumental view of factory la-bor. For them, success could be measured in terms of improved in-come and the things they could buy with it, and extended leisure time and the pleasure they could derive from it. As they saw it, industrial work was principally a means to this kind of individual fulfillment, not part of a craft tradition that conveyed its own standards of value. Hence, these truly modern industrial workers accepted the rational-ization of the work process as long as their earnings improved and their absolute physical and psychological limits were not tested. "It was pretty hard work in Buick in 1916, 1917, and 1918 already," re-called Lauri Niemimen, a metal finisher (and homeowner) who moved over to Fisher Body in 1923, "but still we had such a big price."[54] There is little reason to doubt that the pragmatic individual materialism implicit in Niemimen's recollection shaped the attitudes of most Flint auto workers towards their jobs in the 1920s.

Radical union organizers, who viewed the situation of the auto-mobile workforce quite differently as the epitome of what Marx had called alienated labor, could never really understand, and therefore never reach, their potential constituents. Lester Johnson, a represen-tative of the Auto Workers Union who was unable to establish even a skeleton local in Flint during the 1920s, remained confused thirty years later. After partially blaming his failures on the Communist faction that took over the union's leadership in that period, Johnson remembered,

> of course, that got along in 1925, '26, '27 when there were good times, when the workers did not need an organization. They needed it but they did not *feel* they needed it because they were making good money. They could quit one job and go over and get another job. . . . So even if the communists had not come into the organization it might have petered out.[55]

Indeed, since the union had already been ignored by the vast majority of workers even prior to the Communists' ascendency, it is likely that auto workers' satisfaction with their own individual material progress continued to be ⎍ e fundamental reason for the organizational failures of the period.

Looked at from a Marxist perspective, the professed contentment of Flint's working people during the 1920s appears to be a classic case of "false consciousness." Yet, when it is applied to this particular historical situation, the term obscures much that is significant. Most importantly, if the "false consciousness" of Flint's workers is stressed, the dramatic qualitative improvements in everyday life during the 1920s can easily be underestimated or even ignored. Moreover, emphasis on "false consciousness" obscures the extent to which working people's trade-off between alienated labor and participation in the new consumer-oriented lifestyle was calculated and conscious. Local automobile workers (estimated to be 96 percent of the men and 62 percent of the women employed in local manufacturing in 1925) made significant material gains, despite the uncertainties of an industry tied so closely to consumer confidence.[56] In the first half of the decade, the annual earnings of most auto workers fluctuated dramatically. The postwar depression of 1920–21 cut deeply into workers' take-home pay, but prices also fell rapidly, somewhat cushioning the effects of mass layoffs and short-time. The boom was fully renewed by 1923–24, the years of the first big migrations from the South; and since prices remained rather stable for the rest of the decade, real wages actually improved a bit.[57] This was probably truer in Flint than it was elsewhere, because money wages were less "sticky" in the automobile industry than in most other industries. Brief recessions in mid-1924 and late 1925 again held down the annual earnings of many auto workers, though the impact of these short-lived slumps was not nearly as severe as the depression of 1920–1921. Finally, in the last

FIGURE 3.   Food Price Index, May 1919 – December 1933

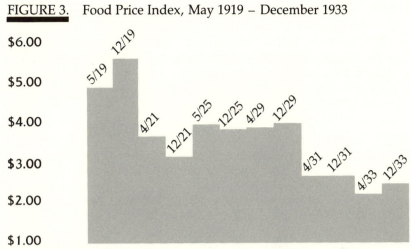

NOTE: Each bar shows the price of a market basket of food (1 pound sliced bacon, 2 pounds round steak, 1 pound coffee, 1 pound butter, 4 loaves white bread, 2 cans of corn or peas, 2 cans pork and beans, 2 cans condensed milk, 1 sack flour) as advertised by Flint's leading food stores in the *Flint Daily Journal*. This market basket survey is not meant to represent a typical, or a balanced diet. It is meant to illustrate the general movement of food prices during the peak of the automobile boom and early years of the Great Depression.

four years of the decade, both the wages and earnings of most of Flint's automobile workforce reached the levels that would be remembered as prosperity in the midst of the Great Depression.

Comparing the annual earnings of Flint auto workers in the late 1920s with the authoritative income standards for a family of five first set down by Paul Douglas in *Wages and the Family* in 1925 gives a clearer picture of the Vehicle City's relative prosperity.[58] First, it seems certain that none of Flint's automobile workforce lived below Douglas' "poverty" line, although a Brookings Institution study done in 1929 found 21 percent of the nation's families did. Moreover, very few, if any, auto workers and their families lived under the "minimum subsistence" standard (sufficient to meet physical needs with nothing left over for emergencies or pleasures). Douglas defined this level as a family of five living on an income of $1,100 to $1,400 per year. In Flint, women workers at AC Sparkplug and the other big plants had the poorest incomes in the industry. During the recession year of 1925, a Department of Labor study found the median earnings of Flint's female auto workers located on the low end of Douglas' "minimum subsistence" scale. However, very few women in the local auto industry were supporting a family of five on their incomes. The majority were young (under twenty-five) and single, and lived at home, or alone in groups in rooming houses. Married women made up another one-fifth of the female workforce in the automobile factories. Typically they told investigators their earnings were needed to supplement their husbands' earnings.[59]

Some unskilled male auto workers also had annual earnings in the "minimum subsistence" range. However, their wages seemed to have improved enough in the late 1920s to have pushed up their living standards.[60] By contrast, the Brookings study of 1929 placed another 21 percent of the country's family units in the "minimum subsistence" category. It is a measure of Flint's great prosperity, that while two-fifths of the nation lived at or below the "minimum subsistence" standard, very few of its industrial workers experienced the material problems associated with extremely low earnings.

Most Flint auto workers had annual earnings during the late 1920s sufficient to give them what Douglas called a "minimum health and decency" standard of living (one that supplied adequate food, housing, and clothing and a modest amount for recreation). Douglas claimed a family of five could achieve this standard of living on an income of $1,500 to $1,800 per year, about what most less-skilled male auto workers earned in the period. However, many workers in the higher semiskilled categories exceeded this level throughout the 1920s by working long, hard hours to maximize on their piece rate pay. Metal finishers, painters, trimmers, and other semiskilled body shop workers commonly exceeded $1,800 annually during the last decade of the boom.[61] On Douglas' scale, the earnings of these workers topped "minimum health and decency," but they did not reach "minimum comfort" (the so-called "American standard"), which began at $2,500 a year. In this era, about 30 percent of the nation's families attained this "American standard" of living, including virtually all of Flint's highly skilled auto workers.

Although this comparison of annual incomes demonstrates the relative prosperity of Flint's industrial working people rather forcefully, it still underestimates the actual material welfare of most auto workers in the second half of the 1920s. First of all, Douglas' definitions of living standards were for the then typical family of five, while the average family in Flint was much smaller than those in most other industrial cities.[62] Many Flint auto workers were either single or recently married in this era, so it was fair to assume that their disposable incomes were much higher than Douglas' definitions would allow. Moreover, many local auto workers' families had more than one income-earner, a pattern that developed in the uncertain years of the early 1920s. By 1925, nearly two-fifths of the city's working women (about 10 percent of the total labor force) were married. Government investigators discovered that most of these married women worked "because the earnings of their husbands were insuffieicnt to support the family."[63] Their willingness to work reflects the higher material expectations raised by life in Flint, not an absolute need, since the earnings of most workers were sufficient to keep their families out of poverty. It was also common practice for auto workers with large families to take in one or more lodgers to supplement their incomes and help with house payments. Indeed, of the nearly nine hundred auto workers' homes surveyed by U.S. Department of Labor researchers in 1925, 30 percent had at least one lodger living with the family.[64] Finally, as has already been noted, many of the semiskilled and highly skilled auto workers in the higher income brackets derived added income from savings and investments. Thus, it is fair to conclude that by the later 1920s, when some new cars still were sold for less than $500 and many local houses were priced at under $3,000, Flint's working people had achieved the ability to meet their basic needs and had set aside considerable disposable income for recreation and other nonessentials. In other words, in real measurable terms, they had the potential to actually become modern consumers.

Besides income levels, there are other strong indications that everyday life in Flint during the 1920s had changed enough to consider the city to be a true consumer-oriented society. The smaller families and the large number of two-wage-earner households foreshadowed developments that became national in scope after the Great Depression. Likewise, the patterns of widespread homeownership and residential sprawl pointed towards the kind of suburban growth that would characterize the full-blown consumer society of the post-World War II era. "The city has spread out and become one of detached houses and small apartments," noted the Labor Department study published in 1929.[65] As working people purchased houses in the fringe areas, or sought lower rents in less conveniently located districts, the central core of old Flint came to contain a progressively decreasing proportion of the city's total population. In addition, during the 1920s, the four townships immediately surrounding the Vehicle City more than doubled in size, becoming the first real suburbs of metropolitan Flint.[66]

As the city spread out over an ever larger area, automobile ownership and use grew accordingly. By the time of the Great Depression, private cars were the principal links between individual households and the rest of the local economy. A survey done in 1936 by city planners (the first time such data were collected) showed that fully two-thirds of Flint's auto workers depended upon the motorcar to get to work. And, more than half of these blue-collar commuters drove to work alone in their own vehicles.[67] Since other circumstantial evidence suggests that the depression forced at least some auto workers to abandon their cars, it seems likely that this pattern of commuting, so typical of modern consumer-oriented America, was established in the 1920s.[68]

The vitality of recreational businesses in Flint prior to the Great Depression was yet another sign that this industrial city had moved into the consumer-oriented era. As early as 1916, the Vehicle City supported fifteen movie theatres and six dance halls. Economic problems drove about half of these facilities out of business in 1920–21. However, by the mid-1920s, the city once again had fifteen flourishing theatres, and the newest ones were far bigger and more elaborate than their pre-war predecessors.[69] Flint's central welfare-capitalist organization, the Industrial Mutual Association, also managed a booming recreational trade. By 1925, its downtown bowling alleys, pool rooms, and dance hall drew from three thousand to five thousand working people every Saturday night. Encouraged by this kind of attendance, the I.M.A. erected a six-thousand seat auditorium in 1929 for shows and other cultural events. Unfortunately, the economic collapse of 1930 quickly turned the facility into a white elephant when hard-pressed workers who had purchased subscriptions demanded refunds.[70]

Perhaps the most convincing evidence of Flint's new consumer-oriented popular culture can be found in the U. S. Department of Labor's study of the city's working women that was conducted in 1925–1926. The government's investigators discovered a genuinely modern kind of individual materialism was guiding the life-shaping decisions of women workers. First, almost all the women in industry had not bothered to finish high school; in fact, only a third had gone beyond eight grades of formal schooling. Interviews with hundreds of working women revealed that jobs in the auto factories were most desired simply because auto workers' earnings were high. Even office work, which could provide earnings comparable to those of most female auto workers, was shunned, because the special courses needed for such work would have delayed the achievement of personal independence and material gratification.[71] The study also showed that the young single women who comprised the bulk of the city's female labor force regularly ate their meals in restaurants (even though Flint was "not an eatery center.") More significantly, these same women placed an extremely high priority on buying new clothes to keep up with the latest fashions, and they often went into debt to stay in style. The report's authors traced this fashion consciousness to the widespread belief that most men "naturally favored the better-dressed girls."[72] It is impossible to demonstrate a direct link, but this kind of thinking must have been influenced by the new style-oriented mass advertising that was proliferating in the newspapers and magazines of the day.[73] Furthermore, the observations of the Labor Department's investigators show just how far the extension of credit to ordinary working people had gone in Flint by this time. Previously, the banks and General Motors had offered loans to workers for houses and new cars. Now, in the mid-1920s, local retailers had set up installment plans for even the lowest-paid group of industrial workers.

Dramatic material improvements in everyday life affected the values of almost everyone in Flint during the automobile boom. Like their female counterparts, most of the men who worked in the Vehicle City's factories embraced a consumer-oriented, instrumental view of their jobs and a strong desire to partake immediately in the "American Standard of Living." Some looked to work their way up through the ranks to more skilled positions, and a few took advantage of the opportunity to advance as foremen or supervisors. For these workers, the company provided training and education at the General Motors Institute; and, as long as the boom endured, these goals generally could be attained.[74]

Yet, most auto workers were not career-minded in the traditional middle-class sense of the term. Extended formal education and long training programs delayed the attainment of the material expectations that were building up during the 1920s, so many auto workers simply avoided them.[75] These modern worker-consumers had already learned to define personal advancement interms of the acquisition of a house (a rather traditional goal), a car, and the other new mass-marketed durable goods that industries like their own were beginning to pour into the American marketplace. For them, high wages and the kind of steady work that increased purchasing power and leisure time pleasures, not white-collar status, were what mattered most about a job. When explaining why he had left a promising position as a store manager to work at Buick after World War I, Arthur Case frankly recalled, "the big money in the factory took me back to the plant again."[76] The individual materialism and instrumental view of work revealed in this recollection were typical of the new consumer-oriented outlook on life that emerged in Flint during the last decade of the automobile boom. As long as the prosperity continued, these values formed an insuperable barrier to the development of independent working-class consciousness and organization. They were, in other words, essential to the politics of normalcy.

5

THE POLITICAL CULTURE OF NORMALCY IN FLINT

There is no reason why Republicanism should offer the prospect of complete equality, or why it should cultivate a distaste for luxury, refinement, prosperity and amusement. . . . People do not wish to be all alike. Each person desires to be the equal of a king or better.—*Flint Daily Journal*, June 9, 1924

Welfare Capitalism and Americanization

Although the common private pursuit of higher material living standards formed the everyday basis for creating a more homogeneous, consumer-oriented society in Flint, the public character of that society was shaped more directly by the same group of progressive businessmen who had led the fight against socialism before World War I. Prior to the Great Depression, these class-conscious business leaders dominated the institutional life of the city. They built up an elaborate network of privately sponsored welfare programs, insurance plans, community action groups, and charitable organizations to make Flint a place where working people could adjust to urban, industrial life without demanding public welfare programs or independent working-class actions. The city's industrial-financial elite also tried to control local politics, but they had less success handling challenges to their control of the Republican Party that arose on the far right and from William McKeighan's rejuvenated, political organization. Businessmen like J. Dallas Dort, C. S. Mott, D. D. Aitken, and William

Ballenger were not autocrats, motivated simply by a will to power and a desire to protect their economic privileges. Instead, their attempt to control social and cultural change after World War I reflected a complicated set of motives, including a genuine concern for the well-being of Flint's working people that was consistent with Mott's earlier reform program and with local paternalistic traditions.

Welfare capitalism in Flint had its origins in the relative intimacy that existed between employers and workers in the turn-of-the-century carriage and wagon industry. As Arthur Pound recalled,

> Employers made a point of keeping in close, personal relations with their men; boosted mutual insurance funds; supported athletic teams and workers' bands; gave away turkeys at Christmas; and tapped the till promptly in case of emergency need.[1]

By the 1920s, the intimacy between boss and workers was gone, but local paternalism had spawned one of the most comprehensive welfare-capitalist experiments in the nation. Skilled workers derived most of the benefits from the Savings and Investment Plan, the General Motors Institute, and the Modern Development Corporation, which were all directly administered by the giant corporation. This distribution was probably intentional. General Motors depended on skilled workers twelve months of the year, and these programs helped to ensure their loyalty by binding their personal finances and advancement opportunities closer to the company.[2]

Skilled and less-skilled workers alike were included in the programs and insurance coverage provided by the Industrial Mutual Association. This citywide organization had its roots in the Flint Vehicle Factories Mutual Benefit Association, a worker-managed mutual insurance plan that was set up in September 1901 at the suggestion of J. Dallas Dort and other manufacturers. The catalyst for this employer initiative had been the formation of the local Socialist Party and a Central Labor Union resolution in favor of organizing all workers in the carriage and wagon factories.[3] Initially, this insurance plan required modest weekly dues that were scaled according to skill, and it provided similarly graduated benefit payments in the event of sickness, injury, or death. For many years, enrollment was not mandatory, but workers were strongly advised to sign up when they took a new job. About three-fourths of the eligible workers did so in 1914. By that year, the organization had already paid out $120,000 in benefits.[4]

In 1912, a year in which the state's first "elective" workmen's compensation law went into effect, the Manufacturers Association (which also ran the central employment exchange) augmented the insurance offered by the Mutual Benefit Association. For an additional annual payroll deduction of $1.20, standard benefits could be extended beyond the usual thirteen weeks up to a maximum period of twenty-four months.[5] Together, the two group insurance plans offered to Flint workers provided a kind of minimum social security, which worked well in normal times. However, in periods of mass distress, the program could not meet the demands for benefits. Of course, unemployment insurance was never offered by either organization, but during the worst months of 1910–1911 and 1920–1921, the worker-dominated board of the Mutual Benefit Association diverted a little cash into a program that distributed meager food and coal allowances to members. Moreover, in the event of some natural disaster, factory managers seemed to have some power to supplement the welfare benefits of their employees. This was certainly the case during the flu epidemic of 1919–1920 which struck down hundreds of workers at every plant. Such activities were well-publicized, and quite naturally prolonged the paternalistic reputation of local management.[6]

Other welfare-capitalist programs were also initiated in this period. In 1910, a Flint Vehicle Workers Club was formed to provide recreational facilities and a small loan service for the local aristocracy of labor. This club strengthened ties between traditional carriage and wagon workers and newly arriving skilled auto workers, but it did not reach out to most factory employees. In 1916, to fill this gap, employers started an Industrial Fellowship League that offered the same kind of services as the Vehicle Workers Club plus educational courses under the auspices of the YMCA. Three years later, the league's industrial training classes were separately incorporated as the Flint Institute of Technology (the immediate forerunner of the General Motors Institute). However, its recreation programs, loan services, and Americanization efforts continued at the "Y".[7] Finally, in 1923, the Vehicle Workers Club, the Industrial Fellowship League, and the various group insurance plans were combined into the new citywide Industrial Mutual Association. Membership in the I.M.A. was made mandatory for virtually all Flint factory workers, including those employed by General Motors. In addition, the giant corporation made the I.M.A. the sole local administrator for the group life and health insurance plans it inaugurated in 1926.

When viewed in retrospect, it is clear that the complex network of welfare-capitalist organizations created in Flint had an important impact on the political culture of the newly emerging industrial order. By anticipating workers' needs for mutual insurance, emergency financial help, recreation, and adult education, Flint's industrial employers gained a degree of control over these programs that would not have been possible under *laissez-faire* conditions. Seen in this light, welfare capitalism in Flint usurped the kind of "friendly society" functions that had often been the nucleus of independent working-class organizations in the past. As the shop newspapers and the *Flint Weekly Review*, the "official voice of local organized labor," constantly reminded them during the 1920s, auto workers did not have to set up their own welfare organizations since employers had already done it for them.[8] Because it had been put into effect as a complement to high wages and tolerable working conditions, welfare capitalism in Flint helped smooth the auto workers' transitions to permanent life in the industrial city while increasing their dependence on business initiatives. It was thus a very significant structural barrier to the development of an independent citywide working class.[9]

It is not enough to judge welfare capitalism as just another industrial relations technique. The author of the most comprehensive study of welfare capitalism suggests that its ultimate goal "was no less than the propagation of an improved American working man."[10] Some aspects of this "improvement," like thrift, industry, and loyalty to the company, were promoted directly by the welfare programs of General Motors and the I.M.A. But other desired civic virtues, especially temperance and patriotism, could be more effectively encouraged by businessmen who had assumed the role of community and political leaders. By the 1920s, there was no shortage of this type of business-class leadership in Flint.

As early as 1909, J. Dallas Dort had led the Local Option group who wanted to impose prohibition on Flint and surrounding Genessee County. Drink was actually outlawed that year, but in 1911, Flint citizens voted to reopen the saloons.[11] Dort continued to lead the campaign against drinking, and in 1916, the city voted with the state majority to reimpose prohibition. Of course, when prohibition took effect in Flint, the illegal sale of liquor continued behind closed doors, much as it did in industrial cities all across the United States. Throughout this period, William McKeighan's rather frequent arrests for liquor-law violations and alleged gambling activities outraged "Old Flint." Yet these well-publicized incidents also lent credence to

McKeighan's claim to the political leadership of Flint's working-class drinkers.[12]

Just prior to America's entry into World War I, new criticisms of deteriorating living conditions in the city prompted a renewal of social activism in the city's business class. Locally, the respected Reverend Bradford Pengelly (of Saint Paul's Episcopal Church) and reformer Lucy Stone stepped up agitation for housing code changes until the businessmen who controlled the city council agreed to make some adjustments. About the same time, Flint industrialists were sharply rebuked for having "not yet awakened to their responsibilities" in a nationally circulated article in *The Survey*.[13] These events, and the war, struck a responsive chord among the automotive elite, especially J. Dallas Dort.

At Dort's urging, the old Board of Commerce was reorganized by his friend and supporter Daniel Reed. The new Board, which included Fred Aldrich, Walter Chrysler, Arthur Bishop, and the Reverend Pengelly as its chief officers, plunged headlong into the war effort. With this organizational assistance, Flint surpassed its quota in both the National War Savings Bond drive and the Red Cross campaigns. In 1917–1918, Dort was a particularly active figure in whipping up local patriotism. Among his own class, he personally circulated a chain letter with U. S. government thrift cards enclosed. Each recipient was to attach one thrift stamp to five cards and send them on to help in "the cause in which we are so righteously engaged at this time—the elimination of the Kaiser and the atrocities he stands for."[14] Within the community at large, Dort formed a choral union that drew huge crowds for the mass singing of popular songs and patriotic anthems. He also endorsed the creation of an "Unconditional Surrender Club," a brainchild of *Flint Daily Journal* publisher Myles F. Bradley.[15] And finally, early in 1918, Dort was one of a group of prominent business leaders who backed C. S. Mott's bid for another term as mayor. As expected, Mott won the primary and then swept to victory at the head of a united Republican ticket. However, he soon retired to accept a commission in the Army's Quartermaster Corps.

Business-class political and social activism did not subside after World War I. Instead, the war seemed to have drawn leading businessmen into permanent roles as community leaders. Though Mott never again ran for local office, he was succeeded as mayor by important business figures who ran virtually unopposed in the general municipal elections of 1919, 1920, and 1921.[16] In other fields, such as the sponsoring of more parks, recreational facilities, libraries, and hospitals, the automotive elite took the initiative. Certainly, this kind of voluntarism was neither extraordinary (when compared to other cities), nor was it completely altruistic. For example, the Mott Foundation, set up in 1926 to put the city's richest man's assistance to the Community Chest, Red Cross, Flint Institute of Arts, and other charities on a "businesslike" footing, clearly served as a tax shelter.[17] Culturally, the constant positive publicity these fund-raising and philanthropic activities received in the city's leading mass media (the *Flint Daily Journal*, the *Flint Weekly Review*, and WEAA, the first and only local radio station, a completely controlled subsidiary of the *Daily Journal*), subtly built up confidence in the social responsibility of business-class leadership. Simultaneously, such publicity reinforced the belief that public problems could be solved by private initiatives. In this way, through the mass media of the city, Flint's business class extended the ideological program of welfare capitalism beyond the factory gates, encouraging the growth of deferential political culture in which working people's only public function was to reaffirm the rule of their economic superiors at the ballot box. "CO-OPERATION MEANS THE CONTINUED PROSPERITY OF FLINT," trumpeted the local Federation of Labor's official newspaper on Labor Day, 1923.[18] It was a declaration that must have warmed the heart of every businessman in the city.

The obvious success of welfare capitalism in Flint supports David Brody's contention that "it was a more vital phenomenon than it has seemed from the modern perspective."[19] By the 1920s, industrial welfare work, community fund-raising, and philanthropy provided local citizens with the highest degree of social security and the widest array of public services they had ever known.[20] For this reason, historical criticism of the manipulative aspects of Flint's welfare capitalism, made with full knowledge of the inadequacies that were exposed by the Great Depression, must be tempered with the recognition that it did contribute to higher living standards and that it was never generally resented.

A vigorous Americanization effort sponsored by leading Vehicle City businessmen in the years immediately following World War I deserves less confidence. The product of parochial xenophobia, excited by the nation's wartime passions and the post-war Red Scare, Americanization was ultimately designed to force the complete assimilation of Flint's first- and second-generation immigrant population. Adult education for foreign-born residents had actually begun during the biggest wave of immigrant settlement prior to the Great War. Elizabeth Welch, principal of the Fairview School in the city's North End, set up night classes in the English language and in civics at her facility as a genuine humanitarian service.[21] Then, about the time the United States entered the conflict in Europe, the Industrial Fellowship League started offering similar courses to immigrant factory workers through the YMCA. D. D Aitken, one of Flint's most influential businessmen and a prominent member of the YMCA board, appears to have been an important booster of this attempt to combine assimilation programs with welfare capitalism.

Although non-English-speaking immigrants represented a distinctly declining portion of Flint's population after the war, demands to Americanize them increased, as newspaper editors and businessmen joined in the anti-radical, nativist hysteria that was then sweeping the nation. In 1919–1920, the *Flint Daily Journal*, the city's primary source of news and local opinion, fed local prejudices by featuring relentless attacks on foreigners, bolsheviks, and other assorted "reds." For months, editorials warned readers about the dangers of bolshevism, a doctrine which the newspaper claimed "impudent and criminal foreigners are seeking to impose on free America!"[22] Throughout this period, news of the counterrevolutionary invasion of Russia and the Palmer Raids received enthusiastic front-page coverage, while cartoonists repeatedly used the stereotypic image of the bomb-throwing immigrant in their work. Fearful that radical activity might break out in Flint, although there was absolutely no evidence of radical activities to warrant such anxiety, publisher Myles Bradley asked for a doubling of the city's police force and for stricter laws against "loafers."[23] He even went so far as to censor the news. In 1919, a year of tremendous labor unrest all across the country, Bradley kept virtually all information about strikes and union activity in the United States out of his newspaper, reasoning that "if the workers of Flint were reading every day of strikes in other cities and employers' acceding to strikers' demands, they would become restless."[24]

The intensity of the *Flint Daily Journal*'s reaction to the Russian Revolution and the postwar strike wave was typical of the way establishment newspapers all across the country responded to these events. Yet, given the conservative history of local workers and immigrants, it seems to have been particularly irrational. The same can be said for businessmen's stepped-up efforts to Americanize Flint's small non-

English-speaking population. In 1920, the YWCA board of trustees (dominated by industrialists and bankers) decided to follow the YMCA example by setting up an "International Institute" that had a single function, conducting classes in English and in American citizenship for foreign-born women. Less than two years later, business leaders who were still unsatisfied with the progress of existing assimilation programs met with the Board of Commerce, and voted to establish a "Cosmopolitan Club" for the purpose of "promoting a very aggressive Americanization program in the north end of the city."[25]

Cosmopolitan Club members actively recruited foreign-born residents for public night school classes in a five-year Americanization course that included classes in English, American history, citizenship, industrial trades, and preparation for naturalization. Flint's leading business-unionist, George Starkweather, lent his support to the program in a 1923 Labor Day editorial. The *Flint Weekly Review* editor noted that "foreigners were getting to be a real problem," and if any of them did not learn English and officially express a desire to be a citizen, "he should be sent back and with him should go his wife and family."[26] The Cosmopolitan Club campaign proved to be extremely effective. In 1924, enrollment in its program topped twenty-one hundred adults. Special English classes were also set up for foreign-born youth. By 1926, former Congressman Aitken could boast, with real justification,

> There is probably no city in the country where there has been such an efficient and successful effort made at Americanization. There are few people in Flint now that do not speak English and who do not practice the customs of the American people.[27]

A One-Dimensional Political Spectrum

Americanization undoubtedly hastened the creation of a more homogeneous society in Flint. However, it also poisoned the city's political atmosphere, upsetting the clear dominance over municipal government that the industrial business class had established during the wartime boom. There were two major reasons for this unforseen turn of events. First, when they made ethnicity a public issue, business leaders drove ethnic voters and a well-organized bloc of black voters back to the political organization of William McKeighan. Secondly, by stirring up nativist sentiments in this period of massive in-migration from rural America, these same business leaders legitimized the political position of a group of Ku Klux Klan adherents who had begun to filter into the city as the economy recovered in 1922–1923.

The revival of McKeighan's power was remarkable. During the immediate postwar period, when his opponents in the industrial business class had been asserting their leadership in public affairs, the former mayor had been in constant trouble with the law. For example, in 1918, McKeighan actually spent two weeks in prison after a conviction for assault (which allegedly occurred at a gambling party). He was released when a State Supreme Court reversed the verdict. In the short run, incidents like this one undoubtedly hurt McKeighan at the polls. However, over the longer run, throughout the 1920s and early 1930s, McKeighan had two strengths: the anti-establishment, anti-prohibition image he had cultivated; and his organization among voters in the white ethnic and black neighborhoods around the Buick plant.[28] In November 1919, when his personal reputation was very badly damaged, these north-side neighborhoods still produced enough votes to defeat a half-hearted attempt by the business class to abolish the ward system, which McKeighan vigorously defended. The coincident recession of 1920–1921 and the growing Americanization movement helped McKeighan to start a political comeback by reviving his appeal among intimidated and unrepresented ethnic and black voters. He restored his organization. In 1922, making his usual campaign as "the Candidate of All the People," McKeighan eked out a victory over several other Republican rivals in the primary on the strength of First Ward (north-side) votes, and then moved on to an easy win in the general mayoral election. A year later, the Republicans were again divided in the primary, and even though a majority cast their ballots against him, McKeighan was renominated for what looked to be a certain third term as the city's chief executive.[29]

Though McKeighan was fiercely resented by the local business elite, his organization's strength in the near north end's First Ward white ethnic and black neighborhoods gave him a crucial advantage over GOP rivals who had to overcome factionalism and widespread apathy in municipal elections. In traditionally Republican Flint, winning the GOP primary, as McKeighan did in 1923, almost always assured a candidate of victory in the general election. However, that year local Democrats nominated a popular sawmill operator, David R. Cuthbertson, who promised "Service, Efficiency, Merit" and lower property taxes, instead of the alleged corruption and mismanagement of McKeighan's administration. At the last minute, automotive business-class leaders forged a bipartisan coalition to defeat the incumbent, and for five days preceding the balloting, the local newspapers were filled with stories and advertisements backing Cuthbertson, while McKeighan's campaign was ignored. The result of this effort was the heaviest turnout in years, and a clear-cut majority for Cuthbertson amidst the usual Republican sweep of all other contests in Genessee County. The Democrat won by a 2,200-vote margin. Local pundits attributed McKeighan's defeat to the lack of support from GOP regulars, to vote-switching in the ethnic precincts, and to a strong effort by a "Women's Campaign Committee" that wanted to oust the mayor over the firing of a policewoman. But perhaps more significantly, for the second time in fifteen years, the business-class elite who usually controlled local politics had ignored party labels to unite in successful opposition to a mayor who threatened their positions by organizing an independent power base among industrial working people.[30]

Mayor Cuthbertson pledged to run the city's business "with the same attention to details tending towards economy that a man would give to his own private business."[31] In other words, as a *Flint Daily Journal* editorial noted, "in reality the Democrat label attached to the mayor means but little."[32] Early in the two-year term (the first two-year term in city history), Cuthbertson lived up to the faith leading Republicans had placed in him. He worked closely with the Republican city council, encouraging extensive construction projects in the downtown business and east-side (Dort Motor-AC Sparkplug) industrial districts. But in April 1924, when Cuthbertson vetoed the GOP-dominated council's decision to create two new wards and then moved to block the Republican city attorney's proposed suit against the railroad that ran the local streetcar service, partisan hostilities emerged, and so did the Ku Klux Klan.

Prominent Republicans led by Myles Bradley, the publisher-editor of the *Flint Daily Journal*, merely attacked the Democratic mayor for usurping the council's power. However, when the local Klan came into the open, it immediately launched a petition drive to recall Cuthbertson and install their own man in City Hall. The precise origins of the KKK in Flint remain hidden. Its rise in a period of rapid in-migration from the lower Midwest and upper South, and its activities as a virtually autonomous local unit conformed to the patterns found elsewhere in the Midwest.[33] The Klan's recall petition charged Flint's mayor with "gross incompetency," "failure to control the liquor traffic and vice," as well as a list of other very vague complaints, including the failure to recognize the requests of the "unselfish class" that made up the "sober-minded electorate."[34] Since Flint had the best record for enforcing prohibition in the state during Cuthbertson's first year in office, it is clear that the Klan's only specific charge was patently false and opportunistic. Indeed, as the subsequent special election campaign showed, the fact that Cuthbertson had appointed a Catholic as chief of police, and that he had hired several married women to fill City Hall jobs seemed to lie closer to the heart of the Klansmen's grievances.

At first the mayor tried to ignore the Klan's charges against him; then he offered facts that refuted the idea that he was soft on vice and prohibition. Neither tactic worked. Finally, Cuthbertson tried to block the recall petition in a Pontiac court, but he failed there too. The day before the actual recall vote, Genessee County Kleagle, Maurice ("Bob") Steenbarger, made a spectacular bid to insure a Klan victory by hiring an airplane to bombard the city with anti-Cuthbertson propaganda. Recall proponents, using the Klan organization, also made sure that they got out their vote on June 12, while Cuthbertson had no such organization behind him. As a result, he was recalled and forced to run in a special election the following month.[35]

Although the effort to replace the mayor was directed by the local Klan leader, Steenbarger, the campaign took on an appearance of greater respectability when Judson L. Transue, a schoolteacher turned banker from upstate New York, was picked to run against Cuthbertson. Initially, several other candidates entered the race, but only one, Homer Vette, a former sheriff and alderman, stayed in the race, vowing to fire Police Chief Cole and clean up the police department if elected. The main contest took place between Cuthbertson and Transue, yet Klansmen and Vette supporters came to blows on a few occasions. Transue kept a low profile, spending much of the month prior to the election "off fishing."[36] However, his backers organized a series of daily mass meetings and nighttime rallies during the final week of the campaign, generating intense interest in the outcome.

Transue posed as a reformer who would restore morality to local government, but his campaign mixed half-truths, lies, and innuendos into a sensational presentation designed to appeal to the fears and insecurities of people who were trying to adjust to a new life in the industrial city. In particular, it pandered to the nativism that had already been aroused by the drive for Americanization. "I have been informed that foreign-born residents comprise a large percentage of the bootleggers in Flint," Transue told a crowd of four thousand people outside the Buick plant five days before the election. He continued, "I feel it is our duty to educate these foreign-born residents regarding our laws. If they refuse to be educated they should be sent back home on the boats on which they came to America." To this typical scapegoat approach, the Klan-backed candidate added a kind of pseudo-populism, making completely unfounded, unspecified charges about the local rich. "I understand that some wealthy Americans in our city are law violators," Transue alleged in the same speech; "They should be punished more severely than the foreigners." It was a good example of what is known today as a "law and order" campaign, and its proposed solutions were as simple-minded as the problems it outlined. After reorganizing the police department, the "reformer" proposed to create a police reserve he described as "a clean-cut body of men to aid in the enforcement of our laws."[37]

In the waning days of the campaign, Cuthbertson received ringing endorsements from the two major newspapers, from J. Dallas Dort, and from other prominent citizens. These probably increased his support among the city's regular Republican majority, although as a Democrat, the mayor got no help from the GOP organization. On election day, thousands of voters who had never cast a municipal ballot turned out, giving Transue a clear margin of victory.[38] When the results were announced that evening, crowds filled the downtown streets in noisy celebration, but in an act some took as a sign of hoped-for responsibility, Klan leaders prevented their followers from parading in their hoods.

The summer and fall of 1924 marked the high water mark of the Ku Klux Klan's influence in Flint. During his first months in office, Mayor Transue lived up to the expectations of his reactionary backers. He fired the married women at City Hall, pushed an "anti-hugging" ordinance through the City Council that forbade certain public displays of affection, and forced a reorganization of the police department's vice squad. He also stepped up the provision of essential services by placing new bonding issues for sewers, water mains, and street-paving before the voters. This last initiative was very well received by the business community, and by the *Flint Daily Journal*, which had demonstrated a willingness to support Transue almost as soon as he took office.[39]

For a short while following Transue's election, the Klan retained its political influence in Genessee County. During the Republican primary in September 1924, Klansmen passed out sample ballots at the polls, and every candidate they endorsed received at least a plurality of the vote. Local voters even gave a plurality to James Hamilton, a longtime supporter of a constitutional amendment to abolish parochial schools, over the popular incumbent Governor Groesbeck.[40] Six months later, during the regularly scheduled municipal elections, Mayor Transue and a Klan-backed slate of candidates ran successfully in both the GOP primary and the general election. William McKeighan resurfaced as an independent in this latter contest, and he gave Transue his stiffest opposition, even though Cuthbertson was also running on the Democratic line. McKeighan openly denounced Steenbarger and the Klan, once again rejuvenating his reputation among many ethnic and black voters. During the campaign, McKeighan reportedly challenged Transue to a public debate. When Transue refused, McKeighan called him a tool of Klan leader Steenbarger. The ex-mayor's old enemies at the *Flint Daily Journal* took up Transue's defense, accusing McKeighan of mud-slinging.[41]

Once more the Klan issue brought a record number of voters to the polls. Transue rolled up comfortable majorities in five out of six wards and he continued in office, but McKeighan's enormous plurality in the First Ward, the home of most of Flint's foreign-born and black voters, made it a close race. The Democrat, former Mayor Cuthbertson, finished a very distant third.[42]

The dominance of the Republicans in the 1925 elections signaled Flint's return to political normalcy. In the later 1920s, local politics lapsed back into a familiar pattern. William McKeighan's political organization and the business-class elite struggled for control of the Republican Party and of the municipal government while fewer and fewer voters went to the polls. Judson Transue hastened the return to normalcy by quickly deserting the Ku Klux Klan. With a full two-year term ahead of him, the mayor sought the approval of the city's big businessmen by reversing all of his campaign positions. There were no more verbal assaults on foreigners or the rich. Even Police Chief Cole kept his job. Meanwhile, Mayor Transue extended city services in a fiscally conservative manner designed to please business leaders and older property-holders.

By the time he came up for reelection in 1927, the mayor had become the establishment's man. D. D. Aitken and William Ballenger headed the list of prominent businessmen who formed a special campaign committee for Transue. However, running in a four-way race in the Republican primary, the incumbent still could not overcome Mc-Keighan's ability to get out the blue-collar ethnic and black vote on the near north side. This election marked the last significant intrusion of the Ku Klux Klan into Flint politics. Embittered by Transue's treachery, Klan leader Steenbarger tried to smear him with charges that he had accepted a bribe to protect a downtown gambling operation. This accusation presumably was made to benefit Lester Mott, an obscure movie theater operator whom Steenbarger was supporting for mayor. When most leading city officials and McKeighan himself denounced the charges and produced evidence to refute them, the issue seemed dead. Yet, in the end, Transue received just a third of the primary vote, an unusually poor showing for a business-backed incumbent.[43]

In the regular election, McKeighan had to fight off a strong challenge by a Democratic lawyer, Charles Adair, who was able to get the endorsement of the *Flint Daily Journal* as the anti-machine, anti-corruption candidate. McKeighan outfoxed his opponents by coming out for nonpartisan elections in a speech before the League of Women Voters. More importantly, on election day, McKeighan's overwhelming majorities in the First Ward's white ethnic and black precincts were enough to overcome Adair's lead elsewhere in the city. McKeighan had secured his third term as mayor.[44]

During the last few boom years, the mayor's numerous opponents among the city's business-class elite relentlessly tried to oust him from City Hall. In November 1927, a recall petition launched by the *Flint Daily Journal's* general manager, J. A. Taylor, failed to win enough support to put it on the ballot. Another petition drive in early 1928 did bring a recall measure to a vote. In this hastily arranged election, the mayor received majorities in all of the city's six wards, but his vote total in the First Ward was extraordinary. One McKeighan organizer claimed all of the First Ward's twenty-nine hundred black votes had been cast against recall.[45]

The automotive business class returned to its alternative anti-McKeighan strategy a few months later when municipal justice Frank Cain formed a charter revision club to lobby for the abolition of the wards and for the appointment of a city manager. The efforts of this club produced genuine business-class unity. Virtually all of the city's business organizations and businessmen's clubs endorsed its efforts. In May 1928, the Board of Commerce collected signatures to put the issue before the voters. Over the summer months, nine charter club members were nominated as a charter review commission, and club members set up branch organizations in all fifty-three precincts in the city. Club members also held thirty-seven neighborhood mass meetings, and they spent unprecedented amounts of money on newspaper and radio advertisments. As one student of the charter revision club has said, "It was in fact a machine to end a machine."[46]

Despite the hoopla, voter participation in the referendum of September 1928 was considerably less than in any of the five preceding municipal contests. Only 38 percent of the eligible voters turned out, approving the creation of a charter-writing commission by a two-to-one margin. This group took a year to prepare the document, which eventually set up nonpartisan elections, a nine-member city commission, and an appointed city manager. In the interim, Mayor McKeighan lost his post to Roy Brownell, a former executive at Durant-Dort and Dort Motors and a founder of the Industrial Mutual Association. Brownell's candidacy was actually helped by George Starkweather's entry into the race. As the publisher of the *Flint Weekly Review*, Starkweather had gained the respect of some McKeighan voters for his consistent anti-Klan positions. In 1929, he divided McKeighan's usual constituency just enough to allow Brownell to unseat the "people's mayor." Voter participation continued to decline in this contest and in the subsequent general municipal election that formally ratified Roy Brownell's triumph. In December 1929, just 16 percent of the city's eligible citizens went to the polls in the special election that actually approved the new charter.

The reorganization of local government in 1930 secured the industrial business class' control of municipal authority for most of the depression decade. William McKeighan's kind of ward-based politics was made irrelevant by the structure of the new nonpartisan city manager system. This was as intended. Yet an unforeseen dramatic shift of increasingly class-conscious blue-collar voters to the Democratic Party (see chapter 6) had an even greater impact on the fate of William McKeighan. After a vigorous but disastrous campaign as the anti-prohibition candidate in the 1932 Republican gubernatorial primary, McKeighan's political career in Flint ended.[47]

Comparing the local politics of Flint in the 1920s with pre-World War I developments brings the practical meaning of normalcy into sharper focus. First, the appearance of the Ku Klux Klan threatened business-class domination of local public life far less than socialism had fifteen years earlier, and thus it did not draw the same kind of united business-class opposition as socialism had. In Flint, the Klan sought moral influence, not real power. In contrast to the pre-World War I socialists, Flint's Klansmen had no clear vision of an alternative institutional structure for local society. Nor did they try to create a party of their own capable of challenging the hegemony of the GOP. Instead, the local Klan-backed candidates within the Republican Party who seemed to share its own narrow, nativist vision of what was true American morality. In this sense, Ku Klux Klan's brand of discontent in Flint merely amplified political trends that had been initiated already by the dominant business-class elite, especially superpatriotism and the demand for the Americanization of foreigners, for a stricter enforcement of prohibition, and for a crackdown on local vice. Of course, in its amplification of these political issues, the Klan offered none of the paternalism that had traditionally softened the way business leaders approached issues of social control. Yet, as the smooth transition of Judson Transue from Klan-backed candidate to establishment mayor revealed, there was no unbridgeable philosophical gulf separating Flint's business class from the majority of those residents who temporarily embraced the local Ku Klux Klan in the mid-1920s. Certainly, this judgment does not mean that Flint's leading businessmen held political views similar to those of the stereotypic Southern Klan. Rather, it is meant to describe the Klan that existed in Flint. As Norman Weaver emphasized in his study of the midwestern KKK, each local unit (like the one in Flint) was virtually autonomous, deriving its specific political character from local circumstances.[48]

The Klan did not pose a fundamental threat to Flint's business-class establishment because it functioned essentially as a social organization, not as a political movement. This point also helps to explain the transitory character of the KKK's presence in the Vehicle City. As a secretive, voluntary fraternity, which consisted mostly of native-born white Protestant migrants, in its time, Flint's Klan met certain social needs of some people who were new to the region and urban life. During the early and mid-1920s, when most newcomers to Flint were arriving from the lower Midwest and the upper South and scattering themselves throughout the city, the Klan's rituals, parades, and picnics, as well as its politics, gave many white migrants a feeling of community and connection with their common rural Protestant past. Hence, as long as its members felt uprooted, the Klan lived on. However, in the later 1920s, as these migrants adjusted to their new circumstances, Michigan Klan membership dropped rapidly, and it never rebounded. By August 1927, when the last big Klororo (statewide Ku Klux Klan convention) was held in Flint, the decline was already evident. Although five thousand people turned out for a barbecue-rally and mass naturalization ceremony in Kearsley Park, only five hundred Klansmen from all over Michigan marched in the torchlight parade that was the meeting's highlight.[49] These figures indicate a dramatic drop in Klan strength in Flint and in the state as a whole. In fact, this convention marked the last public appearance of Klansmen in Flint for forty years.[50]

Judging by their political activities in the 1920s, Flint's leading businessmen certainly regarded William McKeighan as a more serious problem than the Ku Klux Klan. The time, money, and energy they expended on efforts to prevent him from gaining power far exceeded anything done to lessen the influence of the Klan. This conclusion should not be shocking. In this era, when business leaders were making a concerted effort to Americanize local society, Klan politics were much less disruptive than McKeighan and his political machine. As a mayor and political boss who represented blue-collar ethnic and racial minorities, and as a morally suspect public celebrity who flaunted his opposition to prohibition, William McKeighan defied the cultural consensus that the local industrial elite was trying to establish in Flint. Throughout the automobile boom years McKeighan's political power endured because he managed to remain at least a symbolic alternative to business-class demands for social conformity. In this sense, his successes defined the practical political limits of normalcy.

Yet, it would hardly be accurate to describe McKeighan as a representative of a nascent working-class consciousness or a potential political left. During this era, the political spectrum in Flint was truly one-dimensional. Republicans dominated elections (even more so in contests for state and national offices), and businessmen dominated the definition of politics in both parties.[51] As a Republican entrepreneur himself, William McKeighan never directly challenged the basic economic interests or ideology of other Flint businessmen. On the kind of economic issues that created real political divisions elsewhere —like the maintenance of virtually unregulated free enterprise, opposition to industrial unionism, the provision of social insurance and welfare programs through private sources, and the appropriateness of business priorities in public policy making—there was near unanimous agreement among all Flint politicians in the 1920s. Thus, for more than fifteen years following the demise of the local Social-ist Party, political competition in Flint was primarily factional, and trivial.

Instead of focusing the public's attention on the proper role of gov-ernment in a complex, developing industrial society, as both John Menton and C. S. Mott had begun to do before World War I, post-war politicians obscured this critical problem. The politics of normalcy in Flint revolved around personalities, patriotism, nativism, and indi-vidual morality, but not on questions of power, wealth, and social justice. Neither the Ku Klux Klan nor William McKeighan ever ques-tioned businessmen's rights to monopolize political, economic, and cultural decision making. Consequently, despite the appearance of great controversies, politics changed very little of the structure and quality of everyday life in Flint during the 1920s. The actual power to develop industrial society and Americanize its citizens was left in the hands of a business class that was increasingly dominated by men who owed their allegiance to the General Motors Corporation. Ga-briel Kolko has said modern America can "be understood as a class structure without *decisive* class conflict, a society that had limited conflict to smaller issues that were not crucial to the existing order."[52] Though this description is too rigid to apply to all twentieth-century American history, it definitely fits Flint in the era known as normalcy.

In the Absence of Class Conflict: Industrial Relations in the 1920s

In Flint, the automobile boom was an era of revolutionary economic and social change and unusual industrial peace. A large traditional in-dustry, carriage- and wagon-making, completely disappeared, and in its place, a new automobile industry, which employed over fifty thou-sand people in highly rationalized mechanized factories, was created. Yet, throughout this period, there were no serious strikes or indus-trial protests. In addition, every attempt to establish an auto workers union in Flint ended in dismal failure.

There is no simple explanation for the absence of industrial hostili-ties during so many years of Flint's second industrial revolution. The way that high wages and the prospects for improved individual mate-rial living standards, and the emergence of a truly mass-oriented pop-ular consumer culture encouraged workers to embrace an instrumen-tal view of their jobs is an important part of the answer. But it does not tell the whole story. Welfare capitalism also contributed to local industrial peace, though other things surely overshadowed its impact. As Sidney Fine has noted,

> Welfare programs, at best, were of far less significance in determining the attitude of the GM worker toward his job than the wages he received, the hours he toiled, the security of his position, and the conditions under which he labored.[53]

Therefore, to understand the political culture of normalcy fully and the apparent contradiction between the rapid transformation of industry in Flint and the tranquility of its industrial relations, the terms of employment and the conditions of work in the city's automobile plants must be examined more closely.

For more than fifty years, descriptions of work in the pre-depression automobile industry have largely rested on observations originally made by officials and supporters of Detroit's unsuccessful, Communist-led Auto Workers Union. From the publications, correspondences, and records of this ill-fated organization, a stark picture of workers being exploited by low wages, a lack of job security, the speed-up, and dangerous working conditions emerges. The perceptions of Auto Workers Union stalwarts have been compressed and analyzed in more scholarly studies since Robert Dunn first published his *Labor and Automobiles* in 1929, but, as a recent discussion shows, the fundamental critique of "the plight of the auto workers" is still readily accepted as accurate and compelling.[54] Unfortunately, the Auto Workers Union's analysis never reflected the experiences or perceptions of most auto workers; and ultimately that is why the organization consistently failed to enlist the allegiance of any significant group of workers. Throughout the 1920s, it remained a tiny band of radical working-class activists who had no regular contact with workers outside a few plants in Detroit. The AWU's predecessor, the United Automobile, Aircraft, and Vehicle Workers Union, had by contrast claimed as many as forty-five thousand members in 1920 (mostly in widely scattered small shops among skilled workers). However, it completely collapsed in 1921–22. The union was reorganized under a new name by its Communist members in 1923–24, an action that conformed to the "dual union" strategy of the Communist Party-USA in this period.[55] Auto Workers Union members did not share the same popular cultural values as most working people in the automotive production centers. They were a small island of committed union men and Marxists amid in a sea of migrants who generally felt that moving to the city and taking a job in an automotive factory had improved their lives. For these reasons, the Auto Workers Union's descriptions of "the manifold grievances of the workers in the shops" must be treated with considerable skepticism.[56]

In Flint, where the Auto Workers Union unsuccessfully sought new members on several occasions during the 1920s, workers articulated no "manifold grievances" against the company. There simply was no common political consciousness of exploitation in the local automobile industry. Pay scales were kept high enough to attract the best young workers; they kept up with local inflation, and this discouraged union activity. Though earnings fluctuated, in general, material living standards steadily improved during the decade.[57] Uncertainty about employment and earnings, which stemmed from the cyclical character of the automotive market, undoubtedly imposed hardships, especially in the early 1920s. "You can't ever tell how long the work will last in Flint," commented one married woman who was out looking for a job in 1925.[58] But this underlying sense of insecurity seems to have diminished dramatically in the later 1920s as the industry's business cycle stabilized and as the workers became more accustomed to the rhythms of that cycle.

While a few class-conscious workers complained about the inherent insecurity of automobile work, in Flint most workers seemed to accept the seasonal cycle of the industry. These working people ultimately came to view the annual layoffs for model changeovers and the periodic reductions in production schedules as normal features of full-time employment. The notion of "steady work," which cropped up throughout the National Recovery Administration's hearings in Flint in 1934, reveals how something described as a grievance by the Auto Workers Union had actually been deemed acceptable by most auto workers. "I never had a layoff until 1931," explained a machine operator who had started in Flint in 1924, and was the first witness to appear before the NRA committee.[59] Others, including two men whose experiences predated World War I, noted in a very matter-of-fact way that they too had "always worked steady" until the Great Depression. Of course, these workers did not mean they had worked from fifty to fifty-two weeks a year during the automobile boom. Instead, as further questioning showed, their prevailing definition of "steady work" had come to include regular layoffs and slack time.[60]

By the mid-1920s, when the automobile boom was slowing down, most auto workers averaged fifty hours in a five-and-a-half-day week, with weeks in excess of sixty hours not uncommon during peak production periods.[61] Though some skilled workers were employed year-round, the production workforce was usually laid off for two months or more in the fall as factories retooled for the new model year. Looking back on the fluctuating pattern of auto work, labor historians generally have been quick to assume that uncertainty *must have* plagued auto workers throughout the 1920s, but this assumption may not be correct. In Flint at least, as annual earnings rose and industry production schedules were regularized, working people learned to plan ahead, drawing on savings, interest, and occasionally, the expanding pool of consumer credit to cushion temporary unemployment. In some families, the second income of a wife or older child would ease the economic burden of these anticipated layoffs.[62] Hence, as the boom continued in the middle and later 1920s, layoffs did not automatically translate into threats to family survival (as they often had in older, nineteenth-century cities). Long periods without a paycheck surely caused hardships for some working people, especially those who were recent arrivals. Yet others learned to use the released time to make repairs on their houses, to visit friends and relatives, and to pursue urban sports (bowling and softball) and outdoor activities like hunting, fishing, and family picnics. In fact, it seems likely that the opportunity to participate in sports and to make trips back to the country eased the psychological strain of moving from a rural to an urban life. Certainly, routine layoffs provided periods of release from the tensions of the factory.

The pace and discipline of work in the big, noisy plants could be oppressive, but auto workers who settled in Flint accepted these things as a necessary trade-off for being part of the emerging mass consumer culture. Moreover, for several reasons, the detrimental aspects of mechanization and rationalization were not as severe as some union organizers and academic observers imagined at the time. First, despite the stereotype, less than one-fourth of the labor force in most automobile factories were assigned to actual assembly line operations in the 1920s, a distribution that still held true half a century later.[63] Assembly groups and machine operators paid on a piece work plus bonus system were most numerous. Bench work remained important; however, it declined significantly between 1922 and 1930.[64] Piece work pay generally replaced day work after the recession of

1920–1921. It had obvious drawbacks, yet high pay rates, some worker control over speed, and the social interactions among fellow workers made it bearable. Everett Francis, a Fisher Body trimmer and union pioneer in the 1930s, later recalled, "Working in a body plant in the automobile industry up to and through 1929, I would say they could be called good working conditions."[65] The same thing could be said about the other big auto plants in Flint. As long as workers reached their daily piece rate quotas, they were not pressed unmercifully by their supervisors. In fact, by switching to the group piece work plus bonus system, management shifted much of the burden of pace determination and discipline to experienced lead workers.

The heavy flow of new workers into Flint throughtout the automobile boom years also lessened the impact of rationalization on a traditionally volatile segment of the labor force, the skilled workers. Simultaneous expansion and rationalization allowed General Motors to preserve the special status of its skilled workers while filling new, lesser-skilled jobs with inexperienced workers. A contemporary student of this pattern observed,

> the average wage earner with latent ability but no training is employed and taught some one operation, and in the repeated performance of this operation he becomes an expert. Employers assert that this does not remove the necessity for ability but encourages specialization in the individual.[66]

Over the long run, plant managers in Flint were able to build up a young group of production workers who "naturally" associated industrial work with Taylorism; it was all they had ever known. For them, rationalized work could be hard and monotonous, but it was not experienced as a degradation of craft skills. Consequently, the kind of serious labor disputes that could occur when skilled workers were squeezed into lesser-skilled jobs were avoided in Flint and in most other American automobile production centers.[67]

Boom conditions diminished the chances of shopfloor labor disputes in another way too. The general availability of work in the Great Lakes region permitted workers who had grievances about conditions or discipline to "strike with their feet" when problems arose. Young men with their own cars were particularly mobile. Throughout the 1920s, it was typical for a young dissatisfied auto worker (or a fired one) simply to pack up and move on to find another job in another automotive production center. Descriptions of this kind of mobility abound in the United Auto Workers Union's History Project. The background of Herbert Richardson, a union activist in the 1930s, was not uncommon. Born in Saginaw in 1898, Richardson moved to Flint when he finished high school. He took his first job at Chevrolet in 1917, then he quit and moved to another job at the Republic Truck factory in Alma, Michigan. In 1920, Richardson returned to Flint, where he learned a trimmer's skills at Buick. In the next five years, he worked in Lansing, Grand Rapids, and Ionia, Michigan before taking a job at Flint's Fisher Body 2 in 1925. In 1927, Richardson moved over to Fisher Body 1 and remained there until he was fired for strike activities in 1930.[68]

In this era, General Motors did not circulate blacklists or coordinate employee record keeping among its divisions. Neither did the local Manufacturers Association. Thus, Flint's auto workers discovered that they could change jobs easily, even if they had been fired after a bitter dispute with management. For example, in July 1930, when twenty-three workers at Fisher Body 1 were fired for participation in the first plantwide shutdown in industry history, all twenty-three simply crossed town and got jobs at Fisher Body 2.[69] In other words, prior to the Great Depression, serious grievances seldom accumulated in a plant. Those that could not be settled individually by a worker and his immediate supervisors usually disappeared when that worker decided to quit or was fired.

On the shopfloor, there were additional reasons why rationalization seldom provoked industrial hostilities. Although production workers did not strike at the sight of a time-study man in their midst, they could confuse the efficiency experts by holding down outputs to keep a job within their physical and mental limits. Most commonly, groups of workers agreed on a pace and ways to avoid ever appearing idle. As William Chalmers concluded after years of study and actual factory work experience in the later 1920s, "There is no doubt that the workers in the automobile industry as elsewhere attempt to regulate the speed at which they work."[70]

Foremen tried to subvert these worker strategies by appointing people they trusted to the crucial "lead man" positions. The tensions on the shopfloor were real, but they were mitigated by the diffused, personal character of management authority in personnel matters. In most auto plants, including those in Flint, foremen had the power to adjust piece rates, set quotas, improve conditions, and hear grievances. Moreover, as long as the boom endured, lower echelon management's principal personnel problem was turnover, not worker efficiency.[71] Top management urged supervisors and managers to win the loyalty of their employees instead of driving them away with a relentless speed-up. "The factory manager's most important duty then, is training the average workman to realize the importance of his position and the vital part he plays in the manufacture of the article. . . ." explained Chevrolet's general factory manager in the innaugural volume of the management-oriented *Chevrolet Review.*[72]

During the 1920s in Flint, plant managers tried to earn workers' loyalty by promoting a sense of community among their employees. Building on the paternalistic traditions of local industry, General Motors' officials organized company bands and sports teams that participated in citywide competitions, and intramural leagues for the less talented. Shop newspapers, like *The Buick News: Published in the Interest of the Entire Buick Family* and Chevrolet's *Accelerator: For Our Mutual Betterment*, publicized these activities, gave news about welfare and safety programs, and published an endless stream of articles extolling the need for greater cooperation in the factory. In addition, the companies sponsored special events, such as patriotic picnics and displays. One such affair, a "Defense Day" parade in September 1924 drew sixty thousand marchers, fifteen thousand from Buick alone, who were solicited by volunteers who asked workers to show "the whole world that Uncle Sam still had the man power and spirit to back American policies and American traditions."[73]

Managers also tried to minimize uncertainty about layoffs and rationalization. At the shopfloor level, supervisors and foremen could be arbitrary about whom to layoff and rehire, but it seems that an informal seniority system existed in most plants, except where men advancing in age were deemed unfit for work on the line. Even then, older men were not necessarily fired; often they were shifted to jobs requiring less speed, agility, and strength.[74] In the 1920s, length of service raised wage rates and earnings. Under the piece work system, earnings improved as a worker become more proficient at a job. In addition, base rates for experienced workers were raised throughout the decade. By 1928–1929, piece rates for experienced semiskilled workers in Flint were calculated on a base pay rate as high as $1.00 to $1.10 per hour.[75] This trend followed corporate policy. As part of his initial reforms in the early 1920s, GM president Alfred Sloan told his managers to create pay systems that tied wage increases to more carefully calculated productivity gains.[76] In Flint, this policy was implemented by expanding piece work to cover all but the highest and lowest skilled categories of labor. Under that system, as long as the automobile boom lasted, most workers received considerable material incentives to cooperate with management's continuing efforts to rationalize production.

Improving earnings, welfare capitalism, individual geographic mobility, increasingly "steady work," and a general feeling that working conditions were satisfactory prevented the growth of any widespread labor discontent in Flint's automobile industry prior to 1930.[77] However, on occasions when changing economic activities put pressure on management to hold down labor costs, piece work disputes did break out in a few departments in the big plants. This kind of problem most often occurred in the body shops where the tradition of vehicle-building was strongest, and thus where the impact of rationalization was perceived as an attack on skill and status as well as a speed-up. In Flint, four of the five recorded automotive strikes of the 1920s involved piece work disputes in a body shop. Yet, General Motors' management contained all of these protests, even when workers received help from union organizers. This pattern of having relatively few strikes, all concentrated among the body-building workers in the industry, was not unique to Flint. It was true of the whole American industry at the time, and it was even more pronounced in the British motor industry (the world's second largest) during the 1920s and early 1930s.[78]

The first fifteen years of the automobile boom in Flint were virtually free of strikes and union activity. In 1911, when the A. F. of L.'s old Carriage and Wagon Workers Union reorganized itself as the United Automobiles, Aircraft, and Vehicle Workers of America, a few veteran skilled workers expressed an interest in setting up a Flint local, but nothing ever came of it. During the war boom, though living conditions deteriorated, Flint workers apparently had few grievances about the demands made on them in the factories. Central Labor Union dissidents and a handful of other A. F. of L.-affiliated activists were inspired to organize a "Labor Forward" movement that held open weekly meetings in the Carpenter's Hall during 1917. This group endorsed William McKeighan and staged the city's first Labor Day parade that year, but it made no serious effort to unionize vehicle workers. The files of the National War Labor Board contain just a single letter of protest from Flint about low wages for skilled workers and women at Buick. There is no record of any wartime strikes.[79]

In the immediate aftermath of the war, an auto workers' union did manage to gain a foothold in the Buick body shops. Local 9 of United Automobile, Aircraft, and Vehicle Workers of America was established in April 1919 with thirty-three members, mostly skilled topmakers.[80] For the next ten months, union organizers found recruiting difficult. At its peak, in the summer of 1919, Local 9 appears to have had about five hundred signed-up members. In part, workers resisted the opportunity because shop newspapers made it clear that management would not deal with the union. Moreover, information about the union circulated slowly. Both major newspapers, including the Federation of Labor's *Flint Weekly Review*, would not carry UAAVWA announcements, and local police harassed union members who tried to sell the Detroit based *Auto Worker* on the streets.[81] By early 1920, as the postwar boom continued, Local 9 was losing ground. Its remaining members hoped to revive the organization and gain an anti-inflationary wage increase by threatening a strike. Against the wishes of union leaders, about one hundred workers struck on February 2, 1920, when supervisors upped minimum production standards. For two weeks, the strike remained solid. However, it was broken after personal visits by their foremen convinced about two dozen rough-stuff rubbers and backhangers to return to work. In the wake of this disappointment, the UAAVWA collapsed in Flint. As the national organization reported in June 1920, "many of the most active members of Local No. 9 of Flint, Michigan have left the city, rather than work for automobile concerns that are unfair to their workers."[82]

For the next seven years, no effort was made to organize the auto workers of Flint. The open shop prevailed throughout the Vehicle City. Alexander Cook, an A. F. of L. stalwart who arrived at Fisher Body 1 in 1926, recalled,

> There were no union men in the plant at that time. There were occasionally a few building tradesmen, but there was not agreement. *There was not much talk about the need for a union* at that time.[83]

As Cook's comments reveal, the mid-1920s, a period of improving economic conditions, expanded welfare capitalism, and continued public discussion of Americanization, was no time to organize a union. It is not surprising that the only mass job action of the era had nothing to do with union activity.

This remarkable event occurred on Armistice Day, 1925. It had a lot more in common with the super patriotic "Defense Day" celebration (which had been held a year earlier) than a genuine strike. It began early in the morning when several Chevrolet workers carrying two large American flags and rapping snare drums marched through the factory, encouraging many workers to drop their tools. A large group of marchers then continued on following the flags to Buick and AC Sparkplug. Police were warned that a riot was imminent, but General Motors officials got on the phones, shut down all the plants, and rapidly organized a patriotic parade and demonstration downtown. The marchers stopped at City Hall and were addressed by Mayor Transue. There, leadership of the demonstration passed from workers' to management's hands without any protest. I.M.A. director William Power next led what was by then a very big crowd over to Athletic Park for more speeches and the singing of patriotic anthems. The day ended with the circulation of petitions to Congress to have November 11 declared a national holiday. It was a workers' demonstration even the staunchly anti-labor *Flint Daily Journal* could praise.[84]

By the end of the decade, a leveling off of automobile sales began to affect local industrial relations. In 1928, brief job actions by Fisher Body 1 metal finishers in January, and by semiskilled machine operators at AC Sparkplug in March broke the city's long industrial peace. These limited work stoppages successfully blocked management's attempts to cut wages and raise production through piece rate adjustments. As such, they were the first sign that workers would resist efforts to adapt the workshop to the saturation of the new car market, if that meant lower earnings and a speed-up.[85]

A more serious strike by two hundred Buick oil sanders erupted in July 1928. On this occasion, piece rate cuts and an attempt to cheapen long-used materials (oil and sandpaper) prompted these semiskilled workers to walk off the job, put out a picket line, and send to Detroit for help from the Auto Workers Union. Strike leaders also sought advice from local Federation of Labor officials, but they were turned away because the A. F. of L. officials believed that the walkout "was caused and conducted by a group of Communists."[86] For twelve days, the National Conciliation Service officer on the scene accepted this judgement and also refused to speak directly with strike leaders. Conciliation Commisioner Marshman wrote to his superiors, "I felt that if these men were recognized by a representative of the Department they might possibly use it to intimidate others and probably do more harm than good."[87] In the meantime, Auto Workers Union organizers, who had rushed to Flint, used the occasion to hold meetings, distribute literature, and establish a small group of members. Fearing a spread of the strike (which after all involved just four-tenths of one percent of GM's labor force in the city), management gave in to the oil sanders' demands.[88] For a few months after this dispute, AWU organizers continued to make appearances in Flint, but the union's members never formed a functioning local. By year's end, despite the official AWU claim that they were "carrying on a quiet campaign to build up the Flint Local," the Auto Workers Union had disappeared from the Vehicle City.[89]

In May 1929, another piece rate dispute led to a spontaneous walkout by Fisher Body 1 sanders. But whereas the job actions and strike of 1928 had won concessions from surprised supervisors, in 1929, Fisher Body's plant manager overruled his foreman (who was ready to give in and restore the status quo), telling dissident workers he would rather fire them and rely on inventories than settle on their terms.[90] This display of firmness was effective. It ended the strike on management's terms. It also presaged the company's position during the Great Depression that was about to descend on the city. Yet until that time, there were no more departmental strikes in Flint.

The small, widely scattered labor disputes that punctuate the history of industrial relations in Flint during the later 1920s do not give credence to the notion that pre-depression auto workers shared a common set of deeply felt grievances. Though it is tempting to see a trend in these minor incidents, they cannot be called forerunners of the massive labor conflicts of the depression era. These few hundred highly paid semiskilled workers, who at one time or another dared to slow down the pace of rationalization hardly represented "a revolt from below." Tens of thousands of other workers never showed the slightest public inclination to join a union or to go out on strike. In other words, it was the general absence of working-class consciousness and class conflict, not a few isolated piece work disputes, which defined the character of industrial relations in the years of normalcy.

However, something more must be said to fill the void left by that negative description, "absence of working-class consciousness." Among the working people who never struck or joined a union were many workers who consistently turned out for patriotic parades and demonstrations and for company celebrations, like Buick's twenty-fifth anniversary, an event that attracted 125,000 people to

Flint's Kearsley Park just two weeks after the strike by two hundred oil sanders. If sheer numbers are representative, then events like this one or the 1924 Defense Day celebration are a far better measure of the political consciousness of Flint's working people than the history recorded by the Auto Workers Union.

The transformed character of everyday life during the second industrial revolution, including the wondrous mass consumption of a whole new realm of sensory-stimulating technology—telephones, phonographs, photographs, pulp magazines and comics, moving pictures, radios, cars, and even (as the Lindbergh craze revealed), airplanes—provided the essential foundations for business-class dominance of politics and industrial relations in the 1920s. As Warren Susman noted in his extremely perceptive essay, "Culture and Commitment,"

> Americans had begun to believe they had found the American Way of Life and had created a culture and that it was good. Believing so had become part of the culture itself, a response to finding roles to play, and learning . . . how to play them, which reemphasized basic institutions and values and reinforced them in a wide variety of ways.[91]

In Flint, the fusing of those "basic institutions and values" (especially faith in capitalism, Protestant morality, and the flag) with the economic roles working people were expected to play in the new consumer-oriented society was the major ideological achievement of the local business class. Of course, businessmen did not exercise complete cultural hegemony. The brief rise of the Ku Klux Klan and the continuous challenge posed by William McKeighan attest to that fact. Nevertheless, by directing the creation of a true consumer-oriented economy, by implementing extensive welfare-capitalist and Americanization programs, and by dominating politics and industrial relations, Flint's class-conscious business leaders shaped a world view and cultural identity for working people that most would continue to carry with them throughout the twentieth century.

In Flint, it was not long before that newly established world view and cultural identity would be challenged by unforeseen events. Once the Great Depression had undercut the material foundations of normalcy, local politics and industrial relations would be rocked by real class conflict. Yet in the midst of those hard times, Flint's working people could not simply "unlearn" their new social and cultural expectations and values. The everyday experience of normalcy with its steady work, high wages, relatively decent working conditions, and shining material hopes had been too vivid to forget. Instead, encouraged by the popular culture and by leading politicians, individual recollections of life prior to the Great Depression coalesced into a kind of collective memory of the 1920s which paradoxically both energized and set limits on the growth of local working-class consciousness and labor militance.

6

THE GREAT DEPRESSION IN FLINT

> The Buick automobile company is the backbone of the
> industrial life of Flint. . . . In August, the Buick factory
> closed down completely. City officials do not know when
> part-time operations will be resumed. —Official request
> by the State of Michigan for an emergency RFC loan for Flint,
> September 1932

A Sign of Things to Come: The Fisher Body Strike of 1930

The Great Depression quickly undermined the economic foundations
of normalcy in Flint. As a major automotive production center, the
city was extremely vulnerable to the collapse of consumer buying
power that followed the financial panic of 1929–1930. Falling demand
for cars forced local factories to cut the size of their payrolls during the
annual model change, and to put other workers on extended layoffs.
In the biggest plants, the rationalization of production was pursued
with unprecedented vigor. At the same time, wages were cut. Everett
Francis, the Fisher Body 1 trimmer, recalled,

The effects of the depression . . . were felt in our plant early in 1930, when
apparently the corporation anticipated less business because of the stock
market crash and tried to compensate for their loss by cutting the piecework rates of employees and notifying them that they must increase their
pace to maintain their earnings.[1]

In practice, it proved virtually impossible to keep wages up to pre-depression standards because management constantly adjusted base rates and work processes to achieve lower labor costs. So whether they worked or lost their jobs, the industrial working people of Flint almost immediately felt the economic collapse dim the hopes for a better life that they had nurtured in the 1920s.

The critical everyday problems that plagued auto workers during the early years of the Great Depression—unemployment and financial insecurity, declining earnings, and the notorious speed-up—also destroyed normalcy's deferential political culture. In Flint (and in many other industrial cities across the Midwest), the most significant depression-era political development was the organization of a Democratic-voting working class, strong enough to threaten the business-class monopoly over economic and political decision making, and cohesive enough to institutionalize its presence in society. The fact that this emerging working class and the New Deal it helped to foster proved to be neither revolutionary nor socialist, should not obscure its historical significance. Out of the bitterness and violence that marked so many local confrontations during the 1930s, a new kind of political economy (in which the Federal government and organized labor played much bigger roles) was created.

In Flint, angry, disillusioned working people first appeared on the streets in the spring of 1930. Local unemployment had risen very quickly during the winter, especially at Buick. The venerable division's sales had been falling slowly since 1926, and they fell very rapidly after the stockmarket crash.[2] During the Buick model change, many workers were simply released unconditionally. Similar cuts took place at other General Motors divisions. Officially, unemployment in the local automobile industry swelled to 11 percent by census-taking time. In the hard hit construction industry, it topped 25 percent of the local labor force.[3] In Detroit, the Communist leaders of the Auto Workers Union saw a new opportunity for working-class organization in these figures. The AWU claimed twenty-two members in Flint, and it included the city on the list of places where it sponsored unemployment protest marches on March 6. Led by AWU president Phil Raymond, a crowd of fifteen thousand people walked from Chevrolet to City Hall under banners proclaiming, "Don't Starve—Fight" and "Work or Wages." Local authorities, shocked by the sudden demonstration of mass dissent, cracked down instantly. Police dispersed the crowd, arrested all six AWU leaders, and held them without formal charges. When questioned later about these arrests at a congressional hearing, Police Chief Caesar Scarvarda, a veteran of the state police intervention in the copper strikes of 1913 and a close political ally of William McKeighan, answered frankly, "There is not any particular law that we can act on. . . . it was just simply a matter of preventing disorder which would naturally have resulted."[4]

The open display of force, heartily endorsed by the local press, seemed to have the desired effect. The Auto Workers Union was unable to set up a local in Flint. Moreover, the next hunger march on May 1, 1930, drew only twenty-five participants, and again, police arrested all of the AWU organizers arbitrarily.[5] Without testing any other alternatives, a predilection for answering mass protests with repression had been established. Just two months later, it would be confirmed in the first serious strike of the decade.

At nine o'clock in the morning of July 1, 1930, several hundred semiskilled auto workers in Flint's Fisher Body 1 metal finishing and trim departments walked off their jobs. Just a week earlier, management had announced the start of plantwide piece work revisions that raised production quotas and lowered base rates. As Buick's body supplier, Fisher Body 1 was being forced to retrench right along with the car division. Plant manager R. J. Whiting described the program as "wage readjustments required by changes in the models in production."[6] Workers called it a speed-up. Throughout the plant, they were ordered to produce more per day for less pay. Metal finishers and trimmers, two of the highest paid groups of production workers, tried the new system, but they could not earn the one dollar plus per hour that had been customary in the late 1920s. Supervisors ignored their complaints. A few days after the new rates took effect, workers in both departments spontaneously struck to protest the change.

The huge plant remained open that first morning of the strike. Excited metal finishers and trimmers met a short distance away at the Dixie Dance Hall and attempted to get organized. Help came from the outside in a hurry. At the start of the strike, someone (probably a union member) had immediately notified the Auto Workers Union in Detroit. Within two hours, a delegation led by Phil Raymond, the union's Communist president, arrived at the hall, ready to offer advice and recruit new members.[7] Through their hastily selected spokesman, Cecil Comstock, the strikers had already announced that they wanted the piece rate cuts rolled back, but they had no plan of action. Raymond and his fellow AWU organizers provided temporary leadership that quickly escalated this departmental walkout into the industry's first-ever plantwide strike.

Shortly after noon, the strikers moved back to Fisher Body 1. Urged on by Raymond and Comstock, they entered the factory and marched from one department to another, inviting other workers to join them. The speed-up had already dissaffected a large part of this predominantly young workforce, so the strikers received an enthusiastic response to their call for solidarity.[8] In the uproar, most of the first shift joined the walkout. Plant manager Whiting locked out the rest and closed the plant to the second shift. At least 3,600 workers had struck Fisher Body 1. All totaled, the combined strike-lockout idled more than 7,500 persons.[9]

Late that afternoon, while supervisors shut down the plant, a large crowd gathered outside Fisher Body 1. Once assembled, they paraded across town to the Buick plant, where Auto Workers Union organizers hoped to spread the strike. A caravan of automobiles preceded the strikers and their supporters, attracting more people to the demonstration at Buick. By the time the marchers reached the gates of the giant complex, the crowd had swelled to more than fifteen thousand demonstrators. At this point, during the Buick shift change, the Flint police intervened, arresting three AWU officials and "a few local boys" who tried to protect them.[10] To avoid a confrontation that could break the strike before it was organized, Comstock and Raymond encouraged the strikers to disperse and reassemble at the Dixie Dance Hall for a mass meeting. The hall was just outside the city limits, making it a temporary refuge from expected police interference.

This first mass meeting was well attended. AWU organizers circulated through the group, signing up hundreds of new members. The AWU's radicals also dominated the proceedings, offering advice based on prior experience and preparation. A large strike committee of 120 workers and union officials was elected. The whole process of organizing the strike along democratic lines inspired optimism and a willingness to follow up other suggestions made by the tiny band of union representatives. F. R. Palmer, a young worker who had been laid off more than four months during the 1930 model change, remembered, "I was very naive and knew nothing about unionism or unions . . . we had a meeting and elected a committee and did everything very democratically and we felt very confident."[11] Cecil Comstock, a moderate who would not join the Communist-dominated

Auto Workers Union, was elected strike committee chairman, but initially, the union's officials exercised greater influence.

On the second day of the strike, Wednesday July 2, the groundwork for a confrontation was laid. The strike committee issued an expanded list of demands that conformed closely to the official AWU platform. In addition to rolling back piece rate cuts, the strikers now asked management for guaranteed minimum wages for men and women, equal pay for equal work, a guaranteed forty-hour week, and improvements in working conditions.[12] The prominence of women workers' demands here reflected both an Auto Workers Union commitment and the fact that women from the upholstery shops had been active in the strike since the first spontaneous walkout. In an attempt to broaden their base of support, moderates on the strike committee solicited assistance from the Flint Federation of Labor, but they were rebuffed. Local A. F. of L. officials refused to step into the conflict unless the strikers broke all contact with the Auto Workers Union. A friend of George Starkweather who was involved in this appeal recollected, "He [Starkweather] gave me advice. He did not give me any help. He advised me, some of the building tradesmen did too, that it [the AWU] was a left-wing outfit and so on and so forth."[13] Publicly, Starkweather denounced Raymond and the other AWU organizers as "Russians, Bulgarians, and Whatnots . . . a bunch of howling REDS that can't even talk United States good enough so that the average man can understand them."[14]

The rabid anti-communism displayed by Flint's A. F. of L. leaders was not unusual. Rather it represented the official response of all elements of the local establishment to the Fisher Body strike. Plant manager R. J. Whiting refused to meet with representatives of the strikers claiming that "this entire trouble had developed from the activities of foreign agitators and communists from Detroit, Pontiac, and Chicago."[15] He announced that the plant would reopen on Friday, July 3. The strike committee called for mass picketing to block the plant's entrances in the morning. Police Chief Scarvarda readied his men and notified the state police that they might need additional manpower. At five A.M. on July 3, when approximately fifteen hundred pickets turned out at Fisher Body 1, thirty-five state troopers reinforced the local police on the scene. In addition, Governor Green was asked to put the local National Guard on alert.[16] An unprecedented decision to break an auto workers strike with force had been made.

Striking women workers led the long picket line towards Fisher Body 1 shortly after dawn on July 3. Club-wielding state and local police took up positions in order to deny the pickets access to the plant gates. At this point, men replaced the women at the front of the picket line, and they attempted to move ahead. A scuffle erupted, breaking the tension. The police began to use their clubs freely, and the strikers scattered. About twenty persons, including Phil Raymond and Louise Morrison of the Auto Workers Union, were arrested. Fisher Body 1 opened, but of the 1,200 people who reported for work that day, just seventy were production line workers.[17] The violence of the morning raised questions about continued AWU leadership among moderates on the strike committee, but the strike proceeded. Indeed, a combined mass meeting and picnic was scheduled for Sunday, July 6. However, while the plant was closed for the holiday weekend, more repressive measures were used to shatter the strikers' already fragile unity.

Most importantly, Flint police selectively terrorized AWU organizers and their supporters. At four A.M. on July 4, the home of AWU sympathizer John Werner was raided. Policemen arrested Werner and two eighteen-year-old members of the Communist Party's Young Pioneers, who were part of the Auto Workers' organizing team in Flint. A pistol, a mimeograph machine and AWU records and literature were seized. At police headquarters, Chief Scarvarda selected fifty names at random from the 581 union membership cards taken in the raid. These people were picked up and brought downtown for questioning. A U.S. Immigration Service inspector was even called on to search the seized records for the names of those whom the *Flint Daily Journal* described as "non-citizen agitators."[18]

Police-state tactics and the press reports that continued to brand the strike "RED" confused and demoralized many workers. Jack Palmer, the South Dakota–born production worker who was just twenty-two at the time recollected, "It flabbergasted me as a kid because everything I read in the papers stated we were communists or something. I didn't even know what a communist was then."[19] Cecil Comstock, leader of the initial spontaneous strike, was also troubled by the new turn of events. Flint Federation of Labor leaders had told him that the company might meet with a delegation of strikers if they renounced the Auto Workers Union and expelled its official committee. However, if the AWU remained, there was absolutely no chance for negotiations.[20] On Saturday July 5, Comstock ruptured the solidarity of the strike by publicly repudiating the Auto Workers Union, while at the same time he announced the formation of an Automobile Workers Association of Flint. A new executive committee of ten men and one woman was elected at a hastily arranged meeting at the Dixie Dance Hall. One member explained that the AWU organizers had been sent back to Detroit because, "They showed us how to organize ourselves and that is the only use we had for them." This statement was only half true. Most of the union's organizing contingent had not retreated to Detroit; they were in the Flint city jail.[21]

AWU leaders later denounced Comstock's actions as treachery and as "the social fascist policy," but he seems to have had the support of the majority of the strikers.[22] The spontaneous character of the original walkout now resurfaced. At the inaugural meeting of the original independent association, the strikers scaled down their demands to a single idea: a "living wage." Essentially their definition of a living wage recalled the everyday material expectations of normalcy. They described it as,

such wage as will support a family in reasonable circumstances, allowing for schooling of children, paying for homes, life insurance, medical and dental services, and pay for their bills contracted for food, clothing, and other necessities.[23]

For this living wage—a demand that reflected a basic willingness to live within the system if it delivered an "American standard of living"—most of the strikers resolved to continue their protest. Official Flint responded with an offer, and with more force.

Strike committee members met with plant manager Whiting *at police headquarters* on the afternoon of July 5. Mr. Whiting offered to guarantee daily earnings at 1929 rates for six months, but only if workers accepted the increased speed of production. He refused to put anything in writing or to spell out the particulars of the proposed piece rate scale. The strike committee reiterated its demands, this time with specifics about the rates and hours they expected for various categories of work. The parties reached no agreement, nor did they make any further plans to seek one.[24]

The next day, Sunday, July 6, state and local police descended on the Dixie Dance Hall, breaking up a mass meeting that had been scheduled to follow the strikers' holiday picnic. Fleeing workers were pursued relentlessly by state troopers who refused to let them stop and gather. Additional arrests were made. The last remnants of the group were actually chased across the Oakland County line, eighteen miles from Flint.[25]

Monday morning when Fisher Body 1 reopened, police patrolled the streets around the plant, preventing attempts to establish a picket line. Ten more dissident workers were arrested on the official pretext that "all gatherings of the strikers were regarded as 'unlawful assemblies' and were subject to police discipline."[26] About thirty-one hundred workers returned to work on July 7. R. J. Whiting proclaimed the strike over. Strikers were told they could report for work, but some would be called in for "personal interviews." To encourage returnees, Whiting also ordered his personnel director to start taking applications from the unemployed.[27]

This last pressure tactic, a weapon management would be able to use against dissidents throughout the 1930s, finally broke the strike. On Tuesday, July 8, more than five thousand workers returned to their jobs, and no pickets appeared outside the plant. The next day, Fisher Body 1 resumed completely normal operations. Workers found the same conditions they had left. The settlement of grievances was left up to departmental supervisors. Twenty-three strikers, including Cecil Comstock and several women from the upholstery shop, were dismissed. Comstock's association of Flint auto workers simply disintegrated, and Comstock himself left town after a short tenure at Fisher Body 2. Plant manager Whiting was transferred out of Flint soon after the strike ended.[28] As a worker protest against depression-inspired conditions, the strike had failed completely.

Because it produced neither a permanent auto workers union nor a long list of physical casualties, the Fisher Body strike of 1930 has long been overshadowed in the historical record by the momentous General Motors sit-down strike that established the U.A.W.-C.I.O. six-and-a-half years later. Given the traditional interest of labor historians in strikes that either made or broke workers' organizations, this neglect is understandable. Yet, when the lesser incident is considered from a different perspective, as a public indication of how a Great Depression could change society, it takes on the significance of a "watershed" event in local history. The Fisher Body strike dramatically marked the beginnings of an upheaval that ultimately would destroy the political economy of normalcy and replace it with a system that provided a place for organized labor and regulated class conflict.

The institutional dimensions of this turbulent transformation would not become clear for many years to come. Nonetheless, by the summer of 1930, something had changed. When the Great Depression began to undermine the essential economic underpinnings of normalcy, auto workers forcefully demonstrated a willingness to act together to protect the quality of their lives. Resistance to the company's "belt-tightening" policies came first at Fisher Body 1 because of that plant's economic vulnerability, and because its relatively new workforce had no close personal ties to management. As we have seen, from start to finish, the strike reflected an independent indigenous response to the Great Depression, not a commitment to the preformed ideologies of existing labor unions. Both radical and conservative union leaders gave advice and organizational assistance to the strikers, yet neither the Communists of the AWU nor the business-unionists from the Federation of Labor could control the strike. Ultimately, both groups were spurned by workers who were extremely militant, but distinctly nonradical. The unpredictable combination of industrial-based militance and nonradical political independence displayed by the Fisher Body strikers of 1930 previewed the kind of values that would soon unite auto workers all over the city in an effort to establish a local auto workers union.

In 1930, company and city officials were unwilling (or perhaps in some cases unable) to distinguish between the limited material grievances of the strikers and the radical ideology of a few AWU organizers. They treated what remained essentially a limited piece rate dispute as an event that threatened the entire social order. Heavy-handed official repression broke the strike, setting a precedent for its expanded use in later confrontations between workers and management. In this sense, the Fisher Body strike signalled an eventual escalation in the level of industrial violence in Flint.

The city's establishment rallied as a class around Fisher Body management during the dispute. Businessmen, municipal officials, the local press, and even the Flint Federation of Labor denounced the strike, and they all worked together to crush it. To rationalize the repressive tactics used against the strikers, Flint's business-class elite revived nativism and red-baiting. This revival set worker against worker, accentuating the competition for already scarce jobs. By deliberately cultivating anti-communist hysteria during the strike, the city's business class also encouraged a public mockery of justice. As late as July 10, two days after the strike had collapsed, Circuit Court Judge Edward Black still refused to issue writs of habeas corpus for eighteen jailed strikers (some of whom had been held in custody for at least five days without having been charged with a crime). "I do not consider them the equal of any other criminal," the judge told ACLU lawyer Nicholas Olds, "and as far as I am concerned, they can rot in jail."[29] Some of the jailed strikers remained in custody for several additional days. On Friday, July 11, the *Flint Daily Journal* reported that two released "Red agitators" had been kidnapped and beaten after leaving the city jail. The culprits were never found.

In the years preceding the U.A.W.–C.I.O.'s victory in the sit-down strike of 1936–37, Flint's establishment remained actively committed to the task of blocking the organization of dissident auto workers. Indiscriminate red-baiting and the use of force temporarily secured business class dominance. However, as the depression dragged on, that dominance rested more and more on working people's fears, instead of on their deference. For a few years, constant economic insecurity and a systematic extension of General Motors' anti-union efforts prevented another major strike. Yet, once all Flint workers had felt the daily degradation of life and work brought on by the Great Depression, renewed efforts to organize a union to improve conditions gained widespread support. In the longer run, far from removing a "threat from below," the predilection for repression established during the 1930 strike clarified the boundaries between "above" and "below" in Flint. As a sign of things to come, the Fisher Body 1 strike heralded the end of normalcy and the opening of a new era of increased class conflict in industrial relations and politics.

Economic Collapse

The mass market for automobiles disappeared during the Hoover years of the Great Depression. By 1932, the industry's total output had fallen to 1.3 million units, 75 percent fewer cars than it had produced in 1929. Many smaller automobile manufacturers and component makers were forced into bankruptcy. In fact, by eliminating lesser competitors, the Great Depression eventually strengthened the Big Three's hold on the car market.[30] But for a few years, even the big firms had to fight for their survival. General Motors' sales plunged 39 percent in 1930. The following year, GM's sales declined more slowly, although the Buick division's fortunes continued to plummet. General Motors sold 72 percent fewer vehicles in 1932 than it had in 1929. The two divisions with major production facilities in Flint were particularly hard hit. In 1932, the giant corporation's mainstay, Chevrolet, marketed only 384,000 cars and trucks, nearly one million units less than its pre-depression peak. Buick fared even worse. Its sales dropped to just 42,000 vehicles in 1933, an 84 percent decline from the division's best year, 1926.[31]

Declining sales of Buicks and Chevrolets created an economic disaster in Flint. To maintain profitable operations, General Motors' management pursued rigorous retrenchment policies designed to cut costs faster than revenues were falling. In Flint, the company reduced its production schedules and workforce while simultaneously raising the speed of production and the output expected from each worker. Throughout the early years of the Great Depression, wage cuts and speed-ups like those that had prompted the Fisher Body 1 strike were pressed upon all of the company's remaining production workers.[32] Salaried workers also faced layoffs and pay reductions. In addition, some fringe benefits, including the savings and investment plan for blue-collar workers, were terminated.[33] Together, these cost-cutting measures kept General Motors out of the red during the Great Depression. The company even managed to show a small profit in 1932, a year of drastically reduced revenues. Beginning in 1933, General Motors' production, sales, and profits rose steadily, approaching record levels as early as 1936.[34]

In Flint, General Motors' successful retrenchment policies produced a dramatic decline in local business activities, generally lower material living standards, and long-term mass unemployment. Home building, the city's second biggest industry, was devastated by the collapse of the automobile boom. New construction had actually peaked in 1927, but until 1929, Flint builders put up an average of 2,500 new housing units per year. In 1930, they built 360 homes. The following year, the total fell to only 128 new uints. Things then went from bad to worse. During the next three years, from 1932 to 1934, just 45 new housing units were added to the city's housing stock, even though "hundreds" of families still lived in what a contemporary Civil Works Administration survey termed "temporary" buildings.[35] Private construction activity increased slightly in subsequent years. However, as late as 1940, Flint's home building industry remained severely depressed.[36]

Most other Flint businesses also suffered as a result of the cutbacks in General Motors' local operations. Dependent firms, including foundries, machine shops, and small parts makers, were forced to imitate the giant corporation's retrenchments. Some of these companies failed to hold on long enough to see the revival of local automobile production in 1933–34. Wholesalers, retail businessmen, and transportation companies also fell victim to steadily declining demand during the years 1930–33. As the purchasing power of workers was eroded by wage cuts, short-time, and layoffs, many small businesses simply went under. Moreover, as increasing numbers of working people fell behind on the repayment of installment loans and home mortgages, several local financial institutions were driven to bankruptcy.[37]

In Flint, the link between automotive retrenchment and the generalization of depression conditions was clear. The city's request for an emergency Reconstruction Finance Corporation loan in mid-1932 claimed, "With automobile production reduced by one-third in the last two years a similar reduction has taken place throughout other business operations of the city."[38] In August 1932 the Buick Motor Company, which had employed as many as twenty-two thousand people just three years earlier, shut down completely. It was the final blow. Although Buick production and sales would be fully restored under the aggressive new management of H. H. Curtice by 1936–7, the company's closure in late 1932 brought economic activities in Flint to a near standstill. By the end of the year, for all practical purposes, Flint's industrial economy had collapsed.

During the Great Depression, virtually all of Flint's industrial workers endured periods of prolonged unemployment. In the early 1930s, extensions of the annual model change and unscheduled reductions in production affected everyone in the local automobile industry. Although most experienced workers did not actually lose their jobs between 1930 and 1933, with each passing year, they faced longer layoffs, more short-time, and deeper wage cuts.[39] Under these circumstances, the high material living standards of Flint's permanent population of working people were quickly eroded. During the very worst years, 1932 and 1933, many Flint auto workers earned only a few hundred dollars. By 1934, when recovery had begun, NRA investigators found that the annual earnings of the bulk of the automotive workforce (skilled and semiskilled) had fallen to less than half their 1929 levels.[40]

Undoubtedly, falling prices helped to cushion the impact of drastically reduced earnings in the early 1930s, but prices did not fall nearly enough to keep most of Flint's working people out of desperate financial trouble.[41] During the first round of layoffs, many auto workers managed to preserve their living standards in ways they had learned to do in the 1920s. In March 1930, one local personal loan company discovered that fully half its clients were unemployed auto workers. To secure these loans, the company promptly went out and found jobs for all but a handful of those workers.[42] In a brief recession, such short-term measures would have solved most working people's difficulties, yet as the depression deepened, increasing personal and corporate debt only made matters worse.

In 1931, more and more of Flint's permanent working people fell behind on their taxes and mortgage payments. By 1932 many workers had lost their precious homes and all the money they had invested in them. Problems with house payments continued to plague underemployed auto workers in the early New Deal years. More than 1,100 Flint residents forfeited their homes in 1933 and 1934, years when the foreclosure rate was already declining.[43] Automobiles, insurance policies, and other amenities of the new consumer-oriented lifestyle that had emerged during the 1920s were also sacrificed. In this sense, the Great Depression seemed to turn back the clock, thrusting working people into everyday life conditions usually identified with an earlier, more "primitive" stage of industrial capitalism. "In those days," Fisher Body's Jack Palmer later recalled, "we did not worry about payday. We worried about our next meal. That was how hard up everybody was. We worked a few hours a week."[44]

Actually, the industrial workers of Flint who held onto their jobs, even if they worked just a few hours a week, were relatively lucky. Many others were laid off and never rehired. Those with little experience, especially recent arrivals and very young workers and those whom management deemed to be "too old," were particularly vulnerable.[45] Their jobs were "made redundant" in the early 1930s, as hard-pressed plant managers permanently reduced their labor force requirements by shifting more and more of the work load to the most productive, experienced workers. Every major auto factory in the city was subjected to more intense rationalization of production. In some departments new machinery was introduced; everywhere the pace of production was stepped-up. Overall, between 1930 and 1936, General Motors eliminated at least nine thousand blue-collar jobs in Flint, without any loss in productive capacity. The most substantial reductions were made at the city's oldest auto plant, Buick, after H. H. Curtice took over its management. By 1940, when the division exceeded its pre-depression output record by 14 percent, it employed fully one-third fewer workers than it had in the late 1920s.[46]

Ironically, in depression circumstances, what was good for General Motors was not necessarily good for Flint. Reductions in labor force requirements that increased productivity were an essential part of the corporation's successful recovery program, but clearly, they also created severe long-term unemployment problems for the city. Not surprisingly, many workers chose to leave Flint when faced with the prospect of extended joblessness. According to a Civil Works Administration estimate in 1934, the city lost 13 percent of its total population during the first four desperate years of the Great Depression.[47] Recent arrivals left in the largest numbers. It seems likely that many of these people returned, at least temporarily, to some form of rural life. Large numbers of southern-born working people (who formed the biggest group of out-migrants) went back home.[48] All over Michigan, unemployed industrial workers tried to find jobs in the farm labor force as soon as the depression began. Near Flint, a considerable number of working people moved onto small subsistence-sized farms in the rural townships that surrounded the city.[49]

In the later 1930s, as the local automobile industry recovered, the population of Flint's fringe areas was augmented by a large in-migration of newcomers from other states and from other of Michigan. By the end of the decade, the outlying districts of Genessee County had grown nearly 40 percent, while Flint's population remained below its pre-depression peak. Still, the fringe areas did not yet become true suburbs. Instead, prior to industrialization during the 1940s (as part of wartime expansion), most of Flint's fringe areas retained the characteristics of "underdeveloped" agrarian America.[50] On the fringe, "marginal" working people shaped individualistic responses to the Great Depression by combining the everyday life of rural tenants with occasional periods of regular employment in the city's factories. Thus, on a personal level, Flint's fringe areas continued to function as they had in the 1920s, providing a refuge for working people who were not ready to make a permanent commitment to urban-industrial life.[51]

Yet most working people could not simply leave Flint to escape the Great Depression. Tens of thousands had already forged strong personal ties to their homes in the city.[52] Their commitments to urban-industrial life were permanently embodied in the lives they had made for themselves and their families during the automobile boom. Such longtime residents never entertained serious thoughts of leaving the city. As one unemployed Buick worker observed in 1934, "I have been in Flint about twenty years now and *cannot* go any other place."[53]

In addition, many other formerly "marginal" (one is tempted to use the term "migrant") industrial workers eventually settled down during the 1930s. They had very few alternatives. Although some working people could retreat from the industrial depression and find refuge with rural friends and family, a mass exodus back to the land had become impossible. Everywhere one looked in the early 1930s, agriculture was at least as depressed as manufacturing. Moreover, throughout the worst years of the crisis, before New Deal programs like Agricultural Adjustment and Rural Electrification took hold, material conditions in rural America remained more primitive, and therefore less attractive, than those in the cities. Most important, the chance of finding any kind of effective emergency relief programs in the countryside was just about nil. At the same time, flight to other cities offered little real hope for economic improvement. Transient workers discovered that all the previously booming industrial centers of the Midwest suffered from mass unemployment and widespread underemployment during the early depression; and not all of them recovered as quickly as Flint. Consequently, when workers were lucky enough to secure automotive employment, they held onto it, even if the jobs were uncertain, irregular, and increasingly degrading.

In Flint, residential turnover remained very high during the first half of the depression decade. However, once the local automobile industry started its vigorous recovery, the city's population began to settle down and stabilize.[54] The main reason behind this important demographic change is clear. Industrial workers, discontented with local conditions, learned that they could no longer "strike with their feet" as they had done during the automobile boom. Instead, depression circumstances forced workers to endure what formerly they would have rejected. When questioned by NRA investigators about the effects of the stepped-up pace of production, one thirteen-year veteran of Flint's auto shops described the new attitude perfectly. "Of course in normal times [referring to the 1920s] that resentment against the speed-up takes care of itself," explained James Pipes in December 1934, "but today the men will drop dead before they quit their jobs."[55]

The Great Depression trapped many "marginal" working people, compelling them to make a more permanent commitment to industrial life in Flint. On an even wider scale, the depression weakened industrial workers' faith in individual geographic mobility. In this sense, economic collapse was an essential prerequisite for the organization of an industrial working class in Flint. For it not only intensified and generalized the very worst problems of everyday life and work in an automotive production center, the Great Depression also closed a "safety valve" that had previously allowed auto workers to devise their own, individualistic solutions to those problems.

During the Hoover years, when long layoffs, increased short-time, and falling earnings affected everyone in Flint, some working people despaired. In the poorest parts of the city, economic troubles undermined family unity, giving rise to an alarming growth in juvenile crime.[56] Elsewhere, auto workers who had labored long and hard to establish themselves as property-owners, experienced severe emotional stress when forced to give up their homes and savings. NRA investigators commenting on the hearings held in Flint in December 1934 could not help but note how deeply some workers had been scarred by their losses. "So often did it occur, that it should be here recorded," they wrote in their preliminary report, "that witnesses, whose economic plight was tragic, need must be interrupted by us so as to stay the well of tears that surged within them."[57] Nevertheless, it would be wrong to assume that all hope was lost. Without any bargaining power on the job, and with the memory of the repression of 1930 still fresh in their minds, there was not much resident auto workers and their families could do in those terrible years except tighten their household budgets and look for new, political sources of assistance. As a matter of fact, far from becoming apathetic, most working people in Flint focused their attention on relief problems and political candidates when their economic situation deteriorated.

The Relief Crisis and Political Realignment

Despite the extraordinary prior development of local welfare-capitalist services, Flint did not escape the relief crisis that afflicted virtually every city in the nation during the Hoover years. Indeed, welfare capitalism was one of the major casualties of the Great Depression in Flint. In 1930–1931, the Industrial Mutual Association provided food and coal allowances to at least twelve hundred workers and their families, but its benefits were meager and often they lasted just one week.[58] As economic conditions worsened, I.M.A. resources ran short, forcing the organization to curtail its relief efforts in 1932, about the same time that General Motors suspended payments to workers enrolled in its blue-collar savings and investment plan.[59] Contributions to the I.M.A. remained mandatory for all GM workers throughout the mid-1930s. In addition, many supervisors required workers to continue to pay the traditional five-dollar donation to the Community Chest. Both practices were bitterly resented by some workers. After the establishment of the United Automobile Workers Union in 1937, these collections ceased. As a result, the I.M.A. had to drop its newspaper and sell off its clubrooms and recreational facilities in 1939.[60] By that time, union-sponsored newspapers, social events, and recreational activities had already replaced welfare capitalism in many workers' lives.

Just one local philanthropic organization, the Mott Foundation, expanded in the face of depression difficulties. It managed this feat by avoiding direct relief efforts and by opening itself up to new ideas. At the urging of Frank Manley, a former Minnesota high school gym teacher and genuine progressive, the foundation created an ambitious citywide recreation program to control the worst effects of severe youth employment and rising juvenile delinquency. During the New Deal years, Manley's influence within the foundation grew, until he was finally made its director. In cooperation with local government and several Federal agencies, Manley pushed the foundation into the fields of health and adult education. These recreational and educational initiatives broke with the strictly private philosophy of traditional welfare capitalism and philanthropy. In fact, they bore some resemblance to proposals originally made by the city's Socialists before World War I. Then C. S. Mott had opposed them as radical, but in the very different circumstances of the 1930s, he recognized the need for change. Yet the results of this change were hardly socialistic. Through the Manley programs, Mott actually put the resources of the school system and the federal government to work under his private direction.[61] After World War II, Mott Foundation programs gained national recognition, establishing them as models for a new kind of post-New Deal community action "from above." By finding innovative responses to the Great Depression, the Mott Foundation became the most significant survivor of Flint's welfare-capitalist era.

Unfortunately for the people of Flint, when the depression reached its nadir, local charity and welfare capitalism failed to meet even the most basic needs of the unemployed. Private contributions to the city's welfare programs all but dried up during the Hoover years. In 1932, only 7 percent of the nearly $1.2 million spent on relief in Flint came from private sources.[62] However, like local governments all across the country, the city of Flint was not equipped to shoulder the burden of relief alone. By 1932, it desperately needed outside assistance.

Flint had received lots of advice from the Federal and state governments, but, until the winter of 1932–1933, no direct tangible aid.[63] As a result, the city's relief problems had degenerated into a serious local financial crisis. Squeezed by the rising demand for welfare and work relief, and by rapidly falling tax receipts, Flint's municipal government teetered on the edge of bankruptcy throughout Herbert Hoover's last year in the White House.[64] Both of the perennially feuding factions who alternately controlled the new nonpartisan city commission were forced to authorize drastic cuts in regular services and the city's payroll. Yet, neither William McKeighan's "Green Slate" (in power from April 1931 to May 1932) nor the automotive executives who dominated the vehemently anti-McKeighan Civic League (in power in 1930 and most of 1932) could bring the crisis under control. In April 1932, the city had to borrow $100,000 from local banks to meet its current fiscal obligations. In June, it defaulted. Local bankers again came to the rescue, but now, they demanded and got full control of the city's finances. Deeper budget cuts followed, and still the crisis worsened.[65]

When Buick shut down in August, Flint faced imminent financial collapse for the third time in six months, and on this occasion, even the local banks could not help. Luckily, beleaguered city officials and bankers finally had somewhere to turn for outside assistance. Under intense pressure from the public, the president and the Congress had begun to retreat from their defense of local responsibility for relief. In July 1932, they had created the Reconstruction Finance Corporation to pump new money into the banking system and the states where relief problems were most severe. RFC loans bailed Flint out of its immediate troubles in the fall of 1932. The following spring, Franklin Roosevelt's new administration initiated a series of federal emergency relief, work relief, and welfare programs that lifted the financial burden of unemployment relief from local governments. In Flint, and in the nation as a whole, the implementation of these most effective parts of Roosevelt's New Deal ended the relief crisis.[66]

In November 1932, America's working people demanded increased federal relief and recovery efforts by voting Democratic in record numbers. In this sense, the so-called "New Deal realignment" of the country's political balance—a shift from Republican to Democratic dominance of the federal government—seems to have preceded anything Franklin Roosevelt and the Democrats did in office.[67] Certainly, this was true in Flint. There, high unemployment and drastic declines in material living standards sparked a new interest in politics during the Hoover years. As it developed, rising concern about political and economic problems led Flint's workers in two basic directions. On one hand, a small but very influential minority were truly and deeply radicalized by the Great Depression. On the other hand, the vast majority of the city's working people simply turned to the ballot box and to the alternative to Hoover Republicanism offered by the Democratic Party. For the most part, throughout the 1930s and early 1940s, there were no critical tensions between these two movements. In fact, most of the time, the local radicals, who played a very big role in the organization of the U.A.W., supported Democratic candidates at the polls.

In the early years of the Great Depression, informal discussions about politics increased workers' awareness of political issues and of the possibilities of their electoral participation. By 1932, even radical political ideas were being examined wherever working people gathered. "They were living hand-to-mouth," recalled Al Cook, the basically conservative, Colorado-born Fisher Body 1 worker, "and it was getting worse and worse down the line. . . . there was a lot of discussion in cardrooms and certain places that the country is going to have to change its form of government."[68] Although this kind of informal examination of radicalism undoubtedly helped to politicize many of Flint's working people, it did not lead to a massive upsurge of support for actual radical parties. Nevertheless, small groups of Communists and Socialists were formed in Flint during the first half of the depression decade.

The exact origins of Flint's radical groups, and their numerical strength at any given moment, remain shrouded in mystery and factional controversy. However, recent research has clarified some developments. It now seems reasonably certain that between sixty and one hundred people had joined the Communist Party in Flint by 1936. Many of these new party members were foreign-born residents who lived in the First Ward neighborhoods around the Buick plant. The Bulgarian-Macedonian Workers' Education Club in the St. John's Street neighborhood provided a regular meeting place for party members. By late 1934, a small Communist Party unit had been established in the Buick plant. Similar units were established at Fisher Body 1 and Chevrolet in 1935–1936. The Fisher Body unit, led by Walter Moore, Joe Devitt, and Bud Simons—all friends and veterans of the 1930 auto workers strike at the Hayes-Ionia plant in Grand Rapids—was the city's strongest. It would be a primary organizing force in the great GM sit-down strike of 1936–1937.[69]

In May 1935, Flint's Communists felt bold enough to challenge *Flint Weekly Review* publisher George Starkweather to a public debate over the policies of the A. F. of L. in the automobile industry. In July, Max Salzman of the "Communist Party, Flint section" repeated the challenge. Starkweather refused, and he used the invitations as excuses for running a series of page-one attacks on the Communist "vipers" who were undermining already failed A. F. of L. organizing efforts in the auto industry.[70] Yet, the controversy was significant because it gave the local Communist Party a public profile it had previously avoided.

Flint Socialists also made themselves visible in this period. It appears that their numbers grew, in part, through the efforts of Roy Reuther, who set up a Federal Emergency Relief Administration workers' education project in Flint in the fall of 1934. Among those who assisted the dynamic Reuther were Chevrolet workers Kermit Johnson, Tom Klasey, and Ted LaDuke and their wives Genora, Geraldine, and Hester. By mid-decade, these Socialists were holding regular meetings in the Pengelly Building, where they shared a room with two other very small radical groups, the Socialist Labor Party and the Proletarian Party (more of a left-wing reading group than an active political organization). In January 1936, Flint's Socialists felt secure enough to host a three-day meeting of the state's tiny Socialist Party. This meeting gave local Socialists an important morale boost, but the party's influence over electoral questions remained minimal. However, during the General Motors' sit-down strike, Socialists like Roy Reuther and the Johnsons played vital organizing roles.[71]

Other less radical but politically active workers organized in Flint in this period. A Trade Unionists' Progressive Club, similar to organizations in Detroit, Lansing, and Toledo, was also formed in 1935. It consisted of a few dozen nonradical union men, most of whom had been active in the A. F. of L.'s big automotive organizing drive of 1933–1934. This group was initially dedicated to keeping the A. F. of L. alive in the auto plants after it had lost worker support in early

1934. In December 1935, this Progressive Club voted to contact John L. Lewis and the then Committee for Industrial Organization. It continued to meet through 1936, discussing various union organizing strategies and political issues. The club was important because it channeled C.I.O. pamphlets and information to interested groups of auto workers in the plants. However, for the most part, these "progressive" unionists made little or no effort to influence general elections.[72]

The long struggle to organize the industrial workers of Flint and the factional disputes that raged within the auto workers union until 1950 provided Flint's most politicized workers with a kind of self-contained political universe in which to develop their ideas and expend their energies. Throughout the 1930s and early 1940s, many of the leaders of Flint's emerging industrial working class were drawn from these small groups of politically active workers. Generally, these leaders did not immerse themselves in specific election campaigns. Like the bulk of the rank and file, local union leaders, whether they were Communists, Socialists, Progressives, or unaffiliated, usually supported the candidates of the Democratic Party because they perceived the Democrats to be "a friend of labor," who would allow workers to solve their own problems through the union movement. In retrospect, this faith in the Democratic Party may seem to have been misguided. Yet, historically, the reasons why it developed are clear.

In Flint, as quickly as economic conditions deteriorated, voter registrations and participation soared. The surge of new and previously marginal voters to the polls actually started in 1930. In March, a record tewnty-five thousand citizens voted in the city's first nonpartisan primary. A month later, an even larger number turned out to give the automotive establishments's Civic League a seven-to-two margin on the new city commission.[73] Finally, in November, unusually heavy participation in the off-year general elections cut deeply into the "normal" Republican landslide margins in several key races. In Flint, at least, two major aspects of the New Deal realignment—increased voter turnout and the development of a lasting Democratic majority —were already apparent in 1930, long before anyone had heard of the New Deal.[74]

Despite a steadily declining population and the formally nonpartisan character of municipal elections, local contests continued to draw more people into the electoral process during 1931 and 1932. In the absence of any effective relief policy, the relief crisis focused public attention on the problems of local government. It breathed new, but very temporary life, into the old rivalry between the automotive elite and William McKeighan. Rising concern over the administration of emergency relief and the city's budget complicated the already heated controversy between Civic League supporters of the new charter and "Green Slate" proponents of a return to the old mayoral system. Another turnout record was set in April 1931, when new voters swept the "Green Slate" into power on the city commission. After this stunning reversal, both the appointed city manager and the Civic Leagues's mayor-commissioner resigned. "Green Slate" leader McKeighan, who had reached out for working people's votes, billing himself as "Flint's Friend of All Classes and Creeds," seized the opportunity to reestablish a strong mayor-council system that he could dominate.[75]

McKeighan tried to run the city without regard for the new charter. Once the "Green Slate" commissioners had elected him mayor and had approved his appointment of Police Chief Caesar Scarvarda as "acting city manager without pay," McKeighan simply assumed the powers of a strong mayor. A "Green Slate" charter restoring the mayor-council system was prepared in order to legitimize this coup, but before it could be submitted to the voters, McKeighan had to prove that he could handle the city's relief and fiscal problems more effectively than Civic League city management had. It was an impossible task, especially for a politician committed to expanding municipal work relief and welfare to secure the electoral support of disadvantaged blue-collar voters. Under McKeighan, relief expenditures per capita nearly doubled, even though rising unemployment forced reductions in average family benefits beginning in January 1932. McKeighan's most controversial welfare grant, $35,000 to the Negro Community House, may have cost the "Green Slate" some white backlash votes in April 1932.[76]

By early 1932, McKeighan and the "Green Slate" were under heavy attack in both major local newspapers for having driven the city to the brink of bankruptcy. Civic League supporters received a big boost in February, when the mayor, Chief Scarvarda, and ten others were indicted for conspiring to violate prohibition. Although everyone involved was exonerated by a federal jury, the "Green Slate" could not recover from the negative publicity in time for the annual municipal elections. In April, all of the vulnerable "Green Slate" commissioners except McKeighan lost to the Civic League, after a bitter campaign that drew more than forty thousand people to the polls (a record for municipal elections that stood for many years). A few weeks later, when the city ran out of cash, local bankers made the firing of all "Green Slate" appointees a precondition for their first emergency loan to the city. During the bankers' interregnum, the Civic League finally won control of the city's government, but it took a charter referendum (which led to a revision of the system restoring the wards and making elections biennial), several recall petitions, and special local elections in November to settle the issue.[77]

The Civic League's final triumph over William McKeighan was a hollow victory. By autumn 1932, the old deferential politics was breaking down in Flint. As the depression grew more severe, political apathy disappeared. The number of registered voters and voter participation rates had doubled since the late 1920s. Most of the newly activated citizens were working people who hoped to find solutions to the relief crisis and the depression through the ballot box.[78] For three years, they had tested the alternatives offered by the political culture of normalcy, and they had discovered that neither city management nor old ward-style politics could overcome the problems created by a national economic collapse. Herbert Hoover's voluntarism had also failed to provide a practical way out of the depression. In November 1932, the voters of Flint opted for something different, a dramatic (though nonspecific) promise to expand federal responsibility for relief and economic recovery. A remarkable fifty thousand citizens went to the polls (more than twice as many as in 1928), and they voted heavily for the Democratic ticket, headed by Franklin Roosevelt.[79] For the first time in memory, the city's voters had cast a majority of their ballots for Democrats in the races for the presidency and Congress. A long era of one-party Republican politics in Flint was over. After 1932, political attention in Flint would focus more and more on national issues, not local personalities, and it would usually involve genuine two-party competition.

During the next four years, the tangible accomplishments of the New Deal in Flint earned Franklin Roosevelt and the Democratic Party the electoral loyalty of the vast majority of Flint's working people. The new Democratic voters of 1932 had expected Roosevelt's election to produce vigorous and effective relief and recovery policies, and it did. Within a few months of its inauguration, the new federal administration had taken over the city's relief problems and solved them.[80] Within a few years, New Deal welfare programs and federally sponsored public works recreation programs and housing reforms had vastly improved the quality of life in the city. Of course, all the improvements could not be traced directly to Roosevelt's New Deal. A slowly recovering automobile market allowed General Motors to start calling back its laid off workers in 1933.[81] Nonetheless, in the judgment of one student of the period, by 1936 the New Deal had created "a striking improvement in public health" and the "achievement of civic improvements which five years before would have been unthinkable.[82]

It is hard for any American born in the last half a century to imagine the impression Franklin Roosevelt and the Democrats made in those first four years of the New Deal. We have experienced nothing like it since. In Flint, working people who had often voted Republican, or not at all, quickly learned to admire and support President Roosevelt and the Democratic Party. As early as October 1934, shortly after the local Federation of Labor had voted to endorse a straight Democratic ticket and despite his best efforts to dissuade them, a bitter George Starkweather editorialized:

> The working people have it so firmly impressed on their minds that President Roosevelt and the Democratic Administration is for them that you cannot convince them otherwise.[83]

Ironically, throughout 1933 and most of 1934, Starkweather had contributed to this so-called "Roosevelt revolution" in public opinion by featuring long excerpts from the speeches of A. F. of L. leaders who praised the president in the *Flint Weekly Review*. In January 1935, George Starkweather finally succumbed to these changes in the political climate. After two decades as the president of the local labor federation, he was forced to retire from office by a membership that had abandoned both his Republicanism and his conservative business-oriented unionism. Starkweather's replacement was Robert Passage, a militant Teamsters' business agent who had arrived in the city in 1933 determined to organize local coal haulers. In 1934, he succeeded in gaining the respect of the local federation by leading two strikes that forced employers to sign written contracts with their drivers.[84]

The election of Passage over Starkweather at the Flint Federation of Labor was another clear sign that working people in Flint had rejected the political values of normalcy. The Roosevelt administration gained political support among unionized workers because it endorsed changes in federal labor laws that established the right to organize unions and to bargain collectively with employers. Section 7(a) of the National Industrial Recovery Act and the Wagner Act (which Roosevelt finally endorsed with some reluctance in 1935) were especially important to Flint's automobile workers because they were struggling to establish a union of their own in these years. From 1933 to 1937, union leaders (first from the A. F. of L. and then from the C.I.O.) who spoke in Flint never missed a chance to remind the city's workers that the president was on their side in their fight for a union. Though not always satisfied with his performance, Flint's automobile workers generally accepted the idea that Roosevelt was a pro-labor president. During the campaign of 1936, this perception was sharpened by the actions of General Motors management and the U.A.W.– C.I.O. organizers who were in town trying to revive the struggle against G.M. In October, when company officials on the shopfloors suddenly sprouted Kansas-sunflower "Vote for Landon" buttons, the union representatives started their own campaign for Roosevelt inside the factories, claiming his reelection would mean "the preservation of a democratic government, under which labor will be permitted to work out its own salvation."[85] Roosevelt himself made a dramatic last minute campaign stop in Flint to bolster his "pro-labor" image and to bring out the blue-collar vote. It worked. His motorcade through the city's streets drew the biggest, most enthusiastic crowd ever seen in the downtown area. And, on election day, less than two months before labor-management tensions exploded in the union-making General Motors sit-down strike, the largest turnout in Flint history (fifty-three thousand voters) gave the Roosevelt-led Democratic ticket an overwhelming vote of confidence.[86] In terms of political participation and as a spontaneous measure of the expanded electorate's support for the New Deal, the 1936 election marked the high point of the local political realignment.

The dramatic shift in voter support away from the Republican Party (or from not voting) to the Democratic Party took place in every blue-collar precinct in the city between 1930 and 1936. The Buick neighborhoods (William McKeighan's traditional stronghold) and the precincts around the Fisher Body 1 plant on the city's southside, an area heavily populated by southern-born migrants, led this political realignment. For the most part, the city's black voters remained loyal to the Republican Party through 1932, but the poorer black voters who lived near Buick had shifted *en masse* to the Democratic Party by 1936.

The city's tiny black middle class, which clustered in the Thread Lake area, changed their voting preferences more slowly, "and could not be considered 'safely' Democratic until 1948."[87] However, on the whole, strongly Democratic voting patterns had emerged in all but the city's highest income districts by 1936. They would remain essentially unchanged for the next quarter of a century.

Institutionalization of the New Deal realignment in Flint proceeded more slowly. Before this could take place, stable unions, capable of running effective political campaigns, had to be established; and this, as we shall see in the next chapter, was no easy task. Still, a clear pattern of increasingly organized working-class political activity began to emerge in the mid-1930s. In other words, the class-conscious impulses that led workers to fight for unions also led them to try to control the election process, once their unions were organized. As unionization proceeded in Flint, so did the effort to increase the power of working people in local politics and to insure the election of pro-labor New Deal Democrats to state and national offices.

Almost immediately after he won the presidency of the Flint Federation of Labor from George Starkweather in 1935, Teamsters' business agent Robert Passage tried to push the traditionally conservative central labor union into liberal-Democratic politics. This change of policy was announced by the organization's political action committee during the March campaign for circuit court judgeships, in which they backed three Democrats and a Farmer-Labor candidate. A circular issued by Passage explained,

> In the past, the Political Action Committee has thought it their duty to endorse candidates for their various offices and go no farther. . . . It is the duty of the newly formed Political Action Committee to endorse their candidates by getting behind the aforementioned candidates. . . . We are asking the help and support of every member carrying a Union card.[88]

The P.A.C.'s political efforts did not have much impact in 1935. George Starkweather still controlled the *Flint Weekly Review*, and he invariably supported Republican candidates. Moreover, some of Starkweather's longtime conservative supporters on the Flint Federation of Labor refused to follow through with the new political action committee's request to take an active part in the campaign. Instead, these generally older members seemed to concentrate their political energies on finding a way to discredit the Teamster's leader and have him removed from the local federation's top office.[89]

Prior to the successful organization of the United Automobile Workers Union in Flint in 1937, there was no organized working-class presence in local politics. Participation in local elections fell off drastically after the relief crisis of 1932, and this decline allowed the automotive establishment's Civic League to maintain its hold on City Hall.[90] However, the business class' continued dominance of municipal government in the period from 1932 to 1936 was not nearly as significant as in former years because the federal government under Roosevelt had usurped many of its former functions. Moreover, the composition of the nonpartisan city council was already changing in ways that reflected the rising class consciousness of Flint's working people. In 1936, two Civic League commissioners were not renominated because they were alleged to have connections with a locally notorious anti-union terrorist group known as the Black Legion (reputed to be a militant fragment of the Ku Klux Klan). In addition, of three new "Green Slate" commissioners elected that year, two were factory workers who would supposedly represent the interests of industrial working people. In actuality, one of these blue-collar representatives turned out to be a consistent supporter of the Civic League majority.[91]

The establishment of the U.A.W.–C.I.O. gave Flint's emerging working class an institutional base from which political power could be asserted. Even before General Motors recognized the union in December 1936, the U.A.W.'s local organizers complained that a Flint Community Fund questionnaire probing unemployed workers' union and political affiliations was being administered by county relief officials and turned over to General Motors. Naturally, Genessee County Emergency Relief administrators denied there was anything improper about the questionnaire or its uses. Nevertheless, under union pressure, they dropped the offending procedure.[92] More dramatic displays of the union's political power followed the great sitdown strike that forced General Motors to bargain with the U.A.W. In February 1937, city manager John Barringer was removed from office in response to untiring union protests over his use of excessive force during the strike. A few months later, in July, a mass meeting of five thousand auto workers voted to set up political organizations in the wards and to have them affiliate with the local Labor Non-Partisan League. This mass meeting also voted to recall a "Green Slate" commissioner who had supported the firing of the new city manager for having defended the Hotel and Restaurant Workers' unions's right to picket outside a downtown candy store. Shortly thereafter, the recall was accomplished. The local U.A.W.'s widely circulated *Flint Auto Worker* proclaimed,

> It [the recall] should be a warning to all those minority interests in the city who think they can flout the interests of the overwhelming majority of the people and serve only those of big business or their own selfish ones.[93]

Flint's organized working class continued to improve its political position during the years immediately preceding World War II. In 1938, a Genessee County Labor Political Action Committee was formed to fight in the September primaries and November elections. In the primary, this new P.A.C. succeeded in getting five pro-labor candidates on the nonpartisan ballot for the city commission. Intense factional feuding that raged inside the U.A.W. at this time probably hindered labor's campaign efforts in November. Even so, union-backed candidates won two more seats on the city commission (leaving them just shy of a majority), while the Democrats swept most contests in the county.[94] In 1940, a more unified U.A.W. was able to secure its place in Flint politics. That year, union-backed candidates won a clear majority on the city commission that they were able to hold throughout the war. By 1948, when an alliance between the Democratic Party and the U.A.W. was formalized at the precinct level, it is fair to say that the New Deal realignment had become a "permanent" part of the structure of politics in the Vehicle City.[95]

The New Deal realignment endured in Flint because it was institutionally rooted in a powerful working-class organization, the U.A.W.–C.I.O. Moreover, the New Deal realignment in Flint was a significant development. Most importantly, it expressed industrial working people's independence from the political leadership of the local business class. After 1932, business-class factions no longer defined the political spectrum in Flint. Instead, the rapid growth of a blue-collar, Democratic voting electorate created the basis for genuine two-party competition. The fact that this competition revolved around the New Deal's extension of federal assistance to the unemployed, the poor, and the industrial unions (rather than socialism) should not obscure its class-conscious character. Duirng the 1930s and 1940s, politics in Flint pitted a well-organized anti-labor, anti–New Deal Republican business class against an increasingly well-organized pro-labor, pro–New Deal working class.

In retrospect, it is easy to suggest that liberal Democrats coopted

Flint's emerging working class in the 1930s, and prevented it from finding its own, presumably more radical, political identity. Happily, there is no need to resort to such a condescending interpretation. The New Deal realignment in Flint was no trick. The majority of the city's working people were not duped. Rather, Democratic liberals gave shape and substance to the fundamentally moderate reform impulses of a local working class whose "making" took place after a second industrial revolution. This working class had no hidden revolutionary inclinations that were frustrated by the New Deal. Today, half a century later, the trust it placed in federal reforms and industrial unionism may seem to have been mistaken, just as its hero worship of Franklin Roosevelt and John L. Lewis seems naive. Yet, how can we, the children of post-depression prosperity, permit ourselves such judgments? After all, in their own time, that trust and those heroes did help change government and society, making everyday life a little more dignified and humane for most working people. As a closer examination of the long struggle to create a powerful united automobile workers union in Flint will shortly show, the logic of working-class development in depression-bound America lies not in hindsight or social theory, but in the complex experiences of those people who for the first time in their lives organized themselves as a class in both politics and industrial relations.

7

FROM COMPANY TOWN
TO UNION TOWN

Flint was a natural . . . Frankly, we worked just as hard in
Cleveland, Detroit, and in Wisconsin, but things moved
faster in Flint. George Addes, Secretary-Treasurer of
the U.A.W.–C.I.O.

The Struggle for a Union

A new kind of working class was organized in Flint during the 1930s.
It was dedicated to changing American society through the creation
of industrial unions and the establishment of a federal government
that would provide economic security, stimulate economic growth,
and protect collective bargaining rights. This nonrevolutionary, reformist working class did not emerge overnight. Instead, it was
"made" only after the working people of Flint had been immersed in
two long, closely intertwined experiences: the Great Depression and
an extremely difficult struggle to set up an auto workers union. Both
of these experiences were essential to the timing and logic of working-class development. Without the Great Depression there would
have been no struggle for a union, and without the union, there
would have been no lasting working-class consciousness and power.

   In the early 1930s, those working people who had stayed in the city
shared in the unprecedented degradation of living and working stan-

dards brought on by the collapse of the automobile boom. Some workers quickly found a tentative awareness of class in their common fate. The hunger marches and the Fisher Body strike of 1930, and the surge of blue-collar Democratic voters to the polls in 1932, were but the first signs that a majority of Flint's industrial workers were capable of acting collectively to better their lives and their work if they had the opportunity to do so. However, as the failure of the Fisher Body strike demonstrated, the Hoover years were not the time to fight for a union. Spiralling unemployment and the ever-present threat of repression made unionization virtually impossible. Moreover, Flint's size and its notorious repuation as a company town discouraged the kind of radical organizers who remained active in Detroit and other bigger cities. In 1931 and 1932, no attempts were made to unionize Flint workers, nor were there any significant public protests against wage cuts and layoffs. Yet, as soon as general economic and political conditions started to improve in 1933, Flint's workers jumped at the chance to organize their own labor unions.

In the Vehicle City, the rather amorphous sense of class that had begun to emerge from the shared degradation of the Great Depression and the general enthusiasm for Franklin Roosevelt and the New Deal assumed a more concrete (that is to say, institutional) shape during the years from 1933 to 1938, when auto workers fought General Motors for a union. The creation of the U.A.W. was not the only organizational effort of the 1930s, but it was by far the most important. As one longtime Buick worker later recalled, automobile unionism "was the main topic of conversation I would say in Flint for a period of a couple of years. No matter where you went, this is what people talked about, for and against."[1]

The struggle actually began in the second half of 1933, when "external" events combined to create conditions favorable for unionization. Stronger sales of automobiles and the resulting improvements in automotive employment, the inauguration of the New Deal (especially the elaboration of labor's right to organize contained in Section 7(a) of the National Industrial Recovery Act), and the announcement of an automobile industry organizing drive by the A. F. of L. generated an enormous, nearly universal urge to unionize among the General Motors' workers in Flint. As Carl Swanson, a rank-and-file leader in the A. F. of L.'s Federal Labor Union at Buick recollected,

There was no problem at all getting people to join the organization. . . . People were longing for some kind of security in line with their work. We had seen so much discrimination. . . . people who had a lot of service and had been laid off and friends and relatives kept on. It was easy to organize people.[2]

For the most part, the first workers to present themselves to the A. F. of L. joined in small groups that had already formed on the shopfloor. Even after these groups affiliated, many tried to maintain their autonomy and anonymity. Arthur Case, a shopfloor leader who had worked at Buick since 1919, later explained,

> These were AFL members who had signed up with the AFL and had little groups of their own and had received no recognition from anyone, not even the AFL. . . . Their representatives would be something like shop stewards, except you were not elected or recognized by management.[3]

Very often, it seems, such shopfloor leaders had previous organizational experience or someone in the family who had been a union member. For example, Clayton Johnson of Fisher Body 2 and John McGill, a prominent leader at Buick, had gotten their first union experiences as coal miners in the 1920s. Tom Klasey, who helped organize A. F. of L. members at Chevrolet had been an I.W.W. activist in the Pacific Northwest during World War I. Herbert Richardson, a rank-and-file organizer at Fisher Body 2, was one of the twenty-three strike leaders fired at Fisher Body 1 in 1930. A few, like Bud Simons of Fisher Body 1, had been members of the Auto Workers Union and were still actively associated with the tiny local Communist Party. Together, the previous class-conscious experiences of these individuals hastened the task of union-building. At Fisher Body, workers quite naturally turned to the veterans of the 1930 strike for guidance. "We looked for leadership from one who had already demonstrated his leadership by that early 1930 effort," recalled trimmer Everett Francis.[4] As a result of these spontaneous organizational activities, when officials from the A.F. of L. arrived in Flint in the summer of 1933, they found local units already established and prepared for affiliation.

While less-skilled workers were signing up with the A. F. of L.'s federal labor unions, skilled workers, especially tool and die makers and maintenance crews, joined the Flint section of the recently formed Mechanics Educational Society of America, an exclusive union of skilled automobile workers. In those days when the majority of the city's auto workers seemed ready to establish industrial unions, M.E.S.A. appeared to be the best way for skilled workers to protect their special privileges and advance their own particular demands about wages, hours, and working conditions. By September 1933, Matthew Smith, the British-born M.E.S.A. organizer in Flint, claimed that 98 percent of the city's eligible workers had enrolled in the union and were ready to strike for a wage increase from eighty-five cents an hour back to the pre-depression level of $1.50 per hour. These men also wanted to end overtime shifts during the model changeover that kept them in the plants as long as eighty hours a week.[5] Under pressure from Smith and his militant followers in Flint, who had struck on September 22 to take advantage of the model change, M.E.S.A. members all over southeast Michigan downed their tools on September 26. Once the strike spread, Detroit's vehemently anti-union employer's association headed up the industry's resistance. After a month, frustrated M.E.S.A. leaders allowed radical members to hold mass rallies to whip up support among production workers, but these meetings had little effect, since most lesser-skilled workers were on model change layoff. In early November, the beaten strikers returned to their jobs. Although it was a complete failure in the large factories like those in Flint, this first-ever industrywide strike did win M.E.S.A. a few concessions in some of the smaller shops in and around Detroit. There, M.E.S.A. managed to survive for several more years. However, in Flint, for all practical purposes, the organization was dead by early 1934.[6]

Meanwhile, the A. F. of L.'s campaign in Flint was making rapid progress among the less-skilled auto workers. Union organizers used mass meetings and continuous publicity in the *Flint Weekly Review* to spread their message. In general, the A. F. of L. attracted new members because they expected the union to take quick action to remedy their grievances. The militance of many Flint auto workers frightened A. F. of L. officials. One organizer, James Anderson, actually left the city in early November 1933 for that reason. "He is afraid that the AFL is not going to deliver enough support to the Flint area if a strike is forced upon him," William Ellison Chalmers told Selig Perlman, "and he thinks a strike is inevitable."[7] In 1933, it seemed as if Flint's lesser-skilled auto workers were every bit as militant as the skilled workers who had joined the M.E.S.A.

Nevertheless, there were major differences between the two labor organizations. First, the rank and file in the A. F. of L. unions could not depend on their leaders actually to initiate strike actions, as Matthew Smith had for M.E.S.A. Secondly, unlike the several thousand tool and die makers who had joined M.E.S.A. to raise wages and shorten hours, most workers who joined the A. F. of L. sought job security and respect from management. Production workers had lost these things in the Great Depression, while skilled workers usually could still count on them. "It was not the money at the time," recalled Jack Palmer, a victim of the 1930 strike and one of the first enrolled in the A. F. of L. at Chevrolet's Parts and Service Division, "it was the way we were treated in the shop. There was no dignity. The foreman would cuss you and order you around by 'Hey, you' and by number, and we had no respect at all."[8]

The steep decline in sales and the resulting pressure on the automobile companies to cut their labor costs and speed up production brought on the change in management attitudes towards their employees. During the 1930s, all vestiges of the old paternalism disappeared in General Motors' Flint plants. In its place, supervisors and foremen learned to use fear and intimidation to discipline and drive their workers. W. A. Snider, a Buick foreman, related his experience at the NRA hearings held in December 1934. He told incredulous government investigators that his superiors had pounded foremen on the back, telling them to

"Go ahead and get that work out."

"They would pound the foremen?", asked an NRA official.

"Yes sir," answered Snider.

"And you would have to pound the men?", queried the investigator.

"Yes sir. Right on the back," replied Snider. This was known as getting work out with "a sledgehammer."[9]

Other times, management manipulated workers' fears of unemployment to achieve a desired production level. Ted La Duke, a machine operator in Chevrolet's flywheel department at this time remembered,

> It was no uncommon occurrence for a foreman to go down to the man and tell him that he was not getting enough production from his job, and if he could not get it, there was lots of men waiting at the employment office for his job.[10]

The harsh treatment less-skilled workers experienced day after day in the shops sustained their enthusiasm for the new union, even after M.E.S.A.'s strike effort proved completely futile. Early in 1934, when the membership in Flint comprised nearly half of A. F. of L.'s strength among the nation's auto workers, constant pressure from the rank and file forced reluctant union leaders to threaten a general automotive strike. This pressure "from below" increased in February, as more and more Flint workers joined the A. F. of L. units at their plants in anticipation of a showdown with management. By early March, these so-called Federal Labor Unions had organized a citywide council, which claimed to represent forty-two thousand local auto workers. On the eve of the strike deadline, the local council sent representatives to Washington to urge A. F. of L. officials to order an industrial action.[11] Much to the relief of union leaders, a confrontation was averted when President Roosevelt directly intervened to set up a special Automobile Labor Board to deal with the industry's problems. This settlement, which Roosevelt hailed as "a new course in social enginering," satisfied company representatives and the conservative national A. F. of L. leadership, but it satisfied very few of Flint's militant auto workers. Within a month of the March 25 settlement, three-fourths of the Federal Labor Union members in the city deserted the A. F. of L., never to return.[12]

Most Flint working people had not given up on a collective solution to their everyday problems. Sensing the defeatism of A. F. of L. officials like William Collins, who, in the midst of the crisis, had assured the automobile companies, "I have never voted for a strike in my life. I have always opposed them," Flint's auto workers had merely rejected a union that was too weak to help them fight management for recognition and for the restoration of decent working and living conditions.[13] YWCA industrial secretary, Helen Graves, told NRA investigators several months later that the women workers she supervised (including those who had been too afraid to join the union) "were unanimous in thinking that it had been a mistake they had not struck."[14] Among the men, Fisher Body 2's Herbert Richardson best summed up the prevailing mood with his recollection that "everybody said we got sold down the river."[15]

In the aftermath of this bitter disappointment, and in the face of a vigorous anti-union counteroffensive by General Motors, a nucleus of union stalwarts were unable to reestablish the A. F. of L. in the city's automobile plants. Local A. F. of L. organizations were reduced to mere shadows by further defections, and by 1936, the city's auto workers' council was thoroughly infiltrated by company agents.[16] Representatives from the A.F. of L. units continued to hold meetings in Flint in 1934 and 1935, and the *Flint Weekly Review* dutifully continued to support the federation's efforts, but these efforts could not restore the union's lost credibility. Automobile Labor Board elections held in the big factories in early 1935 revealed that the overwhelming majority of the city's auto workers preferred no union to the discredited A. F. of L. In fact, the A. F. of L. received only 12 percent of the nearly twenty-nine thousand votes cast, just a few more than the company unions, called works councils, that General Motors had set up in 1933 to comply with Section 7(a) and block and A. F. of L.[17]

It seems unlikely that the works councils did much to satisfy auto workers' desires to have a real say in the determination of wages, hours, and working conditions. The works councils were dominated by management, and they continued to function only as long as management retained an interest in them. Al Cook, the conservative president of the A. F. of L's citywide auto workers council, who also served on Fisher Body 1's works council, recalled that the employee representation plan "was sort of a farce. They did some things like getting the toilets policed properly." At Buick, some departments showed their disdain for the works council by selecting comic strip characters like Popeye and Mickey Mouse to represent them. Most workers simply refrained from participating. Only the women workers at the AC Sparkplug factory showed any enthusiasm for the works council, even though under the rules of their plan, employee representatives on the council could only speak for their departments and make motions with the consent of their foremen.[18]

Undoubtedly, General Motors' deliberate attempts to intimidate union supporters contributed most directly to the organizational failures from 1934 to 1936. Widespread terror was generated by the mass firings and selective victimizations of M.E.S.A. and A. F. of L. members in 1934; and by the blacklisting, visits by foremen, stockpiling of weapons and tear gas, and incredibly widespread use of shopfloor informers and paid spies that followed. Reprisals were commonplace at all the major plants in 1934. Sixty-four shopfloor leaders were fired at Fisher Body 1 and 2. At Chevrolet, 126 workers were fired, and they appealed their cases to the Automobile Labor Board. One hundred and twenty-three were reinstated. However, when the Supreme Court invalidated the NRA in May 1935, the company fired "practically all the same ones that had been fired the year before."[19] Though General Motors carefully pruned its industrial relations files when it came under investigation by Senator Robert La Follette's Senate Subcommittee on Education and Labor in 1936, enough records survived to show that the company went to extraordinary lengths to repress union activities in its plants. For example, in the eighteen months following the A. F. of L. strike threat, GM spent at least one million dollars hiring private detectives to ferret out union sympathizers.[20]

The threat of unionization gradually forced General Motors to centralize and standardize personnel policies in the 1930s. In Detroit, top company officials liked to stress the cooperative nature of their relations with workers. However, in reality, authoritarianism and repression were standard operating procedure. For instance, Arnold Lenz, general manager of Chevrolet in Flint, told his superintendents and foremen, "We expect you to discharge anyone who is found circulating a petition or soliciting names for a petition inside our plants."[21] To find such union sympathizers, Lenz employed undercover detectives who worked in the plant and the town, while his foremen cultivated the kind of informers most workers branded "stool pigeons." By mid-1936, according to a National Conciliation Service study of management practices at Chevrolet, 3,700 of 7,700 workers had been *directly* affected by some form of anti-union discrimination or harassment.[22] Although Lenz was arguably the most repressive general manager in Flint, the story was essentially the same in all of the city's General Motors plants. Auto workers had to work and live in fear if they were at all critical of the company. Bob Travis, the dynamic United Automobile Workers of America organizer who arrived in Flint in August 1936, described the prevailing mood for the La Follette committee a few months later. "When I first got to Flint," he recalled,

I could not get more than 25 or 30 people together. . . . They were afraid. They knew there were spies in the local union. . . . Therefore it was necessary to organize little home meetings in members' basements.[23]

Always a company town, by 1936 Flint had been turned into a kind of industrial compound by General Motors' anti-union tactics.

Despite its effectiveness in the short run, the giant corporation's authoritarian response to threatened unionization strengthened many workers' resentments and their resolve to strike back when the next opportunity presented itself. Above all else, the treatment auto workers received at work sustained their growing conviction that General Motors was a common enemy. Older workers resented the speed-up and the brutal discipline, which compared so poorly with pre-depression conditions. One beleagured worker explained in a letter to Senator La Follette,

I have worked at Chevrolet for over nine years and have seen the attitude of management towards their employees change from where you used to be a man, to now you are less than their cheapest tool.[24]

Younger workers, whom bosses valued for their speed and agility, felt equally abused, although their sense of what would be acceptable was not as clearly focused as those who had started in the factories during the best years of the auto boom. For these workers, a wrenching personal experience often led to the commitment to collective action. Twenty-five years later, Clayton Johnson could still recall the day, June 30, 1936, when he collapsed on the line at Fisher Body 2, and was yanked up by his foreman and told "to get back on my goddamn feet." As he remembered,

At the time I was only 28 years old. I had the feeling pretty much that if I had to work under these conditions, I would just as soon be dead. . . . I have never felt very kindly towards General Motors since this time.[25]

He was not alone.

Flint's automotive working people also felt degraded by the loss of their homes, their cars, and especially the loss of the "steady work," which, *in retrospect*, increasingly made everyday life back in the 1920s look satisfying, secure, and respectable. Ralph Burney, an unemployed Buick production worker, revealed this common way of thinking in 1934 when he told NRA investigators,

I think a man with a family should have $30 a week. I know I could get by on a lot less than that, but a man wants to live. He wants *to live like he should live and used to live.*[26]

As the depression dragged on, even some of the most conservative, individualistic workers began to recognize the need for a common response to the debased condition of their lives. Frank Davidson, an unemployed Chevrolet toolroom worker who was born in Flint in 1884 and had "always worked steady up until 1930," described his growing consciousness of class this way in 1934. "I was never a radical," he said, "I always like to do my work, and always liked to come and go, but here is what I have found out since 1933, *that you have to be in the group sometime.*"[27] Trapped by the Great Depression, unable simply to quit and move on, as so many unsatisfied workers had done in the past, Flint's automobile workers discovered a collective identity in their rejection of miserable working and living standards (which they blamed on General Motors), and in the shared memories of the decent jobs and lives they had pursued in the 1920s.

For the many who embraced it, this new consciousness of class was primarily a reflection of their own twentieth-century experience. Cut off from older working class traditions by their overwhelmingly rural backgrounds and by the failure of every previous effort to organize an independent working-class institution in the city, Flint's working people reinterpreted their own history during the Great Depression. From a kind of "dialogue" between their current everyday experiences and their remembered past, most of the city's industrial working people drew a common identity and thus a rough set of common expectations, for which they demonstrated a willingness to fight at some point in the depression decade.

The demands of the nearly fifteen hundred A.C. Sparkplug workers who had joined the A. F. of L. by March 1934 exemplify the logic of this historical process. In a letter to plant manager F. S. Kimmerling, A.C.'s union president, Delmar Minzey, stated that the workers' primary demands were a reinstatement of those fired for union activity and a return to wages and production speeds that *"approximate the nineteen-twenty-eight schedule."*[28] In addition, Minzey informed plant manager Kimmerling that the workers also endorsed the union's wider demands for seniority based on length of service, an impartial grievance procedure, union participation in time-study, and a thirty-hour week (to spread the work). At the time, like the rest of General Motors, A.C.'s management ignored these demands, telling workers the company union (the A.C. Employees Association) had all "the machinery for collective bargaining."[29] Nonetheless, the incident was significant because it reveals, in the context of the depression, the way looking backward could generate demands for progressive reforms among workers who had never before acted as a class.

During the relatively quiet months between the national automotive settlement of March 1934 and the beginning of the big sit-down strike in December 1936, continued economic insecurity, intensified shopfloor discipline, and General Motors' outright repression of dissent literally took the fight out of most workers. The small groups of Communists, Socialists, and other politically radical auto workers described in chapter 6 did continue to encourage genuine independent unionism in the big plants, but their efforts were thwarted by the all-pervasive fear of repression, and by the corruption and treachery of the local Executive Board, which was set up to administer the rump of the A. F. of L.'s auto workers' union in the city. By the summer of 1936, Wyndham Mortimer, who had been sent to Flint to report on the condition of the local union by the breakaway United Automobile Workers of America, found that only four of the thirteen members of the executive board could be trusted completely. The others were either inactive or were suspected stool pigeons. In particular, he cited the local board's policy of investigating every single application for union membership as deliberate sabotage. He reported, "It was quite evident from the first that the newly elected Executive Board had adopted a policy of keeping the union small, prevent it from growing so it could be more readily controlled."[30] Given these difficulties, it is not surprising that most Flint auto workers simply gave up the hope of organizing an effective union in the two-and-a-half years preceding the appearance of the new U.A.W.–C.I.O. in the city in late 1936. Nevertheless, events in these years also revealed that important segments of Flint's automotive workforce remained extremely militant as they awaited a second chance to unionize General Motors.

Friction between management and workers did occasionally lead to confrontations in 1934 and 1935. In May 1934, two thousand of Fisher Body 1's five thousand workers struck over piece rate cuts, the firing of union activists, and the refusal of management to meet with worker representatives other than the works council. The strike, which lasted a week, coincided with similar job actions at other Fisher Body plants in the Midwest. It was settled only after General Motors' vice-presidents William Knudsen and Charles Fisher met with the A. F. of L.'s Francis Dillon to arrange terms for a return to work.[31]

A year later, a similar incident occurred after union workers shut down a Chevrolet transmission plant in Toledo, Ohio, a hundred and twenty miles away. The Toledo strike encouraged A. F. of L. stalwarts at Buick to threaten a strike in key departments as a display of solidarity and in support of their own demands. The Buick union (which had approximately five hundred dues-paying members at the time) secretly polled the workers and found a few departments fully behind their efforts, some almost completely opposed, and others badly split over the issue. Despite this news, the members sent representatives to Toledo, got permits to distribute handbills, and passed a resolution calling on Francis Dillon to announce a May 11 strike deadline. The minority who opposed the strike injected red-baiting into the debate, after the local Communist Party distributed handbills that asked workers to show solidarity and join the threatened job action. Dillon used this issue as an excuse for ignoring the Buick local's strike resolution until the deadline had passed, and a settlement in Toledo undercut its original purposes.[32] Although protesting workers gained nothing tangible from the Fisher Body 1 strike of 1934 and the Buick strike threat of 1935, these incidents confirmed two important, widely held impressions: first, that there were small groups of extremely militant workers in the big automobile plants; and secondly, that the national A. F. of L. would not back up militant automobile workers in confrontations with General Motors.

In the second half of 1936, after the new United Automobile Workers union had severed its ties with the A. F. of L. and joined John. L. Lewis' Congress of Industrial Organizations, Flint's frustrated shop-floor militants finally saw a new opportunity to unionize General Motors. Undoubtedly, "external" events, like passage of the National Labor Relations Act (also known as the Wagner Act), the reelection of Franklin Roosevelt) which seemed to imply the enforcement of the Wagner Act), and the opening of Senator Robert La Follette's investigation of General Motors' labor practices inspired confidence among discontented auto workers. But, most importantly, in 1936 the new U.A.W.–C.I.O. began sending organizers to Flint who believed in hard work and rank-and-file militance.[33] After just six months under this new and supportive leadership, local auto workers were ready to fight and win one of the most significant strikes in American labor history.

The organizers who were sent to Flint were political radicals. U.A.W. vice-president Wyndham Mortimer and Bob Travis, the first two to arrive, were Communists and they commanded the respect of the new union's generally radical leadership.[34] Henry Kraus, who had established the *Flint Auto Worker*, a newspaper designed to spread the C.I.O. message, was also closely associated with the U.A.W. Communists at the time. Roy Reuther, head of the local Federal Emergency Relief Administration's workers' education project, was an acknowledged Socialist, with close connections to the union's hierarchy through his brothers Walter and Victor. As political radicals, all these leaders could contact and build upon the tiny cells of indigenous Communists and other radicals who were among the city's most militant auto workers. Yet the success of the new U.A.W.

in Flint cannot be traced simply to the political commitments of the union's representatives. Rather, it was the willingness of the radical organizers to support rank-and-file militants on local issues that ultimately attracted the majority of Flint's auto workers to the U.A.W. As Arthur Case, a prominent Buick activist, later put it, "our main reason for calling in the CIO was we got no action from the AFL at all."[35]

Unlike their A. F. of L. predecessors, the U.A.W.–C.I.O.'s organizers had to earn the confidence of Flint's new working class. In addition, they had to overcome the widespread numbing fear induced by three years of systematic, anti-union repression. To begin, they worked patiently for several months reestablishing contacts between the union and those workers who were known militants. Though Mortimer was pulled out of Flint early by the union's conservative, unstable president Homer Martin, he was able to provide his own replacement, the extremely able Bob Travis, with the names of 122 workers who were known radicals, or at the very least, union activists who had supported strike actions in 1933, 1934, and 1935. Using this list and his own connections with Communist Party members in the big plants, Travis gradually pulled together the nucleus of the union in Flint.[36] To increase the strength of this activist core, the A. F. of L. plant-based locals were abandoned in favor of one big unit, Local 156. Bob Travis informed U.A.W. vice-president Fred Pieper that this plan of organization was "progressing very well" by mid-October 1936. He wrote,

> A great number of meetings are being held in the homes, small towns, halls outside the union hall, and in little house parties. Every possible opportunity is being taken advantage of. . . . Also committees have been set up within the foreign speaking people. . . . The sentiment of Flint is very good. If it is possible for the local to erase this fear from their minds, I am sure Local 156 will be one of the largest in the International.[37]

Banned from advertising in the local newspapers or on the local radio station (which was owned by the vehemently anti-union *Flint Journal*), the union's organizers relied heavily on Henry Kraus' well-written, professional-looking newspaper, *The Flint Auto Worker*, for publicity. By December, Kraus was printing a bi-weekly, fifty-thousand-copy edition that unemployed auto workers led by Communist Party member Charlie Killinger delivered door to door all over the city.[38]

169

Moreover, to overcome General Motors' intimidation of Flint workers, Travis and his associates relied on the emotional power of direct action. They especially encouraged the shopfloor groups that were re-forming at Fisher Body and Buick. In October and November, U.A.W. officials consistently backed up rank-and-file radicals at Fisher Body 1 who called frequent, "quickie" sit-downs to impress management with the seriousness of their grievances. Travis also made converts at Buick by publicly endorsing the demands a committee of shopfloor leaders were making to divisional president, H. H. Curtice.[39] In December, news of U.A.W. strikes against General Motors plants in Atlanta, Kansas City, and Cleveland added credibility to union organizers' pledges of solidarity with local militants. So did Roy Reuther's quick mobilization of U.A.W. support for Flint bus drivers when they went out on strike. Still, most auto workers held back, unwilling to risk open membership and uncertain about the radical reputations of the U.A.W. leadership. By the last week of December, on the eve of the great sit-down strike, perhaps as many as 10 percent of the city's forty-five thousand auto workers had actually signed up with the U.A.W.–C.I.O.[40]

The Great Sit-Down Strike

The story of the union-making sit-down strike against General Motors is a familiar one. However, most often it has been told to emphasize the national significance of the event that ended with General Motors' recognition of the United Automobile Workers union.[41] Looked at from a different perspective, with an eye for its place in the "making" of Flint's working class, the great sit-down strike appears to be just another chapter, albeit the most important one, in the local struggle to remedy the demeaning circumstances of everyday life and work brought about by the Great Depression. "They have come to the mature conclusion it must be done if they and their children are to have a decent life," wrote Mary Heaton Vorse in her report on the women who threw their energies into the picketing and the other strike support work performed by the red-bereted Emergency Brigade.[42] Certainly, this description applied equally well to the men who had initiated the strike and who sat in the plants for forty-three long, cold winter days.

The bitter struggle began on the morning of December 30 when a young militant minority of the workforce shut down Fisher Body 2 without the prior approval of union leaders. This action was taken to protest the firing of three union inspectors. Because they lacked enough members in the city's other big auto plants to conduct a standard strike, local U.A.W. organizers had to endorse the sit-down tactic to support the Fisher Body 2 job action and to spread the strike. Fisher Body 1 activists, led by the charismatic Bud Simons and Walter Moore quickly followed the lead of Fisher Body 2, after Bob Travis told a lunch-hour meeting of union men that the company was moving a key set of dies out of Flint. In combination with other strikes already begun elsewhere in the General Motors' empire, the sit-downs at Fisher Body 1 and 2 soon forced both the Buick and Chevrolet management to cut back their operations for lack of car bodies.

Bud Simons remembered the first forty-eight hours of the strike were "one big mass of confusion," as union oficials tried to develop a coordinated plan of action.[43] During those initial hectic hours, rank-and-file leaders, especially the handful of Communist activists, provided enormous assistance because they had already drawn up some guidelines for establishing strike committees, food supplies, and the like. One striker, Charles Kramer, later recalled that on the first night of the strike,

> Bob pulled the leaders out of the plant for a midnight meeting . . . and said "What do we do?" So five guys in the back of the room took a couple of pieces of paper out of their pockets—"What to do in case of a sitdown."[44]

There had obviously been some preparation. Nevertheless, the strike caught the U.A.W. hierarchy by surprise. They had not planned any action until after the first of the year, when the New Deal Democrat Frank Murphy would take over the governor's office in Michigan. As George Addes, the union's longtime secretary-treasurer explained, "There was no plan. We actually had no choice in the matter, it just developed too rapidly."[45]

In Flint, the strike brought long simmering class-conscious hostilities out into the open. Company officials and local authorities combined to defeat the sit-down by mobilizing all the resources at their disposal. In October and November, company security personnel at each General Motors plant were sworn in as special Flint police officers. Once the strike began, the company sought and got an injunction from Judge Black, ordering the strikers to vacate the plants, but the union discredited the court order by publicizing the facts about the judge's substantial ownership of General Motors stock.[46] In the aftermath of this fiasco, leaders of the city's automotive establishment formed an anti-union Flint Alliance on January 7, 1937. Under the direction of former mayor and Buick paymaster George Boysen, the Flint Alliance condemned the sit-down as the work of an alien, communistic minority, and pledged itself to protect "the Security of Our Jobs, Our Homes, and Our Community." At first, Boysen tried to enroll virtually everbody in Flint (including children!) in the alliance. However, special pressures to sign up were put on nonstriking auto workers by their supervisors and foremen in hopes of creating a massive back-to-work movement.[47]

Despite the pressures, most auto workers did not join the Flint Alliance. Instead (if their actions after the strike are any indication), they stayed on the sidelines, waiting and hoping for a U.A.W. victory. With violence in the streets, constant harassment both on and off the job, and the memories of earlier union setbacks still fresh in their minds, the reluctance of the majority to reveal their loyalties is understandable. Older men with families and most women workers at the AC Sparkplug factory were intimidated, and they tended to avoid open commitments. Consequently, the sit-down strike was carried on by a young, mostly unmarried male minority of the workforce. As one participant later recalled, "The younger guys had the guts and said what the hell am I risking anyway."[48]

The first violent confrontation of the strike occurred on January 11, the same day two hundred of the city's leading businessmen and professionals pledged themselves to the Flint Alliance at a downtown luncheon. City manager John Barringer and representatives of General Motors determined that they could oust the hundred or so strikers on the second floor of Fisher Body 2 by having the company's guards (who were still on duty on the first floor and at the plant gates) cut off the flow of food and heat to the factory. The union responded by calling up reinforcements, and by sending a special "flying squadron" of pickets armed with billies to seize the main gate. When the union men arrived at the plant entrance, the guards retreated, locked themselves in a bathroom, and notified the Flint police they had been captured by the strikers. The police answered the guards' pleas for assistance with an all-out assault on the plant. Using tear gas to disperse pickets on the street, the officers charged the main gate. Twice, the police were repulsed by strikers who threw heavy door hinges and bottles from the second floor while directing a high pressure stream of water from a fire hose on the ground floor. Frustrated and freezing (it was just sixteen degrees farenheit), the police fired into the crowd of surging pickets as they fell back across the Flint River. Fourteen union supporters were wounded by the gunfire, but the day belonged to the U.A.W.–C.I.O.[49]

The events of January 11, known in union folklore as the "Battle of the Running Bulls," boosted the morale of the strikers, strengthening their resolve not to evacuate the plants. "Everyone was in a wonderful uplift," remembered Henry Kraus, "Despite the many who had been wounded and the occasional gas shell that came zooming down the street, all carried the intoxication of a great victory."[50] The battle also had an important effect on the still undecided majority of Flint's auto workers. Victor Reuther recalled, "The drama the [huge crowd of] bystanders witnessed put our point across more cogently than any words could have done, and served to nudge thousands of Flint workers off dead center."[51] Immediately after the police retreated, part of the crowd actually stopped a police car, turned it over, and stripped it. More significantly, for days afterwards, the union signed up new members who wanted to help in the fight. Emotionally, the union victory over the Flint police on the streets in front of Fisher Body 2 was one of the critical turning points of the long strike.

The "Battle of the Running Bulls" had one other important result. In the aftermath of the street fighting, Michigan's new governor, Frank Murphy, a New Deal Democrat with very close ties to President Roosevelt, finally decided to order a contingent of the National Guard into the city. However, much to the chagrin of Flint's automotive establishment, the governor refused to use the troops in their traditional role as strikebreakers. Instead, under Murphy's direction (which Roosevelt endorsed), the National Guard was deployed as a buffer to prevent further violence. For many years, Frank Murphy's decision to let the strike continue formed the focus of the enduring business-class hatred of the New Deal. "He didn't understand. . . ," C. S. Mott told Studs Terkel in 1969,

> He was governor during the sit-down strikes, and he didn't do his job. *He didn't enforce the law. He kept his hands off. He didn't protect our property.* They had no right to sit-down there. They were illegally occupying it. The owners had the right to demand from the Governor to get those people out. It wasn't done. *The same as today.*[52]

Unable to command the armed forces of the state to dislodge the strikers, the company joined in the mediation efforts that Murphy commenced in Lansing on January 14. A verbal agreement that would have ended the strike by granting recognition to "employee organizations" was worked out, with evacuation of the Flint Fisher Body plants and face-to-face bargaining set for Monday January 18. Although union president Homer Martin fully supported this plan, the radicals on the union's Executive Board and the C.I.O's John Brophy were highly suspicious of General Motors' refusal to put anything in writing. Their suspicions were justified. On January 17, the company revealed its true intentions, when vice-president William Knudsen told the press that the Flint Alliance would be recognized as an employee representative, with the same rights as the U.A.W. In response, the so-called "Lansing agreement" was promptly denounced by union leaders, and the stalemate continued in Flint.

As the siege dragged on, the strikers in the plants received invaluable assistance from union members and other supporters (like the women of the Emergency Brigade) on the outside. One restaurant (greatly augmented by a volunteer staff) managed to feed the sit-down strikers with food supplied by the U.A.W., a few nearby farmers, and worker-hunters. Inside the barricaded factories, shop stewards enforced military-like discipline and routine to sustain morale and prevent senseless vandalism. State labor commissioner George Krogstad was extremely impressed by the order and discipline of the men in the plant he visited near the end of the strike. He found the machinery oiled and covered, the floors clean, and generally no signs of damage.[53] The strikers also received an enormous amount of aid from other U.A.W. locals. Unionists from other cities contributed foodstuffs, walked the picket lines, and, on occasion, took their own turns sitting-in in the struck plants. In fact, on crucial days, caravans of U.A.W. members from all over Michigan and Ohio were rushed into the city to reinforce the Flint strikers. In addition, the green berets of Detroit's Women's Emergency Brigade and the white berets of the Emergency Brigade from Toledo were frequently seen walking the picket lines. Altogether, the constant participation of working people from other industrial cities taught many of Flint's workers a lesson in solidarity they would not soon forget. In subsequent months, whenever striking workers elsewhere in the Midwest needed help, Flint could be counted on to provide some form of assistance.[54]

In late January, U. S. Secretary of Labor Frances Perkins tried to mediate the dispute, but she failed because General Motors' president Alfred Sloan absolutely refused to meet with any union or C.I.O. officials until the Flint strikers vacated the Fisher Body plants. By this time, the company was getting desperate. U.A.W. strikes in nine other cities had virtually halted the production of General Motors' cars nationwide.[55] Hoping to force the issue, the company returned to the Flint courts and got a new evacuation order from Judge Paul Gadola. Local 156 responded by taking the offensive. On February 1, union men seized the vital Chevrolet No. 4 engine plant after luring company guards away by creating a disturbance in another nearby Chevy factory. At this point, tensions mounted. City Manager Barringer announced the formation of a special "police reserve" to break the strike. "We will go down to the plants shooting," the overzealous Barringer reportedly exclaimed.[56] At the same time, hundreds of extra pickets rushed to Flint from Detroit, Lansing, and Toledo. To avoid a certain bloodbath, Governor Murphy steadfastly refused city and company requests to enforce the Gadola injunction. Instead, with the direct assistance of President Roosevelt, Murphy finally pressured General Motors' William Knudsen into bargaining with C.I.O. President Lewis and U.A.W. Vice-President Mortimer.

On February 11, 1937, General Motors, the world's biggest open-shop industrial employer, capitulated on the principle of written recognition. Knudsen signed a six-month contract with the United Automobile Workers that called for the evacuation of the occupied plants and a return to work without discrimination. Under this contract, the union was granted the right to be the sole bargaining agent for its members. The union's original list of demands (issued on January 4) established the basis for the negotiations that were scheduled to begin February 16. These included the abolition of piecework, the thirty-hour week/six-hour day, seniority based on length of service, reinstatement of discharged management-union committees to set union members production speed, and the creation of "a minimum rate of pay commensurate with an American standard of living."[57]

The U.A.W. victory in the General Motors' sit-down strike marked a major turning point in American labor history. In Flint, victorious sit-down strikers marched out of Fisher Body 1 to the cheers of thousands of supporters and the strains of "Solidarity Forever." Similar scenes were repeated at Fisher Body 2 and Chevrolet 4. The victory demonstrations culminated with a parade downtown and rally at the Pengelly Building. It was a celebration that Roy Reuther could only "liken to some description of a country experiencing independence."[58]

A Union Town

During the six months immediately following the U.A.W.'s great strike victory, there was no holding back the expression of local working-class demands and solidarity in Flint. At the automobile factories, some workers still believed General Motors would ultimately defeat the union, but most signed up eagerly, hoping to improve their own working conditions and wages. Undoubtedly, the U.A.W.'s performance in the long sit-down strike was its biggest drawing card. Many auto workers, who had been skeptical of all unions since the failures of M.E.S.A. and the A. F. of L. in 1933–1934, rediscovered their faith in the labor movement in early 1937. John McGill, a former A. F. of L. enthusiast who had initially felt that the U.A.W. was "just another fly-by-night organization," later described this typical reaction for the union's oral history project. "Naturally when we saw them stick by the sit-down strikers as they did," he recalled, "why we came back in droves."[59]

By mid-March, only a month after the sit-down settlement, Local 156 had twenty-five thousand Flint auto workers on its membership rolls.[60] This figure represented a clear majority of the city's automotive labor force. Fisher Body and Buick were the centers of the union's strength, while AC Sparkplug seemed the most resistant to the union's appeal. However, even in the best organized plants, some departments had very few union members. In the spring of 1937, the union stepped up its pressure on these pockets of resistance. Sometimes, the methods of U.A.W. zealots were rather heavy-handed. Jack Palmer, one of the prime movers in the organization at Chevrolet's No. 3 Parts and Service plant, remembered,

> We would get in a group and five or six of us would go over to a guy and say, "Now you are either going to join or we are going to throw you in the river." We would threaten them. Maybe some guy would get a little stubborn and then they (management) would send everybody home. But that was the way we organized the plants, through vicious tactics actually. People were scared, a lot of people were good people but they were just scared because maybe they figured this was not going to last.[61]

Despite this very frank testimony, the role of coercion in the U.A.W.'s success in Flint should not be overemphasized. Most shopfloor leaders, especially those from the union's strongholds at Fisher Body and Buick, credited general rank-and-file militance, an effective shop steward system, and frequent victories in "quickie" strikes with sustaining local 156's initial membership drive.[62]

Looking back, Bud Simons, the chief steward at Fisher Body 1, recalled, "Actually when the sit-down strike was over, the struggle began."[63] There were at least three dozen significant strikes at the various General Motors units in Flint in the first few months after the company recognized the union. Most of these strikes occurred spontaneously in the city's Fisher Body and Chevrolet plants. Only one, an early April sit-down involving 130 women workers, took place at AC Sparkplug.[64] For the most part, these "quickie" strikes allowed workers in specific departments to win concessions on the speed of production, pay scales, seniority, and the reinstatement of fired union members. In addition, they helped establish rank-and-file-controlled shop steward systems that reflected the membership's desire to redress longstanding grievances against their supervisors and the company.

The rapid growth of shopfloor democracy in Flint surprised even the most radical union officials. In early March, Bob Travis wrote Henry Kraus,

> The steward system is functioning properly. In fact, too much so. They want to meet every night. Everybody wants to talk. Leaders are popping up everywhere. One of the healthiest situations I have ever seen.[65]

Departments led by young militants were particularly vulnerable to the unauthorized "quickie" strike. At first, Travis and his associates did not worry much about these job actions. Indeed, they seemed to view rank-and-file militance as a sign of the union's vitality, and as a necessary organizing tool. Yet, the repeated (often plantwide) disruptions of production in Flint were endangering the ongoing negotiations between the company and the union. Moreover, after March 13, when the U.A.W. signed an interim contract with General Motors that, among other things, established a grievance procedure designed to circumvent the shop steward systems and prevent wildcat strikes, the continued militance of Flint's rank and file violated official union policy.[66]

Under pressure from their Executive Board, the company, and Governor Murphy, U.A.W. organizers in Flint and even some of the Communist stewards on the shopfloor tried to rein in the young militant members. Meetings were held at the various plants, and the membership dutifully passed resolutions prohibiting unauthorized strikes. But still the disruptions continued. In fact, the number of wildcat strikes actually increased in late March and early April. Travis began to believe General Motors' "hirelings" and "reactionaries within our own movement" were fomenting the strikes to discredit the local leaders and destroy the C.I.O. union.[67] Given General Motors' past anti-union record, such paranoia was understandable. Yet, it seems more likely that the wave of "quickie" strikes in March and April arose from the rank and file's urge to settle their departmental grievances immediately through direct action. Workers who had won respect and changes in conditions by means of their own shop steward system would not give up that system easily even when their contract and union leaders demanded it. Where they could, workers on the shopfloor continued to pressure their supervisors to correct their grievances directly. The shop steward system was maintained informally at Chevrolet for more than a year after the union's leaders signed it away. At Fisher Body 1 it was still functioning as late as 1940.[68]

In late April, wildcat strike activities in Flint finally dropped off. To secure the industrial peace, Travis, Roy Reuther, and Ralph Dale (an enormously popular U.A.W. organizer assigned to Buick) put together a city wide, union-sponsored recreation program to absorb the energies of their restive membership. On May 17, Travis boasted to Adolph Germer,

> So far as Flint is concerned, we have over thirty thousand in the union. We have 54 soft ball teams and up to the present time about 18 hard ball teams, with a recreational director, and a real sports program under way that will tend to counteract a lot of dissension within our own ranks.[69]

Whether or not these union-run activities actually contributed to the decline of wildcat strikes that began in late April is a moot point. However, it does seem remarkable that at this early date the local union's radical leadership turned to recreation for purposes of social control, just as employers had done during the welfare-capitalist era.

In addition to the pressures put on them "from above," other changes in the local labor movement forced Bob Travis and his associates to become more concerned with rank-and-file discipline in the spring of 1937. Most importantly, the split between conservative union president Homer Martin and the radicals on the executive board began to disrupt the unity of the local union because workers took sides in the dispute.[70] Martin, a Missouri-born preacher turned union organizer, was a dynamic speaker and inveterate red-baiter. In 1935, while a part of the A.F. of L. auto workers' organizing team, he had made a series of speeches in Flint that apparently had won him a personal following in the newer plants where many conservative southern-born workers were clustered.[71] In 1937, he opened his campaign to win over a majority of Flint workers by sending a representative to the city to push for the breakup of Local 156 into smaller plant-sized units. This proposal had some support among active union members because it was thought that smaller locals would be more responsive to specific shopfloor demands. Travis himself believed Local 156 would ultimately have to be split up, but he resisted Martin's attempt to do so in 1937 as premature and politically motivated.

Homer Martin blamed the U.A.W. officials in Flint for the wave of unauthorized strikes. This was a mistake, for it alienated most of the militants who were attracted to the idea of smaller locals. In late April, Martin formed a slate of candidates in a bid to win the Local 156 elections, but Travis, Roy Reuther, and Ralph Dale campaigned successfully for their own candidates. To avenge this loss, Martin demoted Travis and ordered Roy Reuther out of Flint. The local union's membership responded by reaffirming their faith in Travis and by hiring Roy Reuther on as an independent organizer.[72]

As time passed, and the affairs of Local 156 became more and more routine, Martin was able to increase his strength among Flint auto workers who remained militant about "bread and butter" issues, but conservative in their politics. He had his greatest followings at Fisher Body and Chevrolet, but he won almost no support from Buick's rank and file. He seemed to secure the backing of many of the original A. F. of L. enthusiasts who had feared the radical political connections of so many U.A.W.–C.I.O. officials in Flint. By late summer 1937, these conservative unionists dominated the organization at Fisher Body and Chevrolet, giving Martin the indigenous support he needed to break up Local 156 and to purge its radical organizers.[73] However, in the interim period, throughout the late spring and early summer, Travis, Reuther, Kraus, and Dale did their best to secure and expand the power of Flint's new working class.

First, another anti-union offensive had to be repelled. Within the space of a week in late April, an Independent Automobile Employees Association and a Protestant Action Association announced their formations and their intentions to drive the U.A.W.–C.I.O. out of the city. The rival union (if one can call this short-lived organization that) claimed an initial membership of six thousand auto workers, and it disavowed all connections with General Motors. Its nominal leaders, auto workers from each of the big local plants, condemned the C.I.O. as irresponsible, alien, and communist. Not many people listened. Its first meeting at the American Legion hall attracted just seventy-five workers, who railed against the U.A.W. and went home.[74] Henry Kraus promptly labelled the group just "another company union failure" in an article in the widely read *Flint Auto Worker*. Bob Travis called it a "stunt on General Motors part," which was "too trivial to worry about," but he confessed he had had to dissuade some union hotheads from taking physical action against its leaders.[75] Unable to draw the U.A.W. into a confrontation or to attract any real rank-and-file support, the Independent Automobile Employees Association quickly vanished from public view.

The Protestant Action Association had an equally short public life, but its very existence reveals something of the sinister quality of class conflict in Flint in the late 1930s. Accoding to *Detroit News* reporter Martin Hayden, who interviewed the group's leaders (a minister and an architect), the P.A.A. had close ties with the Ku Klux Klan and the Black Legion, that shadowy fragment of the Ku Klux Klan dedicated to spreading anti-union terror all across southern Michigan.[76] Publicly, P.A.A. spokesmen admitted their group included K.K.K. representatives as well as members of several other local fraternal organizations. They claimed to be "pro-American," "not anti-anything," but they went on to condemn the U.A.W. as "a group of racketeers" who "can't differentiate between the Russian peasant consciousness and that of the American working man."[77] Luckily, the P.A.A.'s anti-union crusade never really got off the ground in 1937. This fact reflects the enormous changes that had occurred in local society since the mid-1920s when the Klan had briefly dominated the city's politics. Although a small minority of Flint's blue-collar workers continued to flirt with the K.K.K., the creation of a strong, essentially democratic labor movement in the 1930s permanently prevented a resurgence of mass-based ultra-right-wing politics in the Vehicle City.

In the late spring and summer of 1937, Flint witnessed an unparalleled expansion of the labor movement. Inspired by the militance and the success of the U.A.W., workers in almost every industry in the city organized and pressed their employers to sign written contracts that improved their wages, hours, and working conditions. Emotions ran high as retail clerks, waiters and waitresses, downtown office clerks, dry cleaners and laundry workers, and many others staged their own "quickie" strikes and sit-downs. As one auto worker remembered, a kind of contagious enthusiasm for organization swept the city, with workers developing what he called an "if they got a union we can too" attitude.[78]

For a few short months, under the continued leadership of Travis, Roy Reuther, and the other radicals, Local 156 was transformed into a kind of general workers union that offered advice and direct assistance to any group of workers who asked for it. Time and again, U.A.W. organizers, sound trucks, and "flying squads" of pickets were dispatched to aid striking workers. Initially, the local tried to restrict its help to those working people with some connection to the motor vehicle industry. Workers at seven smaller auto parts and accessories manufacturers and mechanics at five automobile dealerships were brought into Local 156 under this policy.[79] However, once this expansion of the union began, it was hard to set boundaries. Roy Reuther, who had provided assistance to striking Flint bus drivers in December, continued to be the most active of the U.A.W. organizers outside the automobile industry. He personally directed a five-week-long sit-in at J. C. Penney's department store that won women clerks higher pay, shorter hours, and affiliation with the U.A.W. as the Retail Clothing Clerks Association. Reuther also organized a strike by seventy-five cab drivers against three different taxi companies. It dragged on for months, and ultimately the drivers were forced back to work without a contract. Usually, the union's organizers were more successful. By mid-June, in addition to these groups, construction workers at Fisher Body, truck drivers who delivered coal to the auto plants, clerks at the city's biggest grocery chains, dry cleaners and laundry workers, numerous waiters and waitresses, downtown postal telegraph messengers, and local utility company workers all had received strike support from the Flint's U.A.W.[80] In fact, almost all these workers were actually enrolled in Local 156, until they could be sorted out into the proper C.I.O. unions.

Working-class women played an extremely important role in the expansion of Flint's labor movement in mid-1937. The red berets of the Emergency Brigade always seemed ready to assist striking workers, especially if other women were involved. For example, on March 31, employees at the downtown Durant Hotel struck, disrupting the state convention of the Daughters of The American Revolution. Within minutes, Genora Johnson and some of her brigade arrived on the scene, organizing pickets and confronting police. At day's end, the hotel's management had capitulated and signed a union contract with their workers.[81] In subsequent months, the Emergency Brigade helped organize the Retail Clerks Association and a local unit of the Amalgamated Clothing Workers union that was able to get all of the city's large dry cleaning establishments to accept union contracts.

The most remarkable woman to emerge from the class conflicts of 1937 had no connection with the Emergency Brigade or the C.I.O. Her name was Betty Simpson, and she was an organizer for the A. F. of L.'s Hotel and Restaurant Workers union. When she arrived in Flint in the early spring, none of the city's hotels or restaurants had recognized the union (although a few like the Durant Hotel had signed with the ill-fated C.I.O. Culinary Workers union). Nonetheless, by the time she was forced out of the city, as part of a conservative reorganization of the local federation, one hundred seventy-five Flint establishments with more than a thousand employees had contracts with the Hotel and Restaurant Workers union. In addition, she had extended the local union to include workers in Lansing, Saginaw, Bay City, and Pontiac.[82]

Betty Simpson's success, like that of the U.A.W. organizers, can be traced to her own militance and a willingness to back local workers on local demands. She seems to have had an extraordinary ability to inspire mass picketing, even if it meant a confrontation with the police. During the peak of a very violent wave of hotel-restaurant strikes (in June and July), she was arrested several times. Once, she was temporarily blinded by tear gas that had been thrown into the sound truck she used to direct pickets.[83] Yet, until December, when national officials cracked down on her activities and broke up the giant regional local she had formed, Betty Simpson continued to lead successful strikes against Flint's hotels and restaurants.

The turning point in the organization of Flint's new working class actually came on June 9, when U.A.W. workers at the Consumers Power Company shut down all generators in the Saginaw Valley, forcing massive layoffs and leaving nearly half a million people without electricity. This strike gained for the power workers recognition, a wage increase, shorter hours, and overtime pay.[84] However, the intervention of Governor Murphy and national union officials also spelled an end to the expansion of Local 156. At the urging of John L. Lewis and Homer Martin, the C.I.O.'s Director of Automotive Organization, John Brophy, was dispatched to investigate the causes of the continued militance of Flint's U.A.W.. Brophy quickly concluded that Local 156 had to be reorganized. By the end of June, Bob Travis and the rest of the local union's radical leadership had been removed from office and transferred to assignments that were deliberately scattered all over the country. Thousands of Flint auto workers protested this purge, but to no avail.[85] A committee of five was put in charge of Local 156's affairs for the rest of the year. This committee, which contained no one from the union's radical "Unity" caucus, cracked down on the militants within the auto plants. It also directed non-auto-worker members to the appropriate C.I.O. unions in their respective industries. In August, Henry Kraus published the last issue of the *Flint Auto Worker* before leaving the city for a position on the West Coast. No new citywide labor newpaper was created to fill the void. Instead, members at each big factory began publishing their own tabloids. By the end of the year, both the reality and the idea of one big industrial union had been expunged in Flint.[86]

Not so coincidentally, the Flint Federation of Labor was also purged and reorganized at this time. During the first half of 1937, its younger members had been swept up in the enthusiasm of the organizing zeal of the C.I.O. Indeed, on more than one occasion, the F.F.L.'s newspaper (under new management since 1936) praised Bob Travis and the other U.A.W. radicals for the work they were doing in the city.[87] In late August, Raymond Bellamy, an official from the national federation, came to Flint to put an end to this heresy. Bellamy set up a temporary regional office in Flint, declaring he would do away with the "public be damned" attitude of labor in an area "where legitimate labor activity has been regimented and coerced by irresponsible and radical groups."[88] At first, this typical conservative A. F. of L. bureaucrat found his task more difficult than expected. Betty Simpson pressed ahead with her militant organizing drive. Moreover, the new, independent-minded editor of the *Flint Weekly Review* refused to knuckle under, and he continued printing praise of the U.A.W. Finally, in mid-October, Bellamy took dramatic action. He intervened in a sit-down strike called by Betty Simpson at the Home Dairy food store, breaking it up before any agreement could be reached. Although organizer Simpson resumed picketing at the Home Dairy a month later, Bellamy had taken the initiative out of her hands. As a very serious recession settled in on the city in late 1937,

Bellamy pushed the F. F. L. back into its old anti-militant ways. Like Local 156, it too had been reformed "from above."

The severe recession of 1937–1938 brought an end to the rapid expansion of Flint's labor movement, but it did not destroy the city's unions or the new working-class consciousness they embodied. In terms of mass unemployment, the first six months of 1938 represented the nadir of the Great Depression in Flint. As early as January 1, 1938, eleven thousand local auto workers had been forced onto the unemployment rolls. By April, as many as 65 percent of the workforce at Buick and Chevrolet were laid off. Twenty thousand Genessee County families were receiving public assistance in early 1938, nearly twice the previous peak (reached in 1934). Fully one-quarter of those families had never been on relief before.[89] Locally chosen relief officials (who had been given more administrative responsibility after Roosevelt's triumph in the 1936 elections) heightened the crisis atmosphere by making rash statements about moving the "unemployables" out of Genessee County and sterilizing all second-generation relief clients. This attack on the needy backfired. Instead of turning the employed against the unemployed, the relief crisis of 1938 revealed the strength of local working-class consciousness. In April, when food allowances for welfare recipients were cut to less than four cents per person per meal, a united front of all the major local labor unions staged a mass sit-in at the county relief offices until the cuts were revoked. Later in the year, continued protests by Flint's labor unions and unemployed council forced the state to remove the most offensive local relief official, welfare administrator, Louis Ludington.[90]

Naturally, the mass unemployment of 1938 put Flint's labor leaders on the defensive. Faced with layoffs and threatened wage cuts, even the most militant of the city's workers looked to protect the gains they had already made, and not to push forward with new oganizing drives. As unemployment soared, just keeping the auto workers union together became a problem. Participation at union meetings and dues collections fell off dramatically as layoffs and short-time mounted early in 1938. U.A.W. officials asked unemployed workers to remain in the union, and they cut monthly union dues in half (from one dollar to fifty cents) to encourage them to do so. Laid-off rank-and-file activists organized auto workers in the Works Progress Administration. This caused some friction with the local unemployed council that tried to build up its membership by lowering its monthly dues to twenty-five cents.[91] At the same time, leaders of Local 156 initiated a dues collection drive among those auto workers who remained on the job. This drive was ultimately successful, but not until mass picketing by paid-up members caused a temporary shutdown of Fisher Body 1 in mid-April.[92]

Not surprisingly, the economic problems of 1938 intensified the factional dispute between supporters of U.A.W. President Homer Martin and backers of the more radical "Unity" caucus. Initially, the recession had seemed to benefit the local Martin forces. In primary elections for the leadership of Local 156 held in February 1938, Martin's slate of candidates won a clear plurality of the votes cast. Encouraged by this success, Martin then moved his personal headquarters to Flint to step up his red-baiting campaign against the "Unity" caucus. Locally, this tactic worked. A large segment of Flint's industrial workers never seemed to shake off the fear of communism that had been a cornerstone of the political culture of normalcy. As Arthur Case, a noncommunist Martin opponent at Buick later explained, this fear was basically irrational, but it was deeply rooted. "None of us really knew what Communism really was," he recalled. Nevertheless, he continued, at a meeting "if somebody at the door said, 'There's Art Case, a Communist, he is going to be talking tonight.' Half the crowd would go home."[93] In March, Homer Martin's handpicked candidate for the Local 156 presidency, Jack Little, received 63 percent of the twelve thousand votes cast, after a campaign highlighted by the union president's red-baiting. The rest of the Martin slate won by similar margins. Elsewhere around the U.A.W. that month, only the Packard local in Detroit gave Martin's men such a clear-cut victory.[94]

Despite their defeat, the local "Unity" caucus (a combination of rank-and-file Communist Party, Socialist Party, and other radical activists) did not disband. As William Genske, a Proletarian Party member and a Martin opponent at the Martin stronghold, Fisher Body 1, later explained, "They continued to attend union meetings. But they were usually outvoted and not listened to."[95] The vigor of the "Unity" opposition in Flint during a year when Local 156 was decimated by unemployment kept Jack Little from imitating the red-baiting excesses of Homer Martin. Indeed, Little seems to have tried to work out an alliance with local Socialists after the union's top Socialists and Communists split irrevocably at the Michigan C.I.O. convention in April.[96] In addition, Little maintained Local 156's reputation for militance by backing the rank and file's demand for a strike vote at Chevrolet and Buick to protest seniority violations and wage cuts. He also formed a special "flying squadron" of uniformed union members in May, after the city commission authorized the creation of a special volunteer police force to serve under the direction of the city manager.[97] In fact, under Little's leadership, only one major change was made in Flint's U.A.W. At the end of 1938, Local 156 was finally broken up into six factory-based locals (Buick–599, Fisher Body 1–581, Fisher Body 2–598, AC–651, Chevrolet–659, and Standard Cotton Products–655). Many "Unity" caucus supporters had long urged this kind of separation. "Each of us felt that we ought to have autonomy to solve our own problems," remembered Martin-foe Norman Bully.[98]

Throughout 1938, Homer Martin's leadership of the national U.A.W. had become increasingly more autocratic and erratic. In the fall, his suspension of the "Unity" opposition on the union's international Executive Board and his subsequent denunciation of John L. Lewis split the U.A.W. In March 1939, a special convention called by C.I.O. President Lewis expelled Martin, and he took his small band of supporters into the A. F. of L. A few Flint auto workers followed Martin out of the C.I.O., but the vast majority remained loyal to Lewis and the union that had fought the great sit-down strike. "Martin's attack on Lewis and the CIO had been a major blunder," Victor Reuther recently explained, "in those days the initials CIO meant more to workers, in terms of loyal and identification, then did UAW."[99]

In June 1939, a desperate Homer Martin tried to capture the loyalty of Fisher Body 1 (the only plant where he still had substantial grassroots support) by calling a strike just before the annual model change. This was another blunder, U.A.W.–A. F. of L. pickets closed the big factory for one day, but once Walter Reuther, the U.A.W.–C.I.O.'s General Motors department director, showed up to mobilize C.I.O. loyalists, the picket lines were broken and the plant reopened. In retaliation, Martin resorted to "goon squad" tactics. He called in men from Kansas City and Saint Louis, gathered his local supporters, and tried to close Fisher Body 1 by force. Men and women workers going into the plant were beaten up in the streets, and an emergency meeting of the C.I.O.'s Local 581 was beseiged in the union hall. Local police allowed this warfare to continue for two days, presumably in the hope that the union would self-destruct. In the meantime, "flying squadrons" of U.A.W.–C.I.O. loyalists from other plants in Flint, Detroit, and Pontiac converged on the union hall across the street from Fisher Body 1. When a stalemate developed, the state police entered the city and ordered both sides to disperse. Martin had lost his bid to control the union at Fisher Body 1, and he was thoroughly discredited among most Flint workers.[100]

A month later, Walter Reuther called a successful tool and die makers strike against General Motors in the midst of the annual model change. It was a brilliant stroke, for it restored confidence in the militance and the solidarity of the U.A.W.–C.I.O. among the great majority of the General Motors workforce, and it earned Reuther the respect of most GM skilled workers. The strike also convinced General Motors management that the union was there to stay. As result, the giant corporation elevated industrial relations to a top function, and it changed its basic policy from one of outright hostility to what one recent historian of the period has called a "tough but fair" labor policy.[101]

In Flint, less-skilled rank-and-file activists played a crucial role in the 1939 tool and die makers strike, organizing production workers who walked the picket lines day and night for six weeks. At Chevrolet, militant production workers led by Jack Little and Jack Palmer used the strike as an opportunity to restart collective bargaining with a plant manager who had withdrawn recognition from the U.A.W.–C.I.O. during the open fighting with Martin's union.[102] Of course, the strike victory assured the loyalty of General Motors' skilled workers to the C.I.O. It also helped establish Walter Reuther as a major contender for the union's leadership. In this sense, it was actually the beginning of a new era of factionalism within the U.A.W.

In early 1940, the U.A.W.–C.I.O. swept every National Labor Relations Board jurisdictional election in Flint. In their U.A.W. Oral History project interviews, virtually all of the city's rank-and-file leaders (including those who had supported Homer Martin up to 1939) had the same explanation for these C.I.O. victories. "Workers had not forgotten '33 and '34 with the AFL walking out on us," explained Buick's John McGill. Tom Klasey, a onetime Martin backer, put it this way, "We had had enough of the A.F. of L. . . . We were going to stay with the C.I.O."[103] In the aftermath of these election victories, the U.A.W.–C.I.O. was quickly built back up to full strength in almost all departments in the major plants. Even AC Sparkplug was fully organized, after the new regional director, Buick militant Arthur Case, hired a full-time women's organizer to do the job.

By late 1940, when the first pro-labor city commission in Flint's history was elected, it is fair to say that the city had been transformed from a company town to a union town. Never again would the local business class be able to dominate the public life of Flint in the same way it had prior to 1930. In both politics and industrial relations, two areas of public life where Flint's business class had held a virtual monopoly over decision making, the new organized working class asserted its power, forcing reforms that modified the character of local capitalism. In this respect, the direct accomplishments of the union in collective bargaining with General Motors seem at least as impressive as the "New Deal formula" that the vast majority of the workers endorsed year after year at the polls. Between 1940 and 1955, by means of national negotiations with General Motors, the U.A.W. got Flint workers not only increased pay, but also paid vacations, equal pay for equal work, a grievance procedure with an impartial umpire, paid holidays, built-in cost-of-living raises, a pension plan, family insurance, and supplemental unemployment benefits. Moreover, at the plant level, union pressures did lead to improvements in working conditions (particularly in health and safety matters) and in work rules (like fixing and extending rest breaks). Of course, the assembly line was not dismantled, and disputes over the speed of work and production standards persisted. Nevertheless, a major change took place in the relations between workers and management. Foremen lost the arbitrary hiring and firing power that had built so much insecurity into the lives of most workers. Finally, on the shopfloor, by reestablishing informal shop steward organizations during the war years, by using the grievance procedure, and, on occasion, by selectively slowing down or stopping the production process, Flint's industrial workers won something else in these years—a self-respect that had been stripped from them in the early days of the Great Depression.

The organization of a working class in Flint in the 1930s was more than an isolated local accomplishment. It inspired similar changes in other company-dominated towns in the Midwest, and it led to qualitative improvements in the working and living standards of automobile workers all over the country. Perhaps Victor Reuther best summed up the significance of what happened in Flint during the Great Depression in his published memoir, *The Brothers Reuther and the Story of the UAW*. "Our solidarity and shared ideals were fortified by the extraordinary qualities of humanity summoned forth among the workers of Flint by the series of emergencies," he wrote,

They endured what seemed an unending nightmare; they suffered terror, broken heads, their families hunger, and extreme risk, not just for another nickel on the hour, but for the dignity and individuality denied them by an arrogant corporation. They won a richer life for millions of industrial workers in other towns and cities. They exhibited the most selfless quality men can possess: the ability to sacrifice immediate material security for desirable but as yet unrealized goals for humankind.[104]

8

THE DECLINE OF CLASS CONFLICT IN MID-TWENTIETH-CENTURY FLINT

> It is pretty hard to sell a man that can buy a $10,000
> home, drive a new automobile, have a television set, on the
> fact that the system he is living under isn't good.
> —testimony of Herbert Donnelly, a former member of
> Flint's Communist Party, before a subcommittee of the
> Committee on Un-American Activities.

The Rise and Fall of the Rank-and-File Movement, 1940–1950

The 1940s were years when the class conflict that had developed in Flint during the Great Depression was increasingly channeled into bureaucratic procedures and institutions. In 1950, a long-term contract fixed what William Serrin described as the "civilized relationship" between General Motors and the U.A.W.[1] By then, the union had abandoned its former mass-based industrial militance. In fact, during the Eisenhower and Kennedy administrations, the U.A.W. became part of both the local and the national establishments. As the sole legitimate representative of hundreds of thousands of workers (most of whom never attended regular union meetings), the union had real power. Yet, after 1950 it seldom resorted to strikes or other industrial actions to achieve its purposes. Given the nonrevolutionary, moderately reformist intentions of most of the auto workers who had helped build up the U.A.W. in the 1930s, perhaps some sort of "civilized" relationship between the General Motors Corporation and the United Auto Workers was inevitable. However, the historical process that integrated this powerful industrial union and at least some of its politically radical leaders into a political economy still dominated by the giant company was by no means simple and direct.

When the Great Depression finally began to give way to the war boom, class tensions eased in Flint, but only slowly and erratically. Throughout the Second World War, Flint remained a hotbed of rank-and-file militance and organized resistance to the C.I.O.'s "no-strike pledge." In 1945, there was even open discussion about the formation of separate labor party at local membership meetings at Chevrolet and Buick. Nonetheless, despite the vitality of the rank-and-file movement, Flint's shopfloor actvists and union radicals could not regain power and independence they had lost from 1938 to 1940. Several closely linked developments ultimately made it impossible for anyone to create a politically independent, workers'-control-oriented auto workers' union in Flint. Changes in company policy and changes in official union policy (both made in light of changes in federal labor policy) steered local industrial relations away from shopfloor confrontations between workers and their immediate supervisors toward a legalistic, bureaucratic system that still essentially excluded the "average" worker from real participation in decisions affecting him/her. General Motors flourished during the heyday of this "civilized relationship"—the 1950s and 1960s—and so did Flint. Only those who believed the U.A.W. would do more to bring power and dignity into workers' lives felt disillusioned.

The initial success of the U.A.W.–C.I.O. in 1937 had caught the General Motors Corporation off guard. Within the company, management had not been prepared to bargain with a union; they had only been prepared to prevent unionization. As a result, there was considerable confusion among company officials about how to respond to workers' demands and how actually to conduct collective bargaining. At the plant level, managers and departmental supervisors had no clear ideas about who to recognize and what issues were to be considered as part of the bargaining process. Top corporate officials in Detroit elevated industrial relations to a major managerial function and set out to define uniform policies and to train managers in collective bargaining techniques, but these things took time to develop. In 1937 plant managers and departmental supervisors had no time to spare. They faced well-organized, militant workers led by shop stewards who frequently called "quickie" strikes and work slowdowns to back up their demands for rapid improvements in working conditions and shop discipline.[2] In Flint the shop steward system was established in all the major plants, and it was extremely effective. In just a few months of face-to-face bargaining with their immediate supervisors, Flint's militant auto workers were able to force significant concessions on work pace, production standards, and discipline from the company. These gains were made at the particular expense of the foremen, who lost their arbitrary hiring and firing powers and thus much of their authority on the shopfloor.

The recession of 1937–1938 and the intense factional feud that split the U.A.W. in those years gave General Motors the opportunity to develop a tough unified response to the union presence in their factories. Although some company officials would still have liked to destroy the union, this was not the main thrust of the corporation's new industrial policy. Basically General Motors' top executives decided they could live with the U.A.W. if, and only if, the union agreed to restrain its militant rank and file and limit the scope of collective bargaining to wages (and benefits), hours, and working conditions (defined narrowly). This "tough but fair" policy meant that the company would henceforth refuse to relinquish its right to hire, fire, promote, and discipline workers. Moreover, General Motors had decided also to oppose all suggestions for joint union-management responsibility over production-related questions. Essentially then, General Motors boldly asserted most of its traditional managerial prerogatives. In all cases, except collective bargaining over wages, hours, and working conditions, it would initiate action that the union could either accept or protest through the established grievance procedure. This management-dominated system is what the company insisted on during contract negotiations in 1940. In return for recognition as the sole bargaining agent for *all workers* (not just those who were members of the U.A.W.–C.I.O.) in those plants where it could win N.L.R.B. certification elections, the union was forced to agree to a sharp curtailment of its own powers.[3]

In Flint, the split between the U.A.W.–C.I.O. and Homer Martin's U.A.W.–A. F. of L. had allowed most plant managers to suspend collective bargaining until the N.L.R.B. elections were complete. In some plants, this suspension of bargaining lasted nearly a year. During the dual union period, General Motors' new industrial relations policy was put into effect in Flint. When the bargaining relationship between management and the five big U.A.W. locals was resumed, it was under the provisions of the strict 1940 contract that stripped shop stewards of all legitimacy and sharply curtailed the powers of the union committeemen who now each represented three hundred to five hundred workers. Almost every local union leader and former activist interviewed by the U.A.W. Oral History Project remembered the split in the organization and the 1940 national contract as giant steps backwards for the workers on the shopfloor. In 1940–1941, while they worked hard to bring all the workers in their plants back into the U.A.W.–C.I.O., both the company and the union's General Motors Department pressured Flint's rank-and-file leaders to suppress what had been their most effective organizing tool and form of solidarity: the shop steward system and direct action on shopfloor grievances. In 1960, Ted LaDuke, an early Homer Martin supporter at Chevrolet who remained loyal to the C.I.O., summed up the prevailing wisdom this way:

> Today, the workers in the shop feel that it was that split that developed in the organization that lost us more than we ever gained back as far as contracts are concerned, as far as working conditions in the shop and the power of collective bargaining is concerned.[4]

The U.A.W.'s new leaders directed the attempt to suppress shopfloor militance in Flint in 1940. With Ford as yet unorganized, and Homer Martin's pathetic A. F. of L. union still challenging the C.I.O. in certification elections all over the Midwest, R. J. Thomas, the new U.A.W.–C.I.O. president, and Walter Reuther, the ambitious head of the union's General Motors Department, were determined not to give the company any more excuses for breaking off collective bargaining. Executive officers from union headquarters in Detroit were sent to Flint, in part to help local officials with the restoration of membership in the plants in which it had fallen off, but also to keep rank-and-file militants in line with the new contract.[5] On September 17, both Thomas and Reuther had to rush to Flint after the discharge of a shop committeeman prompted a wildcat strike that closed down Chevrolet, idling thirteen thousand workers. According to the National Conciliation Service's report on the incident, "the Union agreed to put the plant back in operation" and then negotiate further with the company.[6] Two days later, Thomas and Reuther were again forced to rush to Flint to put down another, even more serious wildcat strike. This one followed a fight between union members and hardcore Martin supporters who refused to join the C.I.O. local at Fisher Body 1. Plant managers responded to the fight (a rather common occurrence in those days) by firing seventeen workers, all members of the U.A.W.–C.I.O. This blatantly discriminatory action led rank-and-file leaders (a group that included the now unofficial shop stewards as well as many local union officials and committeemen) to call a strike that shut down the entire complex. In an additional display of solidarity, the rank-and-file leadership at Buick initiated a sympathy strike that closed that plant. All totaled, the combined strikes kept twenty thousand workers off the job. Thomas and Reuther were able to get everyone back to work on September 20, but as these events demonstrated, Flint's rank-and-file labor movement was far from dead in the fall of 1940.[7]

Fighting between U.A.W.–C.I.O. workers and small groups of Homer Martin supporters caused several other less dramatic strikes at Fisher Body 1 and Chevrolet that year. Invariably, supervisors decided to discipline only members of the C.I.O. majority after these incidents. In response, the unofficial shop stewards would call for a "quickie" strike. There were at least three such wildcat job actions at Fisher Body 1 that were not settled until Walter Reuther had personally intervened. William Genske, one of the plant's shop committeeman at the time, later recalled,

> On each occasion Reuther came down and told the people that they had to live up to the contract. He would just not permit any wildcat strikes. Then it seemed from the standpoint of the people in our plant after Reuther had won his victory in establishing the CIO back in GM that he was determined to sell the company the idea that the UAW was a responsible union. The membership did not always see eye to eye with that because it ruled out a lot of the activities they thought would eliminate some of the problems they were confronted with.[8]

Genske, a shrewd observer who left the shopfloor in the early 1960s to manage the U.A.W.'s regional credit union, was absolutely correct in his assessment of Walter Reuther's strategy and the opinions of the local membership.

At Fisher Body 1, rank-and-file opposition to Reuther's no-strike policy hardened in the waning months of 1940 after eighty-two union men in the north trim department were fired for striking in protest against the disciplining of their unofficial shop stewards. When this happened, Reuther immediately sent officials from the General Motors Department to prevent any sympathy strikes. These officials stayed on in Flint, supposedly to expedite the reinstatement of the fired strikers. This process took several weeks, and even then, most of the eighty-two were placed on probationary status in widely scattered jobs away from the trim department. In the end, all but one striker got their original jobs back, but not until many months had passed. The delays and the unwillingness of the union's General Motors Department officers to press the company for immediate reinstatement, confirmed many Fisher Body workers' suspicions about the inadequacy of the "reformed" system of collective bargaining established in the 1940 contract.[9]

By the spring of 1941, when new contract negotiations began, most of Flint's rank-and-file leaders believed that the 1940 national contract's relatively unrepresentative committeemen system and its tedious grievance procedure could never solve their shopfloor problems. General Motors had been pushing its workers as sales rebounded from the recession of 1938–1939. In the factories, many workers felt victimized by another speed-up and by management's stricter discipline. When the annual contract negotiations stalled early, Flint's big U.A.W. locals voted resolutions calling for a companywide strike. Recognition of shop stewards, improvements in seniority guarantees, and a wage increase were the chief demands, but in addition, both the Buick and the Fisher Body 1 locals resolved to demand the dismissal of Walter Reuther as head of the General Motors Department. Reuther, always a talented manager of rank-and-file discontent, responded by setting a strike deadline for May 15. Yet his commitment to the defense build-up and the kind of "responsible unionism" desired by both the company and the Roosevelt administration made Reuther's determination to press hard for the rank and file's demands suspect. As it turned out, Reuther was able to save face when Secretary of Labor Frances Perkins acted on her own and sent the General Motors dispute on to the new National Defense Mediation Board. This action allowed Reuther to call off the strike, even though members of the U.A.W. Executive Board were angered because they had not been consulted. Buick's Local 599 and Chevrolet Local 659 struck anyway on May 15. These unauthorized actions were ended in a few days, but only after federal mediators had injected themselves into the dispute on the grounds that the struck plants had already started some defense-reflated production.[10] In other words, by the summer of 1941, the rank-and-file movement in Flint found itself making demands that were opposed by General Motors, the union's international officers, and the federal government. This situation would endure until the movement finally collapsed in the late 1940s.

In Flint, conversion from automotive production to war materials production was a long process that began in late 1940 when the first machine guns came down the assembly line at the A.C. Sparkplug factory. Federal plans for war production in Flint (which included the erection of a new aluminum foundry at Buick and a tank plant in suburban Grand Blanc) were well advanced by January 1941, but the actual conversion was not finished until the fall of 1942.[11] Undoubtedly some of the delay was caused by the difficulties inherent in the shift from making cars and trucks to manufacturing aircraft engines, tanks, and other armaments. However, General Motors' well-documented reluctance to abandon profitable civilian production until the country was formally at war accounted for much for the lost time. As Alan Clive pointed out in his excellent study, *State of War: Michigan in World War II*,

> Certainly from mid-1941 onward, thousands of tons of critical materials and countless man-hours were wasted in production of passenger cars. The automakers allowed concern for profit to obscure the very vision upon which the government was depending for the creation of production "miracles."[12]

All totaled, the war boom created an additional twenty-five thousand jobs in Flint, almost all of them in manufacturing. However, before full war production was attained and labor shortages appeared (in mid-1943), many local workers were forced to live through a long spell of unemployment. Employment in Flint's major factories started falling off in July 1941 and bottomed out in January–February 1942 when twenty-three thousnd auto workers were laid off.[13] Unemployment remained a serious problem in Flint throughout the summer of 1942. It took the edge off many rank-and-file leaders' enthusiasm for war work. For example, at the end of June 1942, Chevrolet Local 659's *Searchlight* got itself into hot water with management and Walter Reuther's General Motors' Department for warning workers,

> Until there is a shortage of man-power, we must not increase our individual production. After all our brothers are back we will do our part. To act differently is merely to increase G.M.'s profits.[14]

Of course, unemployment compensation helped to ease the financial burden on out-of-work auto workers. In addition, General Motors established a loan plan that allowed workers with seniority to draw against their future earnings.[15] Nevertheless, when it was compounded by resentment against the C.I.O.'s "no-strike pledge" (made at a White House labor conference shortly after Pearl Harbor) and by suspicions about the U.A.W.'s call for "equality of sacrifice," widespread irritation over the prolonged unemployment helped renew the militance and solidarity of Flint's auto union activists.

The wartime rank-and-file movement in Flint (which most labor historians recognize for the part it played in the drive against the "no-strike pledge" within the U.A.W.) was built upon a class consciousness that could be traced back to the early days of the Great Depression, but no further. Its most prominent leaders, like Buick's John McGill, AC Sparkplug's Bob Carter, and Chevrolet's Don Chapman and F. R. "Jack" Palmer, were elected to local union offices during the war years. Most of them had been active union supporters in the 1930s who remained loyal to the C.I.O. during the years when Homer Martin split the organization. Like the voting memberships that elected them, as a group, the rank-and-file movement's leaders were committed to their shop stewards and to the right to strike over grievances. They were also alienated from the U.A.W.'s international officers, not simply over the no-strike pledge, but in reaction to the suppression of union militants in 1940–1941. John McGill later recalled,

> We had not forgotten about the Fisher Body boys being fired out there and the International Union through the leadership of R. J. Thomas at that time allowing them to stay fired and be put out to other General Motors plants on a so-called probationary period.[16]

Thus, in Flint at least, the rank-and-file movement stemmed from a class-conscious desire to reform the U.A.W. "from below" by returning to the militance and shopfloor level of bargaining that had characterized the union in the 1930s.

Within most of the city's General Motors plants, workers maintained informal networks of shop stewards throughout the war. These shop steward networks had no legal status under the contract between General Motors and the U.A.W. They were not officially approved or recognized by either the company or the union. Nevertheless, they were the most vital part of the local working-class' political culture in the early 1940s. At Buick, union leader Arthur Case remembered,

> A shop steward system was not recognized but we still had it. We tried to set up a shop steward for each ten men in a group and that man contacted the committeeman.[17]

Such shop stewards played a key role in the maintenance of the kind of militant class consciousness that had emerged in the struggle to establish the union. As Arthur Case implied, the shop stewards brought workers' grievances to the attention of the committeeman, or if necessary, before the active membership at local union meetings. They also explained, and very often criticized, company, government, and official union policies in what amounted to ongoing group discussions. In retrospect, these routine shop steward functions (and not the more dramatic but very infrequent wildcat strikes) appear particularly significant. Today we can see clearly that the shop stewards, and only the shop stewards, maintained contact between the union leaders (both international and local) and the majority of dues-payers who usually did not play an active role in union politics. As long as these shop steward systems remained strong, workers on the shopfloor could not easily regard the U.A.W. as a distant disillusioning bureaucracy. Nor could they view the company's and the government's wartime calls for cooperation and sacrifice uncritically. In this sense, the shop stewards created a lively political culture on the shopfloor, which, in terms of developing critical political perspectives, had no counterpart in the wider society.

Although the leaders of Flint's rank-and-file movement were sometimes indiscriminately branded "communists" by the company and a hostile press, they were not. Indeed, after June 1941 when the Nazi invasion of Russia brought the Soviet Union into the war as one of the Allies, the rank-and-file movement found itself opposed to the Communist Party members in the international union and local union leaderships. In Flint, as elsewhere, Communists in the U.A.W. fully supported the no-strike pledge and the "equality of sacrifice" program. Communists were also among the strongest proponents of incentive pay for productivity increases, a proposal that the rank and file condemned as a reintroduction of the old hated piecework system.[18] Where Communist Party members had played a major role in the organization of the union and the life of the shop steward network, their dramatic reversal on rank-and-file policy issues in June 1941 created considerable confusion and bitterness within the local union. This was especially true at Flint's two Fisher Body locals. Yet, during the war neither Fisher Body 1's Local 581 nor Fisher Body 2's Local 598 was "captured" by the rank-and-file movement. In 1944, the rank and file controlled the local union offices at Buick, Chevrolet, and AC Sparkplug, but the two Fisher Body locals remained basically loyal to the international union leadership and the no-strike pledge. In fact, in 1944–1945 when wildcat strike activity peaked at Buick, Chevy, and AC Sparkplug, there were no comparable job actions at the Fisher Body plants, despite the fact that worker discontent with the no-strike pledge was growing, especially at Fisher Body 1. Although such a conclusion is somewhat speculative, it is hard to resist the idea that the continued influence of the Communist Party within the Fisher Body locals helped to keep their memberships from participating in wildcat strikes.[19]

The growth of the rank-and-file movement as a political force within Flint's U.A.W. from 1943 to 1945 was closely related to the spread of wildcat strikes that expressed many members' discontent with working conditions, War Labor Board grievance procedures, and the no-strike pledge. Unlike Detroit, Flint was never the scene of a massive wave of wildcat strikes. However, there were at least a dozen significant walkouts in the city between February 1942 and the end of the war. None of them directly concerned wages, even though anger directed against the War Labor Board's policy of holding increases to no more than 15 percent of their January 1, 1941 levels (the so-called "Little Steel formula") was widespread. Disputes over production standards and company discipline provoked the majority of Flint's wartime wildcat strikes.[20] In addition, there were several recognition strikes in the new facilities and smaller (non-General Motors) factories. The most important of these, at the new Grand Blanc tank plant in July 1942, was started by union activists who had been transferred from Fisher Body 1's welding department. The tank plant's management did not recognize the union, even though its workforce overwhelmingly favored unionization. Three young union welders decided to challenge the company's policy by working to rules laid out in the Fisher Body 1 contract. They were fired. To protest this harsh discipline, the rest of the U.A.W. members struck the plant. This strike closed the new tank plant for nearly two weeks. It was finally settled when War Labor Board mediators arranged a certification election (which the U.A.W.–C.I.O. subsequently won by a seven-to-one margin).[21]

Most of Flint's wartime wildcat strikes occurred in mid-1944 among assembly workers at Chevrolet and Buick. Long hours, mandatory overtime, and the seemingly endless delays (from three hundred to four hundred days) in the official grievance procedure finally exhausted the patience of thousands of war-weary working people. At both plants, disgruntled workers were led by their unofficial shop stewards and by local union officers who had recently joined other dissidents within the U.A.W. to form a unionwide Rank-and-File Caucus. The caucus was organized in the spring of 1944 after the union's Executive Board voted to suspend local union officials who supported wildcat strikes. Its leaders were Robert Carter of AC Sparkplug's Local 651, John McGill of Buick Local 599, and Eddie Yost of the powerful Ford Local 600. In Flint, the caucus also had the support of Chevrolet Local 659 officials and its membership.

In September 1944, the Rank-and-File Caucus challenged the no-strike pledge at the union's annual convention in Grand Rapids. The debate over the pledge was a bitter one that saw both sides threaten to bring disabled veterans to the microphone to make their case. When the votes were cast, neither the leadership resolution favoring the strike ban nor the minority resolution to repeal it had gained a majority. However, the caucus did force the convention to submit the no-strike pledge to a membership referendum. At the same convention, the AC Sparkplug's Bob Carter ran against R. J. Thomas for the union's presidency, while Buick's John McGill contested the second vice-president's spot. With no real organization to back them, both Rank-and-File Caucus leaders were handily defeated. Then, in the early months of 1945, the referendum on the no-strike pledge drew a response from less than a quarter of the membership. Although all of the major U.A.W. locals in Flint except Fisher Body 2 Local 598 voted to repeal the pledge, the unionwide referendum approved the no-strike policy by a two-to-one margin. The significance of this vote is hard to estimate since, as Ed Jennings has pointed out, more workers actually struck in 1944 than voted for the pledge in February 1945.[22] Nevertheless, this series of political defeats completely demoralized the Rank-and-File Caucus. John McGill later recalled, "I more or less just gave up and figured I was batting my head against a stone wall."[23] It was the end of the unionwide effort to repeal the no-strike pledge.

The collapse of the Rank-and-File Caucus left the leaders of the rank-and-file movement in Flint politically isolated in their struggle against the union leadership. However, in the short run, it did nothing to dampen the the militance and solidarity of workers on the shopfloor. In fact, Flint's biggest wildcat strike took place in March 1945, a month after the collapse of the Rank-and-File Caucus. It began when an AC Sparkplug committeeman was laid off for alleged violence against a foreman. Forty to fifty workers, all women, immediately struck in protest. At this point, local union officials intervened and got the women back on the job within an hour. Nonetheless, two days later on March 26 the company discharged eight of these women and suspended five others. When news of these reprisals spread through the unofficial shop steward network, 13,000 of the plant's 17,500 workers walked out, with the support of the officers of Local 651. The next day, at a mass meeting, more than 2,200 strikers listened to the pleas of federal mediators to return to work, and then voted narrowly to continue the strike. On the evening of March 28, another larger mass meeting was held at the I.M.A. Auditorium. This time, Walter Reuther (who had been picking up support in Flint for his opposition to incentive pay and his recent public expression of doubt about the no-strike pledge) convinced a majority to vote to end the walkout.[24]

By the end of the war, most of Flint's auto plants were seething with discontent. Rank-and-file leaders at Buick, Chevrolet, the AC Sparkplug factory, and Fisher Body 1 wanted to reassert their power on the shopfloor, raise wages, and correct what they saw as the deficiencies of the U.A.W.'s "responsible" relationship with General Motors. The active members of the union backed these leaders. From June to September 1945, following Germany's surrender, the U.A.W. Executive Board was bombarded by resolutions from the various Flint locals urging, among other things: a special convention to repeal the no-strike pledge and to prepare for an industrywide strike, union participation in reconversion to prevent a new speed-up, no reconsideration of the old contract, the institution of an official shop steward system, the creation of a national chain of labor-oriented newspapers, and even the formation of a separate political party modeled along the lines of the British Labor Party.[25] These last two items were contained in resolutions passed on August 12 and September 15 at regular (and thus rather small) meetings of Buick's Local 599. There is no other indication in the records that demands for a labor press and a labor party ever again officially came up at Buick. However, rank-and-file activist "Jack" Palmer kept these ideas alive within Chevrolet Local 659 until he gave up the struggle against Walter Reuther's leadership in the late 1940s.

The demands formulated by Flint's rank-and-file movement in the waning months of the war represented the kind of shopfloor militance and political independence that Walter Reuther could not afford to ignore. To quell this discontent and the discontent of many other General Motors locals, he called for a companywide strike in October 1945. Reuther wanted General Motors to grant a 30 percent across-the-board wage increase and simultaneously to freeze the prices of its cars. To prove his claim that the company could afford those demands, he also asked General Motors to open its books, and the negotiations with the union. It was a bold strategy designed to win over the politically active, militant rank and file *and* the consuming public. In addition, it was also clearly designed to help Walter Reuther win the union presidency in 1946.[26] In Flint, the call for a strike was answered with great enthusiasm. Every union local in the city voted overwhelmingly for the strike in late October. When General Motors refused to be intimidated, Reuther set the strike deadline for November 21.

Local rank-and-file movement leaders began preparations for the strike early, happy to follow the international union into a confrontation with the automaking giant. They formed a citywide strike committee and elected AC Sparkplug's Bob Carter as its chairman. Once the deadline had passed, there was no hesitation in Flint; well-organized pickets hit the streets immediately. On December 1, when U.A.W. President Thomas wavered and agreed to GM's request to reopen the parts and accessory divisions to accomodate consumer demands, his office was flooded with protests from Flint, like the one from the AC's Local 651 which read, "Our plant is down 100 percent and we intend to keep it down 100 percent until our just demands are won."[27] The next day, Thomas backed away from his offer and told the company that only those plants that voted to reopen would do so. None in Flint did.

The strike dragged on for 114 days. From the workers' perspective, it was not totally successful. The union accepted a disappointing 18.5

cents per hour wage increase in March, after insisting it would go no lower than 19.5 cents per hour in January. The union failed to get General Motors to consider opening its books or the negotiations. It also failed to get the company to link wage increases to price stability. In fact, within two months of the strike settlement of March 13, 1946, GM had raised it prices an average of eighty dollars per car. Yet, from the union's standpoint, there were a few bright spots. The company's long list of demands (which amounted to nothing less than a repeal of all the contract concessions granted during the war years under National War Labor Board supervision) was rejected. Also the strike settlement did include national contract concessions on total benefits, vacation pay, and a restoration of the overtime premium that had been lost in the war. Even so, the union could not claim that it had expanded the scope of collective bargaining in any meaningful way beyond what General Motors had defined as acceptable in 1940. Flint's rank-and-file leaders tried to get the international's Executive Board to continue to refuse the 18.5 cents offer, but it was a futile effort. After sixteen weeks without a paycheck, most auto workers were ready to return to work, and the union's leaders knew it.[28]

In Flint, the long strike ultimately weakened the rank-and-file movement. When it was over, many rank-and-file workers seemed ready to reconcile themselves to Walter Reuther's leadership of the U.A.W. His wartime stand against incentive pay, his public expressions of doubt about the no-strike pledge, and his willingness to confront General Motors as soon as Japan surrendered had earned Reuther the grudging respect of many militant auto workers. Even Jack Palmer, later a vehement Reuther opponent, conceded in his U.A.W. Oral History Project interview that "Reuther was a big hero after the strike."[29] As a result, when the General Motors Department head announced he would run for the union's top spot in 1946, the rank-and-file movement in Flint split. The division was most serious at Buick, the longtime stronghold of local anti-Reuther forces. John McGill, who had run against Reuther for the second vice-president's position in 1944, endorsed him in 1946 over the protests of other Buick rank-and-file leaders like Ed Geiger and Marlin Butler.[30]

Geiger, Butler, and a majority of the rank and file at Buick and Fisher Body 1 remained hostile to Walter Reuther for two reasons. They could still remember his suppression of the shopfloor militants in 1940–1941, and they still felt loyal to George Addes, the perennial secretary-treasurer of the U.A.W. and leader of the Executive Board's

"Unity" (now anti-Reuther) caucus. "It came from the days when we could not talk to Homer Martin and nobody would do anything for us," recalled Arthur Case, "George Addes did go out of his way to come in here and help us."[31] Without a doubt, some of Addes' support in Flint came from members of the recently re-formed Communist Party shop units who approved of his well-known political association with the Communists in the "Unity" caucus. However, too much can be made of this kind of connection. In the Vehicle City, George Addes' enduring influence stemmed mainly from his well-deserved reputation as a good union man who never forgot that it had been shopfloor militants who had created the U.A.W. in 1936–1937.

In March 1946, Walter Reuther was narrowly elected president of the U.A.W., while R. J. Thomas was forced to accept one of the vice-presidential positions. Reuther had campaigned as a liberal anti-Communist, accusing Thomas of being a "stooge" and "tool" of the Communist Party.[32] This approach won him the unqualified support of the Association of Catholic Trade Unionists (who were numerous in Detroit but not in Flint) and the small group of Trotskyites in the union. He also received very favorable press coverage, including feature articles in the Luce magazines *Time*, *Life*, and *Fortune*. Nonetheless, after his election, Reuther's political position in the union remained very tenuous. The majority on the Executive Board and all the other union officers were still members of the "Unity" caucus led by Addes and Thomas. Thus, with the next convention scheduled for November 1947, Reuther had only eighteen months to consolidate his power. He used them well.

During 1946–1947, Walter Reuther created what John McGill later called "a machine . . . that just could not be beat."[33] Basically, he accomplished this feat by combining relentless red-baiting attacks on his opponents with the promotion of loyal supporters to positions in the international union bureaucracy. Such tactics were not new, but as Roger Keeran has recently explained, "the Cold War, and the anti-Communist hysteria that developed rapidly in 1946–1947 gave Reuther's anti-Communism a potency unknown in earlier years."[34] At this time, unionists in Flint were spared most of the excesses of Reuther's campaign because he concentrated his initial efforts on more promising locals, especially those in Detroit. However, when Chevrolet Local 659's vice-president Jack Palmer arranged a debate between Reuther and R. J. Thomas, the new U.A.W. president showed up with ten bodyguards who forced Palmer to change the ground rules and step down as moderator of the affair. For Jack Palmer, it was a disillusioning lesson that prefigured the treatment he would receive the following year when he ran for Local 659's presidency.[35] Yet, viewed in retrospect, incidents like this one cease to surprise. For as longtime labor reporter Stanely Brams discovered after years of covering Detroit, close-up knowledge of Reuther the politician "dulled some of the shine and gloss that you could see attached to him when you stood farther away."[36]

By November 1947, although Thomas and Addes could still command substantial loyalty in Flint, and in the U.A.W. as a whole, their left-wing "Unity" caucus was soundly beaten. At the convention, Reuther was easily reelected, while his men won eighteen of the twenty-two seats on the Executive Board, both vice-presidential positions, and the secretary-treasurer's spot George Addes had held down since 1936. For all practical purposes, this overwhelming defeat finished the the the "Unity" caucus as a force in the U.A.W.

Having consolidated his power at the top, Walter Reuther next turned to the elimination of the remaining opposition to his brand of anti-communist, "responsible unionism" at the local level. Again, he used the familiar combination of red-baiting and the promotion of his supporters to achieve his ends. Indeed, now that he was assured the backing of the Executive Board, Reuther was able to move more aggressively to remove potentially dissident international union officials and intervene directly in local union elections. For example, Gib Rose, one of the leaders of the sit-down strike at Chevrolet No. 4 and a member of the international union's regional staff since 1941, was removed from office for his unwavering loyalty to the Addes-Thomas faction. So were William Genske, Carl Bibber, and several other well-known Addes-Thomas backers. In addition, a few other "suspect" officials, like Joe Sands, were transferred out of Flint. Naturally, Reuther replaced these "Unity" caucus appointees with people he could trust to be loyal to him. Fisher Body's Everett Francis, Chevrolet's Terrell Thompson and Bill McCartney, and Buick's Norman Bully all rose in the union hierarchy this way. These personnel changes (what some Reuther opponents still call a "purge" today) had important long-range effects. First, they obviously strengthened Reuther's position in Flint, making it increasingly difficult for local rank-and-file leaders to challenge the policies of the international union. Secondly, they were an object lesson for the young, bright, ambitious members of the union who looked forward to getting out of the shop. After 1947–1948, it was clear that you had to become part of the Reuther "machine" to advance in the union bureaucracy.[37]

In 1948, Flint's rank-and-file movement made what turned out to be its last united stand against Walter Reuther's domination of the U.A.W. by suggesting its own agenda for national contract negotiations. This final effort was led by Jack Palmer, who had succeeded Don Chapman as Chevrolet Local 659 president after Chapman deserted the rank-and-file movement to become Reuther's candidate for regional director. Palmer proposed a twenty-five cents per hour basic wage increase plus the incorporation of a quarterly cost-of-living adjustment in the next national contract. The cost-of-living adjustment, also known as the "escalator clause," had first been suggested by the union's small Socialist Workers Party contingent in 1945–1946. Then, the idea had been rejected by both Reuther and the Addes-Thomas factions as something that would actually freeze wages at current levels. By 1948, however, when nearly every economist was predicting double-digit inflation, those fears had vanished among most of the union's left-wing membership. Indeed, as both Walter Reuther and GM president Charles Wilson discovered, the escalator clause had tremendous appeal.

To press his case, Jack Palmer formed a united front with the four other major local union presidents in Flint (Bob Carter of the AC Sparkplug's Local 651, Joe Berry of Buick's Local 599, Larry Finnan of Fisher Body 1's Local 581, and Bill Connally of Fisher Body 2's Local 598). In January, Palmer went on the radio to publicize what became known as the Five Presidents' program. Moreover, the influential *Detroit News* headlined the proposal, giving it additional exposure to the auto workers of lower Michigan. The response was overwhelmingly positive. Ford Local 600 (representing eighty thousand workers), Briggs Local 212, and four other Detroit locals voted to endorse the Five Presidents' program. All totaled, U.A.W. locals with more than two hundred thousand members had joined the "revolt from below" initiated by Flint's Jack Palmer.[38]

To quash this remarkable insurgency, Walter Reuther traveled directly to Flint. He spoke out vehemently against the Five President's program, claiming it undermined a secret (and better) strategy the union was preparing for the upcoming contract negotiations. he reiterated the old argument that an escalator clause would tend to freeze workers' wages, and he pointed to the failure of the petroleum workers' cost-of-living experiment with the Sinclair Oil Company as an example of the difficulties the U.A.W. would get itself into if it followed the Five Presidents' suggestions. Most importantly, Reuther branded Jack Palmer and the escalator clause "Red," using quotes from a *Michigan Herald* story favorable to the Five Presidents' program as "evidence" of its Communist origins. Later, a still bitter Jack Palmer recalled, "Reuther quoted from the Communist Party newspaper, and then from my radio address, and then said, 'These are the people who are trying to destroy our union.' "[39] Reuther's charges were unfounded. Although Jack Palmer had often shown an affinity for the ideas of the Socialist Workers Party, he had never been a Communist Party member or a so-called "fellow-traveler." In fact, during the war, Palmer had opposed the Communists' stands on most major policy issues. Yet as so many Americans found out during this period, truth was irrelevant in a red-baiting campaign like the one Reuther launched against the Five President's program. The accusation of Communist Party connections alone, coming from an authority figure such as the U.A.W. president, was enough to discredit the rank-and-file revolt and it led in a few months time to Palmer's defeat in the local union elections.

Nevertheless, the mass appeal of the escalator clause had not gone unnoticed. In May 1948, after ninety General Motors plants had voted for a strike, company president Charles Wilson put the cost-of-living escalator and productivity-related increases on the bargaining table in the context of a proposed three-year contract that he hoped would establish labor peace in the industry. The motives behind Wilson's apparently statesman-like offer were simple. GM had just completed its reconversion process and it was making record profits (reportedly 28 percent return on investment, six times the wartime norm).[40] Another long strike in 1948 would set the company back, and perhaps even allow its competitors to increase their share of the booming postwar car market. On the other hand, Wilson knew a long-term contract with the U.A.W. would assure GM of continued industry leadership and put its industrial relations on a more stable, predictable basis.

At the time Wilson made this notable offer, Walter Reuther was recuperating from an April 20 attempt on his life, and he could offer no effective resistance to the escalator clause.[41] Union negotiators, still wary of long-term contracts, rejected the three-year proposal made by Wilson, but they did sign a two-year pact that included cost-of-living raises, productivity-based wage increases, and better fringe benefits on May 29. Two years later in 1950, these experimental formulas were extended in an unprecedented five-year contract that seemed to have permanently fixed the "civilized" relationship between General Motors and the U.A.W.

In Flint, the rank-and-file movement collapsed during the two-year term of the 1948 contract. Although many of the rank and file continued to play an active role in local union affairs, and some of the informal shop steward networks survived, the men who had led the resistance to "top down" bureaucratic unionism gradually lost heart. By 1950, when Norman Bully (who was by then a member of the General Motors Department national negotiating team) returned to Buick to seek the opinions of active unionists on the advisability of signing a long-term contract, he found most of them "heaving a big sigh of relief because we were going to have labor peace for five years."[42] When sentiments like this predominated at what had always been the heart of Flint's rank-and-file movement, a long era of working-class militance had come to an end.

The Limits of Working-Class Consciousness in Mid-Twentieth-Century Flint

For fifteen years, from 1933 to 1948, the automobile workers of Flint, Michigan, demonstrated a consistent commitment to industrial unionism based on shopfloor organization and militance. To be sure, not all of Flint's tens of thousands of auto workers supported the U.A.W.–C.I.O. or the local rank-and-file movement, but over those years a substantial activist minority aroused and sustained a widespread class-conscious willingness to struggle against General Motors for improvements in working and living conditions. Ultimately, it was this militant class consciousness that inspired the creation of the U.A.W. during the 1936–1937 sit-down strike and later fed the growth of the rank-and-file movement during the early 1940s. Why then, we must finally ask, did this militant class consciousness disappear so rapidly after World War II? Why was bureaucratic industrial unionism established so easily once Walter Reuther became U.A.W. president?

The tough-minded new industrial relations policy inaugurated by General Motors in 1940, and the U.A.W. leadership's subsequent attempts to prove that they ran a "responsible" union provide part of the answer to these questions. Indeed, from the perspective of many of the pioneer union activists themselves, it was the Reuther political machine with its co-optation and red-baiting of rank-and-file leaders that did the most to undermine militant working-class consciousness in Flint. However, as we have also seen, the "civilized relationship" between management and labor was not easily imposed on workers from above. In fact, during World War II and its immediate aftermath, the attempt to impose such a relationship in Flint actually fueled rank-and-file discontent and shopfloor militance. Perhaps then, we should look elsewhere, to the underlying economic, social, and political changes brought on by the war, for a fuller explanation of the disappearance of working-class militance in mid-twentieth-century Flint.

In recent years, some historians have proposed that sociological and demographic changes brought on by the war boom eventually undermined the solidarity and political radicalism of the C.I.O.[43] For instance, the suggestion has been made that World War II broke up the primary work groups that formed the backbone of the new industrial labor movement in the 1930s. Of course, something like this did happen in Flint. The local rank-and-file leaders interviewed by the U.A.W. Oral History Project recalled the draft, the transfer of workers to new war plants (including the one built for Buick near Chicago), and the shifting of workers to new jobs within the same plant as having caused some breakdowns in their communications with the membership. Yet these men placed little emphasis on this type of disruption. Actually, the success they had in building up the local rank-and-file movement indicates that new primary work groups formed quite easily under the constant pressures of war production. As David Brody has pointed out, the work group "by no means withered away" during the war or even "under the influence of the postwar labor management settlement." Moreover, it is clear why work groups endured. Professor Brody continued,

> Wherever they came into regular contact on the job, wherever they recognized a common identity, factory workers formed bonds, legislated group work standards, and, as best they could, enforced these informal rules on fellow workers and supervisors. Work-group activity was an expression of the irrepressible social organization of the shopfloor.[44]

Given these facts of industrial life, it seems just as likely that the dispersion of experienced, unionized work group members throughout the greatly enlarged wartime workforce promoted rank-and-file organization rather than destroyed it. Certainly, the U.A.W. activists transferred from Fisher Body 1 to the new Grand Blanc tank plant in 1942 acted as catalysts for the expansion of the union's organization in Flint.

The large influx of blacks and women into the industrial workforce during the war years is another often-cited reason for the rapid demise of working-class militance and radicalism in the later 1940s. Racism and sexism, it is frequently contended, divided the working class from within, and in James Green's words, "obviously created serious problems not only in terms of union solidarity, but in terms of shopfloor solidarity" too.[45] Without a doubt, a great many of Flint's white male workers resented the noticeable increase in blacks and women employed in the local war industry. This is not surprising. From 1908 to 1941, the essentially racist and sexist hiring policies of General Motors had reinforced the prejudices most white males brought with them to Flint during the automobile boom. These prejudices surfaced in every major plant in the city after 1941, even though management tried to restrict new black and women workers to the limited job categories that had been open to them traditionally.[46] Local union officials and rank-and-file activists were divided over these issues, but not nearly as much over women working as over the hiring and upgrading of black workers. For example, in 1942, while some local leaders like Buick's Arthur Case adhered to the U.A.W.'s official progressive race policy and fought to open production jobs to black workers, Federal Fair Employment Practices Committee investigators reported that others, including the incumbent regional director Carl Swanson and Chevrolet Local 659's President Terrell Thompson, refused to forward discrimination complaints "because they are unsympathetic with the requests of these black workers."[47]

Without going into further detail, it can be stated categorically that racism and sexism were both important problems that did, at times, divide Flint's industrial working class and its leaders. Nevertheless, these problems were not a primary cause of the decline in local working-class consciousness in the later 1940s. Although the number of blacks and women employed in industry in Flint roughly doubled during the war years, the absolute increase was not enough to disrupt the basic patterns of discrimination that had always existed at GM and in the city as a whole. Personnel managers continued to channel blacks and women into traditionally race- and sex-segregated job categories. Most new women workers found industrial openings at the AC Sparkplug factory and the smaller (non–General Motors) plants that had always hired lots of women.[48] Similarly, most new black workers got jobs at Buick, Chevrolet, and the AC Sparkplug plant, plants that had always kept some black workers on the payroll. Fisher Body 1, the facility with the most southern managers and workers, hired only one hundred blacks during the war, and then laid them all off in 1945. In fact, all across Flint, following the "last hired, first fired" rule, layoffs fell heaviest on blacks and women in 1945–1946, while the postwar rehiring boom favored returning white male veterans with pre-war seniority.[49] In other words, demographic changes in the wartime labor force were simply not extensive enough or permanent enough to account for the dramatic postwar decline local working-class militance.

Political developments, not sociological or demographic changes, were the most important reasons for the decline of militant working-class consciousness in Flint after World War II. The successful suppression of the unofficial shop steward system by the company, the federal government, and the union destroyed the institutional basis for working-class militance in the postwar period. Had the shop steward principle been supported by the U.A.W.'s leaders, and had shop stewards been given a primary role in the collective bargaining process (as, for example, in Britain's automotive unions), a militant form of working-class consciousness could have been sustained. A healthy shop steward system would have kept alive the workers' struggle to control the shopfloor. It would have preserved the independent political arena created by the working class of the 1930s for the next generation of auto workers. Instead, under both R. J. Thomas and Walter Reuther, an increasingly hierarchical international union looked for ways to suppress shopfloor organizations and rank-and-file militance in order to prove itself "responsible" in the eyes of General Motors and the federal government. The dues check-off system inaugurated in the 1946 contract dealt a final blow to Flint's unofficial shop steward networks. The check-off eliminated the last vital function of the shop steward, dues collection. With the dues check-off in place, local union officials no longer needed to rely on shop stewards to keep members up to date. In a sense, their funds now came "from above" instead of "from below." Thus, the stewards lost the institutionalized support of local union officials, and without that support, the remaining shop steward networks withered away.

In Flint at least, there can be no doubt that the U.A.W.'s failure to fight for the shop steward system created by its most dedicated members was an immediate and principal cause of the decline of working-class consciousness and militance.

The deliberate moderation of the U.A.W.'s role in electoral politics also contributed directly to the decline of working-class consciousness in postwar Flint. Undoubtedly, this political development also reflected the essentially conservative desire of U.A.W. leaders for "respectability," something only those with a well-established status in society are in a position to bestow. Beginning in 1940, the year union-backed candidates won a clear majority on the city commission, local union leaders decided not to press the advantage their numbers at the polls seemed to give them. Carl Swanson, the U.A.W.'s regional director at the time, later explained how the goal of legitimizing the union's place in local society took precedence over all other aims. Despite their majority on the commission he recalled,

> We did not go in and dominate the picture. We did not appoint labor people to every position that was to be appointed, such as mayor and city manager.[50]

In fact, from 1940 to 1944, the union supported a prominent Democratic businessman, William Osmond Kelly, as the commission's appointed mayor.

In 1946, the renewed factionalism in the U.A.W. temporarily broke local labor's united front. When the Democrats renominated State Representative Casper Kenny, a member of Buick's anti-Reuther Local 599 and an alleged Communist Party member, the county Political Action Committee endorsed the Republican candidate. Kenny was defeated. In the aftermath of this setback, the Buick local launched a vigorous attack on the P.A.C. Unity was restored by 1948, when the entire local labor movement tried to oust Sixth-District Republican Congressman, William Blackney, a strong supporter of the anti-labor Taft-Hartley Act. A heavy Republican turnout in Lansing and the district's rural areas gave Blackney just enough votes (800 out of 146,200 cast) to hold onto his seat. Naturally, this defeat disappointed local labor leaders. Nevertheless, 1948 marked a final turning point in the institionalization of the local New Deal realignment. With the Cold War raging at home and abroad and Republicans gloating over Taft-Hartley, the U.A.W. had formalized its ties with the Democratic Party by providing a precinct-by-precinct organization of campaign workers who could insure a heavy turnout of working-class Democrats at the polls. In subsequent years, this electoral "machine" was perfected, ensuring the union an enduring, powerful voice in Flint politics.[51]

The electoral alliance between the U.A.W. and the Democratic Party insured the "permanence" of the New Deal realignment in Flint, but it did not represent true independent working-class politics. While union officials often got to act out the role of local power brokers, they could never really challenge decisions made by either the U.A.W. or by national Democratic Party leaders. Over the long run, the U.A.W.–Democratic Party alliance tied the political lives of Flint's organized workers to institutions that were committed to repressing (or co-opting) every sign of independence and radicalism that might appear among the rank-and-file.

To a great extent, both the suppression of the local union's shop steward networks and the formation of the political alliance between the U.A.W. and the Democratic Party succeeded because of a third crucial political development: the revitalization of anti-radical nativism in the early years of the Cold War. Undoubtedly, this revival of what John Higham has called the "equation between national loyalty and a large measure of political and social conformity" stemmed in part from the intense nationalism generated "from above" during World War II.[52] Four years of unceasing patriotic appeals by *all* the powerful public voices of American society—the president, elected representatives, government officials, big businessmen, union leaders, the clergy, and celebrities from Hollywood and the radio—challenged the image of an America politically divided into hostile classes that had formed in the minds of many working people in the 1930s. Yet exactly how this propaganda effort altered the political consciousness of workers remains unclear. A comparative perspective highlights the problem. In the 1940s, all across Western Europe, popular anti-fascism clearly strengthened the political left; but in the United States, the patriotic crusade against fascism was turned into a mass movement against the political radicals with astounding ease. Why?

Some recent labor historians think that wartime nationalism acted directly on the individual worker's political consciousness. They argue that the patriotism aroused during World War II divided working people's loyalties, blocking a transformation of on-the-job militance into a truly independent working-class radicalism. To quote James Green again,

> the class struggle begun in the 1930s continued on the shop floor, where militance often won out over patriotism. . . , but in the realm of political society, where the worker saw herself or himself primarily as a citizen, patriotism or even jingoism became more important than class consciousness.[53]

Certainly, this summary makes sense of events in Flint, where auto workers established a militant rank-and-file movement, while at the same time dutifully registering their support for the anti-radical U.A.W.–Democratic Party alliance at the polls. Yet, it seems questionable to conclude that the patriotic appeals that fell on deaf ears as far as adherence to the no-strike pledge and "equality of sacrifice" went would be so extremely persuasive on their own in the political arena. Indeed, it seems dubious to assume, as many labor historians have done, that there was some inevitable progression from shop-floor militance to political radicalism that wartime nationalism somehow inhibited.

It must be remembered that a political commitment to the Democratic Party and the "New Deal formula" was an essential part of the working-class consciousness that had emerged in Flint during the 1930s. The war did not change this working-class commitment, even though it did recast the character of the national Democratic Party. After 1941, the Democratic leadership continued to try to safeguard the gains made by working people in the previous decade, but it also took on a new role as creator and guardian of the modern national security state. If long-term voting patterns are a valid indicator, then we must conclude that the vast majority of Flint's industrial working class accepted this change. Although there were a few defections to Henry Wallace in 1948 (especially in the increasingly black precincts around the Buick plant), and although a few score workers did join the local Communist Party in the postwar period, as a whole, Flint's industrial working class continued faithfully to support the Democratic Party at the polls throughout the 1940s, 1950s, and early 1960s.[54] Thus, it is fair to conclude that wartime nationalism did not block a political radicalization of Flint's working class so much as it reinforced workers' already well-established moderate political inclinations.

Still, something more needs to be said about the reasons why anti-radical nativism reemerged so easily in Flint in the late 1940s. The key word here is "reemerged." Wartime nationalism and postwar red-baiting did not create popular anti-communism. It simply revived anti-communism, just as it revived the mass consumer culture to which anti-radical nativism had been intimately linked sine the 1920s. Again, we must recall the historical sources of working-class consciousness in Flint to fully appreciate how working people could be both militant in industrial relations and profoundly anti-radical in-politics. As we have seen, a collective memory of everyday life in the 1920s had been the catalyst for the emergence of local working-class consciousness in the early years of the Great Depression. In the 1940s, as conditions that resembled the remembered (and imagined) prosperity and security of the 1920s were restored in Flint (albeit through a reformed political economy), the popular culture and values of normalcy "naturally" resurfaced in Flint. Anti-radical nativism was not exactly imposed on the local working class. There was in fact a convergence of values among union leaders, politicians, and most auto workers. As Nelson Lichtenstein has said of the C.I.O. as a whole in this period, "Official anti-Communism powerfully reinforced the recrudescence of anti-radical chauvinism that was simultaneously at work within popular working class consciousness."[55] Ultimately then, it was the successful restoration of the mass consumer economy upon which the whole political culture of the Cold War years in Flint rested.

Flint's economy boomed again in the postwar era as General Motors expanded its operations in the area to satisfy the pent-up demand for new cars and trucks. Reconversion brought an increase in the capacity of the city's existing automotive plants. It also included the conversion of the Grand Blanc tank plant built by the government during the war to civilian production. By the mid-1950s, General Motors was employing up to eighty thousand workers during peak production periods, nearly a one-third increase over the pre-depression high.[56] This rapid expansion of automotive production had much the same economic multiplier effects as had the first great automobile boom in Flint. New supplier firms, machine shops, and other small industrial companies were attracted to the city and its nearby suburbs. In addition, as wage levels increased, retail sales and services expanded. Of course, all this economic activity fueled a revival of the local construction and housing industries.

As the local economy boomed, Flint's population grew too, from just over 150,000 in 1940 to nearly 200,000 people in 1960. The continued growth of Flint's suburbs was even more impressive. In 1940, the entire Flint metropolitan area had contained about 185,000 individuals; by 1960, more than 265,000 persons lived there. Moreover, during the 1960s, while the central city's population did not grow, continued in-migration of industrial workers and some white flight to the suburbs pushed the population of metropolitan Flint over the 330,000 mark, almost twice what it had been in 1929–1930.[57]

In the postwar era, high wages and the promise of steady work drew both white and black working people to Flint, just as they had much earlier in the century. By 1957, weekly wages in the Vehicle City were 37 percent higher than the national average. The consistently rising wages of the city's enormous unionized workforce accounted for most of this differential. The U.A.W. contracts of the period brought not only higher base pay rates, productivity-related pay increases, and the cost-of-living escalator, they also greatly increased the workers' sense of security ith provisions for pensions (1949), low-cost family insurance (1950), and supplemental unemployment benefits (1955). All these benefits augmented the federal social security system set up during the New Deal. Working people who entered industry after 1941, during the years when the local economy was almost constantly expanding, easily accepted the idea that this automobile boom and the consumer-oriented culture it encouraged were permanent. Older workers were not so sanguine. This generation gap within the local working class was widely recognized during the first serious postwar recession in 1957–1958 when approximately twenty thousand Flint auto workers were laid off. AC Sparkplug's Bob Carter, who was the union's regional director at the time, told reporters,

The old guys remember the Depression years when there were a hundred applicants for every job, and everybody was fighting just to stay alive. . . . These men are worried. The younger ones who don't remember the 1930s clearly take a more cheerful view.[58]

Taking "a more cheerful view" meant spending money, indeed borrowing money to spend on a house, a car, a television set, and all the other consumer goods that American industry was pumping out at the time. Very often, for these Michigan auto workers, it also meant the pursuit of outdoor pleasures like fishing, boating, and hunting. In other words, like the young workers of the 1920s, the auto workers of Flint who had entered the industry during and after World War II adjusted to the demands of their work life by committing themselves to the accumulation of things and the individual pursuit of leisure-time pleasures that were themselves a part of enormous consumer-oriented industries. Most of these working people had no time for union affairs. As time passed and the consumer economy continued to expand, to them the U.A.W. became a distant bureaucracy, not a vital expression of a class consciousness. "It did mean a great difference in our union," Buick's Norman Bully told interviewers in 1961,

> Because there we had people primarily from out of state who had never been in contact with the union and had no knowledge of the conditions in these plants prior to the union. Therefore, they did not feel the same deep sense of loyalties to the union.[59]

Or, as another class-conscious veteran of the 1930s put it, "Today's attitude is not what we can do together but what is the union and the committeeman doing for my five dollars a month."[60]

The decline in militant class consciousness among older auto workers that followed the collapse of the local rank-and-file movement and the absence of any class consciousness among most younger workers combined to produce another remarkable era of labor peace in Flint. For nearly two decades, beginning in 1950, there were no serious strikes in the Vehicle City. Indeed, Flint seemed to present a model of labor-management harmony to the nation. In articles like *U.S. News and World Report's* "Labor Peace: It's Wonderful" (July 1950), *Look's* "All American City" (February 1954), and *Coronet's* "Happiest Town in Michigan" (June 1956), the national news media used Flint as an example of how the country had transcended the bitter, divisive class conflicts of the 1930s and early 1940s to enter a new era of consumer-oriented normalcy. Such publicity further legitimized the "civilized relationship" between General Motors and the U.A.W., and it furthered the alienation of Flint's auto workers from their own union. As these and other widely circulated reports presented it, the U.A.W. was just another part of a system over which the "average worker" correctly perceived he or she had no real control. Only the most dedicated class-conscious veterans of the organizational struggles of the years from 1933 to 1941 could resist this conclusion, because they knew from experience that there were alternatives, that things could have been different. These activists retained their interest in union affairs, and when it came time for them to retire, they created an organization of U.A.W. Pioneers who have tried hard to keep the militant class consciousness of the early U.A.W. alive. During the 1970s, these U.A.W. Pioneers accomplished several notable achievements, including the staging of an elaborate, well-attended Fortieth Anniversary celebration of the great sit-down strike, the successful lobbying of the state government to place historical markers commemorating the sit-down strike, and the launching of a Flint Labor History Project in conjunction with the Political Science Department at the University of Michigan-Flint.

In retrospect, it is clear that the U.A.W. leadership's political alliance with the business-class liberals in the Democratic Party, and its suppression of the rank-and-file movement and the shop steward system that was its heart and soul, left Flint's postwar working class with no institution vital enough to counter the claims of mass consumerism and leisure-time pleasure on the attentions of the individual worker. In a very real sense, the collapse of the union as an independent force in politics and as a militant presence on the shop-floor cut most workers off from the values (especially industrial militance and workers' control) that were rooted class-conscious experiences of the 1930s and early 1940s. Under Walter Reuther's leadership, the U.A.W. ceased to act as if it was part of a militant working class, nor was it perceived as doing so by anyone but the most reactionary American conservatives. Such a union could not transmit working-class consciousness to new generations of auto workers; indeed, as we have seen, it became a barrier to such a transmission. In the long run, although the working-class consciousness that had emerged in Flint during the Great Depression still burned in the minds of many of the older generation who were there at its making, a bureaucratic U.A.W. and a Democratic Party increasingly divorced from its New Deal heritage could not make younger working people feel its power.

9
CONCLUSIONS

It is hard to generalize with confidence about the character of an entire society, especially a society as large and diverse as the United States, on the basis of a single case study. Yet this history of Flint, Michigan, prompts some interesting speculation about the way popular commentators and scholars have usually presented the larger history of twentieth-century America. Certainly, as a local study, it amplifies and sheds new light on the significance of the second industrial revolution in establishing the parameters of both class conflict and consensus in modern American culture and politics. Here, events including progressive reform, the failure of socialism, welfare capitalism, Americanization, normalcy, the rise of Big Labor, the creation of the New Deal "welfare state," and the emergence of a Cold War culture have not appeared as discrete historical episodes. Rather, each of these events has been seen as linked to a pattern of political-cultural response to the central development of twentieth-century social history; the creation of, and ongoing attempt to sustain, a true mass consumer-oriented society. Without completely dismissing the usual

221

chronology and its emphasis on the turn of the century, World War I, and the unique characteristics of each decade since the 1920s, this history suggests a different kind of periodization, one that ties events more directly to the developmental patterns of the second industrial revolution.

This book has tried to define all of the last ninety years as a single historical era. In addition, it tentatively has identified several shorter, significant periods within this era. They are the automobile boom (to 1929), the first great crisis (encompassing the Great Depression and World War II), Cold War prosperity (after 1946), and now, a second great crisis (since the defeat in Vietnam and OPEC oil boycott). This chronology, based on what might be called for lack of a better term the "stages" of the second industrial revolution, provides for the history of Flint (and I believe for all America) the kind of underlying, unifying theme that has been sadly lacking in all too much twentieth-century history. In addition, (although discussion of this point is beyond the scope of this book), the boundaries of this chronology seem to conform roughly to that other central development of modern American history; the establishment of, and attempt to sustain, the nation's role as *the* great power in world affairs. In other words, as an organizing concept, the second industrial revolution appears to have possibilities that transcend even the fields of economic, social, and political history.

A second far-reaching implication of this case study of Flint stems from the way it has enabled us to see national events emerge, not only in terms of broad trends in the wider society, but also as the result of specific decisions that have had a real impact on the everyday lives of people in a particular local history. Moreover, working at this local level, we have been able to identify class patterns in these decisions and their effects, patterns that becomes less distinct when we shift our focus to try to take in the full sweep of national events. Indeed, if the historical experience of Flint teaches us anything, it is that classes have happened, and continue to happen, in modern America.

In this respect, what seems to stand out most in the history of Flint since 1900 is the uninterrupted existence of a politically self-conscious business class strong enough, not only to protect its own immediate economic interests, but to also actually shape fundamental social and political values. If we look at the business class in action at the local level, as we have done here, it appears to be far and away the most powerful influence on the way American society grew during the first stage of the second industrial revolution. When observing the transformation of a small Michigan county seat into one of the world's most important automotive production centers, the connections between the economic power of the business class and its ability to direct social and political change are unmistakable. In the Vehicle City, control of the second industrial revolution through investments in new technology, the creation of large fully integrated companies, the implementation of true mass production, and the making of mass markets for new consumer durables yielded far more than profits; it also conferred the power to make key decisions about the long-run character of society and politics.

During the first third of this century, the formative years of America's second industrial revolution, the flexibility and innovativeness of the business class that emerged in Flint, like those that emerged in other key industrial cities, was especially striking.[1] Whenever it was challenged by discontented working people or unforeseen economic and social events, Flint's business class found a way to manage the problem. It answered the Socialist Party threat with progressive reform, early industrial unionism with welfare capitalism, and rapid population growth with Americanization and the city manager system. Only the Great Depression—the complete breakdown of the mass consumer-oriented economy produced by the second industrial revolution—led to political and cultural changes that were, initially at least, beyond the control of this business class.

Yet even this description of the early twentieth-century business class' influence on the character of modern Flint fails to acknowledge the full and lasting ramifications of its accomplishments. Most importantly, during the automobile boom, the progressive business class in Flint (and, in fact, in all of America) offered working people both the dream of and access to a new, more affluent and more secure way of life. And most working people embraced it. Erich Fromm once wrote,

> In order that any society may function well, its members must acquire the kind of character which makes them *want* to act the way they *have* to act as members of the society or of a special class within it. They have to *desire* what objectively is *necessary* for them to do.[2]

In Flint, as in the rest of American society touched by the automobile boom, the business class constructed a "culture of abundance" that convinced working people to do what had to be done in order for the second industrial revolution to proceed. Undoubtedly, this was the business class' greatest achievement. Even in the depths of the Great Depression, most working people did not give up the dream of this new way of life. Instead, to use a formulation Warren Susman published just before his recent death, "Many who might have chosen the socialist way went instead with the hope of the culture of abundance."[3]

Of course, Flint's business class was itself transformed by the economic, social, and political events set in motion by the second industrial revolution. By the end of the 1920s, the real locus of business class power in Flint had been shifted from the group of resident entrepeneurs who had built up an automobile industry in their hometown to corporate managers who seldom, if ever, spent any time in the Vehicle City. After World War II, Charles Stewart Mott and the Mott Foundation continued to pursue the same kind of progressive-paternalist policies that had characterized the business class' political and social activities during the first automobile boom. However, the real power to make life in Flint either prosperous or depressed rested with General Motors' executives who increasingly looked at Flint as just another production center instead of as the birthplace of their company.

General Motors' top management still exercises this kind of power in Flint. Cutbacks in GM operations there since the start of the current crisis in 1974, including major decisions like the permanent termination of the Buick foundry and automatic transmission operations, the severing of administrative and financial ties with the General Motors Institute, and the planned shutdown of Fisher Body 1, made Flint the unemployment capital of America in the early 1980s. Little decisions, such as the purchasing of Oldsmobile and Pontiac instrument panel clusters from a Japanese firm rather than from the AC sparkplug factory, have also contributed to the dismal quality of life in contemporary Flint. By 1983 literally hundreds of homes and businesses lay vacant in Flint, their boarded-up windows and doors a visible reminder of the nearly 20 percent decline in the city's population that occurred between 1974 and 1982.[4] General Motors President F. James McDonald has defended his company's retrenchment in Flint as a return to the policies of Alfred P. Sloan: but as many old-timers remember, when he took over the company's top spot, Sloan went out of his way to reassure the people of Flint that GM would never forget its hometown, by expanding production there, establishing the General Motors Institute, and investing in the downtown Durant Hotel. Compared to those actions, General Motors' recent cutbacks and President McDonald's warning—"If the workforce can do something about it then fine; but if they can't, then they have to face the consequences" —have seemed extraordinarily hard-hearted, especially since the corporation has continued to make billions of dollars in profits annually. As a result, after nearly three-quarters of a century, the dependent relationship between the local business class and the General Motors Corporation has been openly questioned in Flint. In 1982, while Mott Foundation President William White complained publicly about General Motors as "an absentee-landlord," the city's economic development director Jack Liztenberg declared, "we could make Flint a good town again for *small* business."[5] It is still too soon to predict whether or not this kind of alienation will lead to a permanent breakdown in the alliance between small local businesses and big multinational business in Flint (and other similarly devastated older industrial cities), but should such a rupture occur, it would surely represent a dramatic new development in American political culture.

Whether or not a new working-class consciousness will emerge out of Flint's contemporary problems also remains to be seen. As this study shows, such a development is possible. A self-conscious working class was "made" in Flint in response to the Great Depression and the violence a then desperate business class used in an attempt to repress it. Even though the "making" of this working class followed the second industrial revolution, it was a true historical class, dedicated to struggle against the longstanding business-class monopoly over economic, social, and political decision making. There can be no denying that this class (and indeed the working class that emerged all over the United States in the 1930s) was militant. Yet, at the same time, except for a tiny minority of radical activists who could never command the political loyalty of the majority, the working class of the 1930s was not revolutionary. It did not seek the overthrow of consumer-oriented capitalism because, with the aid of the mass media and especially of Hollywood films, working people continued to dream of and, as in Flint, actually remember the culture of abundance. Industrial unionism and the New Deal formula, two enduring legacies of that working class, did not produce all the gains that militant workers of the 1930s had hoped for; nevertheless, these major institutional reforms did make life more secure, more comfortable, and more dignified, things that are all too often dismissed as insignificant by today's impatient radicals.

The making of a working class in Flint in response to the breakdown of consumer-oriented capitalism in the 1930s suggests that the deep pessimism of the New Left cultural critics of the 1960s was at least partly mistaken. When it is healthy and expanding, advanced consumer-oriented capitalism may indeed create "a pattern of one-dimensional thought and behavior," as Herbert Marcuse once explained.[6] But what happens when the flow of new products and pleasures into working people's everyday lives slows down or stops altogether? What happens when the system cannot deliver more goods and leisure time, when living standards decline instead of rise continuously? If past events in Flint—a city that experienced a second industrial revolution before the Great Depression—are any indication, then new possibilities for the creation of significant reforms may open up.

Flint's recent economic difficulties have not been comparable to the Great Depression. Admittedly unemployment has been severe, but even in the depths of the most recent 1981–1983 recession, the local auto industry kept tens of thousands of workers on the payroll. Therefore, it is not surprising that those who have suffered most in recent years—discouraged working people placed on indefinite layoff—have turned to a traditional solution to their problem; they have moved on to other places in this huge country where economic conditions remained relatively favorable. Even so, within the Vehicle City, there have been a few signs of common consciousness emerging from the common experience of economic insecurity and hardship. The organization of a group called the Committee for Full U.A.W. Employment under the leadership of Georgia Elam, an unemployed Chevrolet worker, was one such sign. In August 1982, this group picketed every General Motors plant in the city, calling for an end to overtime and the purchase of parts and components from non-GM sources. Interestingly, this group of out-of-work auto workers demonstrated a sense of history by calling for sit-down strikes to put pressure on management (and the union) to heed its demands. Unfortunately, neither the company nor the union leadership has shown any real willingness to cooperate with this group.

The Quality of Work Life program now in place at Buick was initially viewed as another sign of a new consciousness emerging in

Flint, although it clearly posed less of a threat to the "civilized relationship" between the company and the union than the independent organization of unemployed auto workers. Written into the 1973 contract at the suggestion of union vice-president Irving Bluestone, the Quality of Work Life idea was something that could be implemented only if local unions took the initiative. In 1975, Local 599 president Al Christner decided that the best way to stop the drastic decline in the Buick workforce (down nearly two-thirds from its post-World War II peak) was to begin a program that would bring workers and management together in an effort to modernize the huge but aging facility. That fall, for the first time ever, Buick's general manager and the officers of Local 599 met in face-to-face conferences. The result was the Quality of Work Life program that aims to create regular worker participation in departmental decision making (including the redesign of the production process), and greater job security through guaranteed job retraining whenever technological changes make older jobs obsolete. By 1983, five departments were fully involved in the Buick Quality of Work Life program, the first of its kind at General Motors. In those departments, absenteeism and grievances fell dramatically while the quality of the product rose.[7]

Despite its apparent well-publicized success, many supervisors and workers at Buick and the other General Motors facilities in the city resisted the Quality of Work Life idea. Some managers saw it as a threat to their authority, and many workers wonder if all the extra time put into the program will really make their jobs more secure. General Motors relentless reduction of its workforce in Flint in the 1980s seems to have provided an answer for many local auto workers. As rank-and-file discontent rose throughout Flint in the fall of 1984, unhappy Buick workers voted Local 599 President Christner out of office. Four other local union presidents, who had been involved in starting QWL experiments, suffered a similar fate in the same elections. Consequently, the future of the Quality of Work Life reforms in Flint remains in doubt.

These events in contemporary Flint seem to confirm Nelson Lichtenstein's recent observation that,

> Unions have again become an arena for political debate, and the issues with which the early CIO grappled—the quality of daily work life, union democracy, and the political independence of the labor movement—have again been brought forward on the social agenda.[8]

Yet, somehow, his assessment seems too optimistic. While this history of twentieth-century Flint has demonstrated that workers in a consumer-oriented society can create a class-conscious movement for progressive social change, it has also shown that the obstacles standing in the way of such a movement today are enormous, greater even than those faced by the C.I.O. in 1936–1937. As we have seen, during the late 1940s in the midst of a Cold War crisis, big business, big government, and newly organized big labor combined to suppress the kind of spontaneously created local working-class institutions that might have (we can never be sure) sustained the independent collective identity that workers had made for themselves in the previous decade. Over the past forty years, there have been many changes in America, but the nation has not fundamentally transformed either its institutional arrangements or the basic cultural values produced by the second industrial revolution. Nor has it ended the Cold War. Thus, in the near future at least, there seems little hope of establishing an independent, nonhierarchical, politically progressive labor movement in the United States like the one that emerged in Flint in the aftermath of the great sit-down strike.

LIST OF ABBREVIATIONS

ACLU	*American Civil Liberties Union*
A. F. of L.	*American Federation of Labor*
AWU	*Auto Workers Union*
C.I.O.	*Congress of Industrial Organizations*
C.L.U.	*Central Labor Union*
CP	*Communist Party*
F.E.R.A.	*Federal Emergency Relief Administration*
F.F.L.	*Flint Federation of Labor*
FPL	*Flint Public Library, Flint, Michigan*
GM	*General Motors*
GPO	*Government Printing Office*
HOLC	*Home Owners Loan Corporation*
I.M.A.	*Industrial Mutual Association*
I.W.W.	*Industrial Workers of the World*
K.K.K.	*Ku Klux Klan*
M.E.S.A.	*Mechanics Educational Society of America*
MHC	*Michigan Historical Collections, University of Michigan.*
N.L.R.B.	*National Labor Relations Board*
NRA	*National Recovery Administration*
NRC	*National Records Center, Suitland, Michigan*
P.A.A.	*Protestant Action Association*
P.A.C.	*Political Action Committee*
RFC	*Reconstruction Finance Corporation*
UAAVWA	*Union of Automobile, Aircraft, and Vehicle Workers of America*
U.A.W.	*United Auto Workers Union*
WEAA	*Flint's local radio station*
WPA	*Works Progress Administration*
WSU	*Walter Reuther Library, Wayne State University*
YMCA	*Young Men's Christian Association*

NOTES

Preface

1. Immanuel Wallerstein, "The Rise and Future Demise of the World Capitalist System: Concepts for Comparative Analysis," *Comparative Studies in Society and History* 16 (September 1974):389.
2. James Henretta, "The Study of Social Mobility: Ideological Assumptions and Conceptual Bias," *Labor History* 18 (Spring 1977):167.
3. George Dangerfield, *The Damnable Question: A Study in Anglo-Irish Relations* (Boston, 1976), xix.
4. E. P. Thompson, "The Peculiarities of the English," *The Socialist Register* (1965):335.
5. David F. Noble, *America by Design: Science, Technology, and the Rise of Corporate Capitalism* (Oxford, 1977), xix.

1. Introduction

1. Joseph Schumpeter, *Business Cycles: A Theoretical, Historical, and Statistical Analysis of the Capitalist Process,* abridged ed. (New York, 1964), 246ff.
2. Eric Hobsbawm, *Industry and Empire: The Pelican Economic History of Britain Volume 3, From 1750 to the Present Day* (London, 1969), 172.
3. Harry Braverman, *Labor and Monopoly Capital: The Degradation of Work in the Twentieth Century* (New York, 1974), 166–167. For a perceptive discussion of this development in the United States, see Noble, *America by Design,* 3–19.
4. From Frederick Taylor, *Shop Management* (1903), quoted in Braverman, *Labor and Monopoly Capital,* 113.
5. For a specific comparison see Ronald Edsforth, "Divergent Traditions: Union Organization in the Automobile Industries of Flint, Michigan, and Coventry, England," *Detroit in Perspective: A Journal of Regional History,* 5, 3 (Spring 1981).
6. Hobsbawm, *Industry and Empire,* 117.
7. In Germany, state-approved cartels speeded up industrial concentra-

tion. Similar "rationalization" schemes were promoted by the Conserva- tive British governments of the interwar period. In the United States, regulatory laws and commissions were used to block anti-trust action, and in Japan, the government actually invested in new industries before selling off its holdings cheaply to encourage concentration. In France, governmental intervention in the economy was minimal prior to 1945. For details, see Robert A. Brady, *Business as a System of Power* (New York, 1943), 23–29 and 83–97; Charles P. Kindleberger, *Economic Growth in France and Britain* (Cambridge, 1964), 185–190; and William W. Lock- wood, *The Economic Development of Japan: Growth and Structural Change* (Princeton, 1968), 503–509.

8. This point is explained at length in Ralph Miliband's *The State in Capital- ist Society* (New York, 1969), especially chapter 4, "The Purpose and Role of Governments."

9. Geoffrey Barraclough, *An Introduction to Contemporary History* (London, 1967), 35. The author dates the transition period as 1890 to 1960.

10. The relevance and limitations of the first four terms are discussed by Henri Lefebvre in *Everyday Life in the Modern World*, trans. Sarah Rabino- vitch (London, 1971), 45–66. The idea of a "post-industrial society" re- ceives an even-handed treatment from Robert Heilbroner in *Business Civilization in Decline* (New York, 1976), 63–78.

11. Barraclough, *An Introduction*, 50.

12. E. P. Thompson, "The Poverty of Theory," in *The Poverty of Theory and Other Essays* (New York, 1978), 46.

13. Heilbroner, *Business Civilization in Decline*, 27.

14. For a concise example of dissent on this point see Ernest Mandel and George Novack, *The Revolutionary Potential of the Working Class* (New York, 1974).

15. T. B. Bottomore, *Classes in Modern Society* (New York, 1966), 23.

16. Ibid., p. 24.

17. Braverman, *Labor and Monopoly Capitalism*, 403.

18. Paul Sweezy, *Modern Capitalism* (New York, 1972), 142.

19. Bottomore, *Classes*, 99–100.

20. Arthur Marwick, *Class: Image and Reality (In Britain, France, and the United States Since 1930)*, (New York, 1980), 18.

21. E. P. Thompson, *The Making of the English Working Class* (New York, 1963), 9.

22. As Professor Thompson has commented, "That historical investigation cannot deal in absolutes and cannot adduce sufficient causes greatly irri- tates some simple and impatient souls. They suppose that, since histori- cal explanation cannot be All, it is therefore Nothing. . . . This is a silly mistake. For historical explanation discloses not how history must have eventuated but why it eventuated in this way and not other ways." ("The Poverty of Theory," 50).

23. Marwick, *Class: Image and Reality*, 361.
24. Thompson, *The Making*, 10.

2. The Transformation of American Society in the Automobile Age

1. Lawrence Gustin, *Billy Durant: Creator of General Motors* (Grand Rapids, 1973), 41–48.
2. James J. Flink, *The Car Culture* (Cambridge, 1975), 34. Professor Flink estimates that the total costs of not banning horses in New York City alone reached one hundred million dollars a year in the early 1900s.
3. John B. Rae, *American Automobile Manufacturers: The First Forty Years* (Philadelphia, 1959), 103.
4. Sinclair Lewis, *Babbitt* (New York, 1980), 23.
5. Robert S. Lynd and Helen Merrell Lynd, *Middletown: A Study in Modern American Culture* (New York, 1929), 254–256. My evidence for the rapid emergence of automobile-centered consumerism in Flint in the 1920s is presented below in chapter 4.
6. Except where noted, all statistics are from *The Statistical History of the United States from Colonial Times to the Present* (New York, 1976).
7. Lynds, *Middletown*, 260.
8. Warren James Belasco, *Americans on the Road: From Auto-camp to Motel, 1910–1945* (Cambridge, 1981), 96.
9. The Lynds' evidence for this view is presented in *Middletown*, 80–84. Eli Chinoy's *Automobile Workers and the American Dream* (Garden City, 1955) shows how this pattern was strengthened after 1945; see especially 126ff.
10. Thompson, *The Making of the English Working Class* (New York, 1963), 13.
11. Stephen Thernstrom, *Poverty and Progress: Social Mobility in a Nineteenth-Century City* (New York, 1972), 165.
12. Flink, *Car Culture*, 55.
13. Henri Lefebvre, *Everyday Life in the Modern World*, trans. Sarah Rabinovitch (New York, 1971), 100–104.
14. George S. May, *A Most Unique Machine: The Michigan Origins of the American Automobile Industry* (Grand Rapids, 1975), 333–335.
15. Stephen Meyer, *The Five Dollar Day: Labor Management and Social Control in the Ford Motor Company, 1908–1921* (Albany, 1981), 195.
16. Flink, *Car Culture*, 58.
17. Thorstein Veblen, *The Theory of the Leisure Class: An Economic Study of Institutions* (New York, 1953, Mentor edition), 69–70. See Alfred D. Chandler, Jr., *The Visible Hand: The Managerial Revolution in American Business* (Cambridge, 1977), chapters 7 and 11 for details.
18. Ed Cray, *Chrome Colossus: General Motors and Its Times* (New York, 1980), 221 and 367.

19. Emma Rothschild, *Paradise Lost: The Decline of the Auto-Industrial Age* (New York, 1973), 40.

20. Paul Baron and Paul Sweezy, *Monopoly Capital: An Essay on the American Economic and Social Order* (New York, 1968), 135–7.

21. Meyer, *Five Dollar Day*, 200.

22. Flink, *Car Culture*, 18; and Rae, *American Automobile Manufacturers*, 119.

23. William Plowden, *The Motor Car Politics, 1896–1970* (London, 1971), 107. It is interesting to note that even in 1913 approximately one-fourth of the cars built in Britain were being turned out by the Ford Motor Company.

24. "Automobile Progress Edition," *The New York Times*, special supplement, February 2, 1919. Also see Flink, *Car Culture*, 93–94.

25. Rae, *American Automobile Manufacturers*, 153.

26. C. E. Griffin, "The Life History of Automobiles," *Michigan Business Studies*, I, 1 (1926):2; and Flink, *Car Culture*, 142–143.

27. Gabriel Kolko, *Wealth and Power in America: An Analysis of Social Class and Income Distribution* (New York, 1962), 14.

28. Walter Chrysler, *Life of an American Workman* (New York, 1950), 197.

29. The combined number of establishments in the motor vehicle, parts, and bodies industries rose from just 57 in 1904 to 2,515 in 1919. In the following decade, the consolidation of operations and the elimination of marginal firms left only 1,154 establishments in the field; however, the average number of wage earners in each establishment was multiplied nearly fourfold, from 53 to 192 workers. See William Ellison Chalmers, "Labor in the Automobile Industry: A Study of Personnel Policies, Workers' Attitudes and Attempts at Unionism" (Ph.D. dissertation, University of Wisconsin, 1932), 12–13.

30. For more details see John B. Rae, *The Road and Car in American Life* (Cambridge, Massachusetts, 1971), especially 49–50; and Flink, *The Car Culture*, 140–141 and 160.

31. The United States Bureau of the Census considered places with fewer than 2,500 residents "rural" and everything else "urban." Traditionally it also listed towns with populations over 8,000, but unfortunately the category was dropped after 1930.

32. Harry Braverman discusses the significance of the decline of urban agriculture in *Labor and Monopoly Capital* (New York, 1974), 272–277.

33. E. P. Thompson, "Time, Work-Discipline, and Industrial Capitalism," *Past and Present* 38 (December 1967):97.

34. Lynds, *Middletown*, 251.

35. Braverman, *Labor and Monopoly Capital*, 357–380.

36. Lynds, *Middletown*, 487ff.

37. Hugh Grant Adams, quoted in Irving Bernstein, *The Lean Years: A History of the American Worker 1920–1933* (Baltimore, 1966), 83.

38. Bernstein, *Lean Years*, 84.

39. This problem is discussed (though not resolved) in David Brody, "The Old Labor History and the New: In Search of an America Working Class," *Labor History* 20 (Winter 1979):112–126. David Montgomery's review essay, "To Study the People: The American Working Class," *Labor History* 21 (Fall 1980):485–512, reveals the actual dearth of studies of post-World War I developments in everyday life and their effect on the organized labor movement.

40. Robert Reiff, "Alienation and Dehumanization?" in *Auto Work and Its Discontents*, edited by B. J. Widick (Baltimore, 1976), 46.

41. David Brody, *Workers in Industrial America: Essays on the Twentieth-Century Struggle* (New York, 1980), 62ff, and Albert W. Niemi, *U.S. Economic History* (Chicago, 1980), 274.

42. Cray, *Chrome Colossus*, 236.

43. Charles Loch Mowat, *Britain Between the Wars 1918–1940* (Boston, 1971), 268–269.

44. Thomas Cochran, *200 Years of American Business* (New York, 1977), 126.

45. Lynds, *Middletown*, 82n.

46. See Stuart Ewen, *Captains of Consciousness: Advertising and Social Roots of Consumer Culture* (New York, 1976), 34–48.

47. Lynds, *Middletown*, 87.

48. Lefebvre, *Everyday Life*, 56. Lefebvre describes this ideology as having "bereft the working classes of their former ideals and values while maintaining the status and initiative of the bourgeoisie," and as having "substituted for the image of the active man that of the consumer as the possessor of happiness and rationality."

49. The definition of the "New Deal formula" is drawn from David Montgomery, *Workers Control in America: Studies in the History of Work, Technology, and Labor Struggles* (Cambridge, 1979), 161.

50. Flink, *Car Culture*, 230–231.

3. The Early Automobile Boom in Flint

1. The others included Wagon Works' Vice-President George Walker, Treasurer William Ballenger, and Directors Charles Begole and Charles Cummings. By this investment, all of them became charter members of Flint's automobile establishment. See George S. May's more elaborate account in *A Most Unique Machine: The Michigan Origins of the American Automobile Industry* (Grand Rapids, 1975), 194–199.

2. The first cars produced in Flint were actually made by A.B.C. Hardy's Flint Automobile Company in 1903. Hardy could not attract the backing of local banks and businessmen, however, and without capital or volume sales, the venture quickly failed. By January 1904, the Flint Automobile Company had already closed its doors. See May, *Unique Machine*, 194–196.

3. The Detroit factory was apparently closed down late in 1904, about the time William C. Durant was taking managerial control out of David Buick's hands.
4. May, *Unique Machine*, 201. Also see Bernard A. Weisberger, *The Dream Maker: William C. Durant, Founder of General Motors* (Boston, 1979), 92–93.
5. David Buick was squeezed out of the company, unable to pay off the debts he had contracted through the years of unprofitable experimentation. When he resigned in 1906, Durant reportedly gave him a large sum of money (perhaps as much as $200,000), but over the years he gradually lost it all in a series of bad business ventures. David Buick died in Detroit in 1929, a pauper.
6. The title was printed on the labels of cigars distributed at a 1911 banquet honoring Durant. See Weisberger, *Dream Maker*, 161.
7. Weisberger, *Dream Maker*, 99.
8. Quoted in Gustin, *Billy Durant: Creator of General Motors* (Grand Rapids, 1973), 77. The directors of the Flint Wagon Works stayed with Buick in the same roles. The Durant-Dort Company put up at least $100,000 itself. W. A. Paterson and W. F. Stewart, owners of the city's other prominent vehicle-making firms, contributed heavily and became Buick directors. Among Flint bankers, Robert Whaley (who first backed Durant in 1882) and D. D. Aitken (former congressman and mayor) of the Citizen's Commercial Bank; John J. Carton (Buick's attorney and a prominent Republican) and George Walker (the Wagon Works' vice-president) of the First National Bank; and three of Durant's relatives (uncles William Crapo and James Willson and cousin W. C. Orrell) as well as chief cashier Arthur Bishop, all of the Genessee County Savings Bank (where Durant himself was a director), each put up some of Buick's original capital requirements. Flint Smith, heir to the city's original lumber boom fortune and a director of the Union Trust and Savings Bank (along with Paterson and Stewart, the carriage makers), also contributed and he was made a Buick director. Also see Weisberger, *Dream Maker* 93–99; May, *Unique Machine*, 204–206; and the Genessee County Biography File, Flint Public Library (hereafter cited as FPL).
9. After crediting every conceivable asset in September 1905, Buick's attorney, John J. Carton, was still left with sixty thousand dollars he could not account for. He finally credited this to unpatented engine improvements made by Walter Marr, and used his political influence to get the necessary state approval.
10. Part of the stock given Durant when he came into Buick (perhaps as much as $350,000 worth) was probably tied to a promise to provide access to this Jackson factory. However, on April 24, 1905, the directors of Flint's three banks got Durant to sign an agreement to discontinue Buick

operations in Jackson as soon as a new plant could be opened in Flint. Weisberger, *Dream Maker*, 96.

11. The profits of the Oak Park Development Association have never been made public, but each person involved accumulated a substantial fortune in this period of rapid expansion. Throughout the automobile boom in Flint, connections between the car companies, the banks, and the real estate developers remained very tight. See May, *Unique Machine*, 213; Gustin, *Billy Durant*, 80–84; and Frank Rodolph, "An Industrial History of Flint," an unpublished manuscript written by the *Flint Daily Journal*'s librarian in 1940, 495–502; Rodolph's manuscript can be found in the Automotive History Collection, FPL.

12. Quoted in Gustin, *Billy Durant*, 43. Ultimately, in its peak years just after 1900, the Durant-Dort Carriage Company made its own wheels, axles, paints, varnishes, and buggy tops, in addition to assembling a diverse line of horse-drawn vehicles. During this era, Durant-Dort not only owned several factories in Flint, it was a a multinational corporation that controlled plants in Toronto, Canada; Atlanta, Georgia; Pine Bluff, Arkansas; and mills in Tennessee and Arkansas. In its best year, 1906, Durant-Dort manufactured 56,000 vehicles in Flint alone, and perhaps as many as 150,000 nationwide.

13. Imperial Wheel, the Flint Varnish Works, and Flint Axle Works were already Durant-Dort subsidiaries in 1905. As Buick grew, the first two were immediately absorbed by the automotive giant. The Varnish Works remained separate until 1918, when it was purchased by DuPont and turned into Buick's sole paint supplier. W. F. Stewart, a company that had started making carriage bodies in 1868, was bought out by General Motors in 1908 and immediately incorporated into Buick operations. Armstrong Steel Spring maintained its formal independence until it was purchased by General Motors in 1923. See May, *Unique Machine*, 214; Gustin, *Billy Durant*, 123; and Arthur Pound, *The Turning Wheel: The Story of General Motors Through Twenty-Five Years* (Garden City, 1934), Appendix 4: "General Motors' Subsidiaries," 453ff.

14. The Flint Wagon Works (producing 35,000 vehicles per year) and W. A. Paterson's (producing 23,000 units) also hit their peak productions in these years. Between them, Flint's three leading traditional vehicle makers thus turned out more than 100,000 wagons and carriages per year at the very same time that the Buick Motor Company was being built into a major producer of rival vehicles.

15. For the city's fiftieth anniversary celebration, a sign carrying the title, "The Vehicle City," was erected across Flint's main thoroughfare. See the photograph on page 232 of *The Book of the Golden Jubilee of Flint, Michigan 1855–1905*, which was published locally. For the New Yorkers' first impressions of Flint, see Clarence Young and William Quinn, *Foundation*

for Living: The Story of Charles Stewart Mott and Flint (New York, 1963), 1–3; and May, *Unique Machine*, 216–217.

16. Bishop apparently carried some of Durant's notes off the books at the Genessee County Savings during this period of rapid expansion. Later, in 1915, Durant named Bishop a director of General Motors. See Arthur Pound, "General Motors' Old Home Town," *Michigan History* 40 (March 1956):90–91; and May, *Unique Machine*, 206.

17. Weston-Mott sales rose from $200,000 in 1903 to more than $2 million in 1908–1909 and $5.5 million in 1909–1910. Initially capitalized at $500,000 in 1906, Weston-Mott tripled that figure by 1908 to finance continuous expansion. See Young and Quinn, *Foundation for Living*, 30ff.

18. Details on the stock exchanges that took place between C. S. Mott and General Motors can be found in Pound, *The Turning Wheel*, 489–490.

19. AC Sparkplug produced 2,000 sparkplugs per day in 1912. During World War I, with the help of government contracts, its capacity was increased to 50,000 sparkplugs every twenty-four hours. In the 1920s, AC Sparkplug diversified its line of automotive parts and components when it moved into the larger facilities of the defunct Dort Motor Company. By this time, with more than eight hundred mostly young single females on its payroll, the AC sparkplug had become the city's biggest employer of women. See Pound, *The Turning Wheel*, 456–460; and Women's Bureau Survey Material, RG 86, Bulletin 67, National Archives.

20. May, *Unique Machine*, 208–209.

21. Output figures for 1910 are in dispute. For example, see Gustin, *Billy Durant*, 87; and Alfred P. Sloan Jr., *My Years With General Motors* (Garden City, 1964), 445–447.

22. McLaughlin served as chairman of the board of General Motors of Canada until his death in January 1972. May, *Unique Machine*, 206–210.

23. The creation of the sport of motorcar racing was one of the automobile industry's earliest and greatest public relations coups. Over the years it has provided the industry with a self-sustaining source of tremendous advertising value as well as a leisure time pursuit that reinforced the consumer consciousness of the automobile's millions of fans. Racing heroes like "Wild Bob" Burman became living symbols of particular products and of the kind of excitement "automobility" seemed to hold out. The Alfred P. Sloan Museum in Flint has extensive collections of material on Buick's early racing teams.

24. The complex details of these unsuccessful negotiations are revealed in Weisberger, *Dream Maker*, 117–133.

25. From Durant's unpublished memoirs, quoted in Gustin, *Billy Durant*, 138.

26. For details on the negotiations between Durant and Leland and a complete list of General Motors' initial acquisitions see Gustin, *Billy Durant*, 120–123.

27. In addition to Buick, W. F. Stewart Bodies, Michigan Motor Castings, Champion Ignition, the Oak Park Power Company and the Randolph Truck Company were all brought under the General Motors banner in Flint by 1910.
28. General Motors' dividends increased 150 percent during 1909 on profits of more than $9 million. Most of this profit came from cash sales of Buick and Cadillac cars. Unfortunately, some of the other companies bought by General Motors turned out to be nearly total losses. The Heany Lamp Companies, which Durant purchased for $7 million, proved to be his biggest blunder when patents it claimed were shown to be fraudulent. More costly than Buick and Olds combined, Heany Lamp could not compete profitably with General Electric. See Gustin, *Billy Durant*, 132–137; and Weisberger, *Dream Maker*, 140–141.
29. Gustin, *Billy Durant*, 132.
30. By 1909, there were more than six hundred salaried employees at Flint's industrial establishments. *Thirteenth Census of the United States Volume 9, Manufactures*, (GPO, 1912), 577. Also see Young and Quinn, *Foundation for Living*, 37.
31. Stephen R. Williams, "The Rise and Fall of Piano Box City," an unpublished paper dated 12/6/73 in the collection of the Alfred P. Sloan Museum, Flint. This and the other unpublished papers cited below were prepared by students at the University of Michigan-Flint for Dr. Richard Meister's urban history course.
32. Williams, "Piano Box City," "The Flight of Time," and "All Flint Held its Breath in 1910," anonymous, undated articles from the *Flint Journal*, Sloan Museum.
33. The details of General Motors' 1910 financial difficulties have been rehearsed by many competent historians. See Pound, *Turning Wheel*, 126ff; Gustin, *Billy Durant*, 136ff; Flink, *Car Culture*, 63–65; and Weisberger, *Dream Maker*, 147–52.
34. This composite picture of the recession of 1910 in Flint is drawn from the *Flint Journal*'s "All Flint Held its Breath in 1910"; Pound, "General Motors' Old Home Town," 91; and Young and Quinn, *Foundation for Living*, 38–40.
35. Gustin, *Billy Durant*, 140; and "All Flint Held its Breath in 1910," *Flint Journal*.
36. Walter Chrysler, *Life of an American Workman* (New York, 1950), 135.
37. Chrysler, *American Workman*, 135–36.
38. Chrysler, *American Workman*, 137.
39. Rodolph, "An Industrial History": 260–261; and Sloan, *My Years with General Motors*, 466–467.
40. The financial maneuvers that Durant used to recoup General Motors are detailed in Pound, *The Turning Wheel*, 152–159; Gustin, *Billy Durant*, 162–182; Weisberger, *Dream Maker*, 185–201; and very succinctly in

Flink, *Car Culture*, 64–66. When Durant began trading shares of Chevrolet for General Motors, Chevrolet consisted of the manufacturing operations in Flint as well as other factories in Tarrytown, New York; Oakland, California; Missouri; St. Louis; Atlanta; and Canada. In other words, in its holding company structure, it closely resembled Durant's previous major ventures, Durant-Dort Carriage and General Motors of 1908–1910.

41. Although Dort and Durant separated their finances in 1913, the two men apparently remained friends for many years. See Gustin, *Billy Durant*, 158–159.

42. *Dort Doings* Volume 2, Number 1 (War Memorial Number), Sloan Museum.

43. John Ihlder, "Flint: When Men Build Automobiles Who Builds Their City?" *The Survey* September 2, 1916, 550–554. In this article, one of a series on war boom towns, Ihlder was very critical of local industrial leaders for their failure to anticipate the housing shortage.

44. Flint's first cigarmaker opened his doors in 1875. In 1898, eight companies were turning out 4.6 million cigars. By 1905, there were twelve firms in this prosperous business, yet none would survive the 1920s. Flint, the Genessee County seat, also became an important agricultural center, as lands that had been cleared during the lumber boom were put into food production. In 1905 there were two major grain mills, several creameries, a pump factory, a broom factory, and several other small implement makers located in Flint. See *The Book of the Golden Jubilee*, 92–96; and Lawrence R. Gustin, *The Flint Journal Centennial History of Flint* (Flint, 1976), 107ff.

45. *Flint Flashes: The Voice of the Exploited Worker*, April 4, 1912 has an article discussing the local party's history. Scattered issues of this Socialist newspaper published in Flint between 1911 and 1912 are almost the only insider sources on the local movement. Surviving copies may be found in the Sloan Museum, Flint.

46. Like every other attempt at unionizing automobile workers prior to the 1930s, this effort failed. Early automobile union failures in Flint are discussed in chapter 5.

47. "Research Notes," Box 3, Edward Levinson Collection, Archives of Urban and Labor History, Walter Reuther Library, Wayne State University (hereafter cited as WSU). These notes are based on Levinson's reading of the *Journals of the Carriage and Wagon Workers Union* and the *Flint Flashes* (including issues now lost).

48. The lack of evidence may, of course, stem from the inadequacy of the remaining sources. See the *Flint Flashes*, April 4, 1912 for a complete list of local Socialist election results from 1901 to 1912.

49. "Notes," Box 3, Levinson Collection, WSU.

50. "Notes," Box 3, Levinson Collection, WSU. This description of the So-

cialist platform is based on material from the 1911 issues of *Flint Flashes,* which are no longer available.

51. "Notes," Box 3, Levinson Collection, WSU. Menton's union record is used by James Weinstein in his *The Decline of Socialism in America 1912–1925* (New York, 1967) as exemplifying working-class participation in Socialist electoral successes; see his note on p. 43.
52. "Notes," Box 3, Levinson Collection, WSU. The election and its aftermath are described in considerable detail in Harold Ford, "The Year of Living Dangerously," *Michigan Voice* 7 (September 1983):6.
53. This summary is based on Levinson's "Notes," and Ford, "Living Dangerously," 6.
54. Ford, "Living Dangerously," 6–7; *Flint Flashes,* March 23, 1912.
55. All quotes are from Ford, "Living Dangerously," 7.
56. *Flint Flashes,* March 23, 1912. This experience led Trafalet to quit the automobile industry permanently.
57. Pound, "General Motors Old Home Town," 91. Pound arrived in Flint in 1902, married the daughter of the city's original wagon maker, W. A. Paterson, and stayed on for a number of years editing *The Arrow* and writing and collecting material for his book, *The Iron Man in Industry* (Boston, 1922), a study of the effect of automatic machine tools on industrial work and production.
58. Young and Quinn, *Foundation for Living,* 47. Because of the entrepreneurial bias of most of Flint history, records of Mott's political career have been preserved far better than those of the Socialists.
59. From Mott's first public statement after winning the 1912 primary. Young and Quinn, *Foundation for Living,* 46.
60. Young and Quinn, *Foundation for Living,* 48–50; Ford, "Living Dangerously," 7.
61. The accompanying article went on to explain that Weston-Mott had never paid city property taxes on the full value of its holdings, much to the benefit of the company's only stockholders, C. S. Mott and the General Motors Corporation. See *Flint Flashes,* March 23, 1912.
62. *Flint Flahes,* March 23, 1912. Nash was charged with keeping boys under the age of eighteen at work for more than fifty-four hours a week. He pleaded guilty and was fined five dollars.
63. *Flint Flashes,* April 6, 1912.
64. This summary of Mott's first year as mayor is based on Young and Quinn, *Foundation for Living,* 52–59.
65. The official tally gave Mott 4,290 votes to Menton's 2,341.
66. These achievements were reviewed in a retrospective article, "Ordinance Record Reflects the City's Progress for Over Quarter Century," *Flint Weekly Review,* May 14, 1926. Also see Young and Quinn, *Foundation for Living,* 60.
67. Young and Quinn, *Foundation for Living,* 63.

68. Though nominally a weekly, the *Flint Flashes* had been published sporadically since John Menton's first electoral defeat in April 1912. Declining revenues from advertising and subscriptions were the principal cause of the difficulties. Without the Central Labor Union's subsidy, it could not pay its bills.

69. Specific examples of this kind of activity are outlined below in chapters 4 and 5.

70. Quoted in Young & Quinn, *Foundation for Living*, 76. This sketch of George Starkweather's career is based on materials found in the Genessee County Biography File, FPL.

71. Young & Quinn, *Foundation for Living*, 64–66.

72. John Menton made a brief but unsuccessful return to local politics in 1930. Running without the Flint Federation's support in the first nonpartisan elections for the new city commission, Menton failed to win one of the nine available seats. Then in July, Menton circulated nominating petitions for the state legislature as a Republican. However, he did not gather enough signatures to make the primary ballot. See the *Flint Weekly Review*, February 7 and July 11, 1930.

73. Ihdler, "Flint," 555. Photographs included with this article in *The Survey* reveal dramatically the underdeveloped state of the city at this time.

74. Ihdler, "Flint," 549.

75. The candidates' public statements are quoted at length in Young & Quinn, *Foundation for Living*, 71.

76. This description of McKeighan is by the Mott biographers, Young & Quinn, *Foundation for Living*, 71–72.

4. The Economic and Social Foundations of Normalcy in Flint

1. John Ihdler, "Flint: When Men Build Automobiles Who Builds Their City," *The Survey*, September 2, 1916, 550.

2. For a complete list, see note 13, chapter 3.

3. Frank Rodolph, "An Industrial History of Flint," an unpublished ms. in the Automotive History Collection, FPL. 261–262. Like his predecessor, C. W. Nash, Chrysler found Durant's free-wheeling, personal style of leadership irksome. Durant recognized this problem, and to keep his talented manager, he had offered Chrysler a three-year contract in 1916 that paid $10,000 a month in cash and $500,000 at the end of *each year* either in cash or in GM stock.

4. *Fourteenth Census of the United States*, Vol. 9, *Manufactures*, 684.

5. Quoted in an interview with L. Frey, National Recovery Administration, "Hearings on Regularizing Employment and otherwise Improving the Conditions of Labor in the Automobile Industry," held in Flint, Michigan, 1 (December 1934):287, in the National Archives (hereafter

cited as NRA hearings). Also see "Hiring Policies in the Automobile Industry," a Works Progress Administration National Research Project prepared by Blanche Bernstein (New York City, 1937), Box 2, Levinson Collection, WSU.

6. The fact that some workers became landlords was revealed in the NRA hearings held in Flint in 1934. For example, at that time Carl Michael, a forty-one-year-old Buick metal finisher, told investigators how he had bought up five houses between 1919 and 1929, only to lose them all in the early depression. See NRA Hearings, 2 (December 1934):508–515.

7. "Memo: Buick Employees to Have New Dormitory," (undated) and Carolyn Rose, "The Attempt of GM to Aid in Easing the Housing Shortage in Flint, Michigan," (an unpublished paper dated November 30, 1971), Sloan Museum.

8. Alfred P. Sloan, Jr., *Adventures of a White Collar Man* (New York, 1941), 105.

9. Durant's other achievements included the acquisition of five important automotive accessories makers, grouped as United Motors, and the creation of the General Motors' Acceptance Corporation to extend consumer credit.

10. See Gustin, *Billy Durant: Creator of General Motors,* (Grand Rapids, 1973), 204ff; and James J. Flink, *The Car Culture,* (Cambridge, 1975), 116–19 and 124–26.

11. In 1949, the Justice Department opened an antitrust suit against the DuPonts for their acquisitions of General Motors stock. The case was dismissed by a lower court in 1953, but the suit was upheld upon a final appeal to the Supreme Court in 1961. In order to cushion the blow, a compliant Congress then passed a special law allowing the DuPonts to sell their sixty-three million shares of General Motors, worth $2.7 billion, without a tax loss.

12. Fisher Body 2, as it came to be known (because it was the smaller of the two plants), produced Chevrolet bodies for the Flint assembly plant. Statistics compiled from "Report to the Stockholders of the General Motors Corporation . . . December 31, 1921," p. 9; and the *Flint Daily Journal,* March 28, 1924.

13. The General Motors Institute was officially created in 1924 when the Flint Institute of Technology was absorbed as the core of the corporation's new training center. The Flint Institute had been set up in 1919 at the urging of the general managers of both Flint's Chevrolet and Buick operations to train needed skilled workers. When it expanded in 1924, the General Motors Institute offered classes in Buick-authorized service, in technical trades like tool and die work, and a four-year college level "Co-operative Engineering" curriculum. By 1928, more than five hundred carefully screened high school graduates were enrolled in these

management training courses. See Albert Sobey, "General Motors Institute," *Foreman's Magazine* 3 (March 1923); and Clarence Young and Robert Tuttle, *The Years 1919–1969 . . . a History of the General Motors Institute* (Flint, 1969).

14. An ill-fated attempt to organize automobile workers during the postwar recession is discussed in the next chapter.

15. Yearly industrial employment averages kept by the Flint Manufacturers Association are given in Robert C. Schmitt, "The Future Population of Metropolitan Flint," Institute for Human Adjustment, University of Michigan, (Ann Arbor: 1947), 30. Estimates for the 1929 peak vary. Information on General Motors' divisions can be found in "General Motors Scrapbooks" (Chevrolet Division Vol. 1, Buick Motors Division, Vol. 1, and Fisher Body Division), Automotive History Collection, FPL.

16. Arthur Pound, *The Iron Man in Industry*, (Boston, 1922), 77–79.

17. Richard Meister, "The Rise of Two Industrial Cities: A Comparative Study of Gary, Indiana, and Flint, Michigan" (an unpublished paper originally presented at the Duquesne University History Forum, October 28, 1971), 6. A copy of the paper may be found in the Michigan Historical Collections.

18. In 1928, Mott was president of the Industrial Savings Bank and its subsidiary, the Bankers Trust Company of Flint. In 1929, these banks merged with Bishop's old company, Genessee Savings, to form Flint's biggest financial institution, the Union Industrial Trust and Saving. At the time, Bishop was also president of the First National Bank and Trust. Mott's resources were so great in this period that he could personally put up $3.6 million in cash to cover funds embezzled by bank subordinates, a story that made national headlines in 1929. See Walter Dunham, *Banking and Industry in Michigan* (Detroit, 1929), 158–61; Rodolph, "An Industrial History," 286; and Clarence Young and William Quinn, *Foundation for Living*: The Story of Charles Stewart Mott and Flint (New York, 1963), 100–101.

19. Durant Motors was founded in January 1921 after Billy Durant raised $7 million in forty-eight hours from sixty-seven friends. A modern factory was built in Flint, but it was never used to full capacity. Many small local investors bought shares in Durant Motors in 1922–1923, confidently expecting their hometown hero to make them rich. Although Durant Motors captured perhaps as much as one-fifth of the national car market in its best year, Durant lost interest in the company in the late 1920s, and he liquidated it in 1933. Many Flint investors never forgave him.

20. Between 1910 and 1930, Burton, Flint, Genessee, and Mount Morris townships more than quadrupled in size. However, unlike the surburban growth of the post-World War II era, this expansion was not a result of flight from the city. The first Flint suburbs were actually settled by

newly arriving working people who could not afford the cost of a home in the city. See I. Harding Hughes Jr., "Local Government in the Fringe Area of Flint, Michigan," Institute for Human Adjustment, University of Michigan (Ann Arbor: 1947), 3–5; and Leo F. Schnore, "The Separation of Home and Work in Flint, Michigan," Institute for Human Adjustment, University of Michigan, (Ann Arbor, 1954), 46. Also see Schmitt, "The Future Population of Metropolitan Flint," 6–8.

21. The exodus from the Michigan countryside continued throughout the boom years, but it could not keep pace with expansion in the cities. Between 1920 and 1930, 40 percent of rural Michigan's population aged ten to twenty in 1920 moved to the cities, extending the trend of the previous decade. See "The Labor Market in the Automobile Industry," a WPA National Research Project prepared by Blanche Bernstein, February 1937, Box 2, Levinson Collection, WSU.

22. As a percentage of the total population, Flint's foreign-born population peaked in 1910 when just over 6,600 immigrants made up 17 percent of the population. By 1930, Flint had nearly 21,000 immigrant residents, but they made up just 13 percent of the population. In 1929, the largest "new" immigrant groups were comprised of an estimated nine thousand Poles, two thousand Hungarians, and fifteen hundred Russians. See File "Statistics—Population," Michigan Room Information Catalog, FPL.

23. Quoted in "Hiring Policies in the Automobile Industry," Levinson Collection, WSU. Missouri natives, who made up about half the new Southern-born population, were clustered at Chevrolet, because the factory's personnel manager came from that state and liked to recruit back home. See Interview with E. C. Paget, NRA Hearings, 1, 205; and Elmer Back to Henry Kraus, February 22, 1937, Box 10, Kraus Collection WSU.

24. In the 1920s, approximately 2,700 blacks and 8,000 whites from the South settled in Flint in these patterns. White southern migrants lived in fairly heavy concentrations on the city's south and west sides, but they did not form the same kinds of tightly knit communities as their black counterparts. Erdmann Beynon, "The Southern White Laborer Migrates to Michigan," *The American Sociological Review* 3 (June 1938):337–341; and Meister, "The Rise of Two Industrial Cities," 9–10.

25. Interview with Larry Huber, director UAW Region 1–C, February 22, 1977; notes in my possession. The roles of the few union veterans and the second-generation workers in the organizing drives of the 1930s are presented in detail in chapter 6 below.

26. Given the boomtown conditions that prevailed in Flint, it is not surprising that the majority of early arrivals were young males. In 1920, there were 129 men for every 100 women in Flint. However, by 1930 this ratio

had dropped to 109 to 100. In that last year, 47 percent of Flint's population was twenty-five years old or younger. See Meister, "Two Industrial Cities," 9.

27. Flint neighborhoods were described, classified, and mapped according to income levels, occupational groups, ethnic and racial composition, and type of dwelling by the Home Owners Loan Corporation (HOLC) in the mid-1930s. Although these figures were compiled after depression-related out-migration had slightly lowered the city's total population, it seems fair to assume that HOLC's data represent prior settlement patterns. See HOLC Survey File, 1935–1940, RG 195, Box 23, "Flint, Michigan Master File, July 18, 1937" in the National Archives.

28. Beynon, in "The Southern White Laborer Migrates to Michigan," reported that only 18 of the 2,737 southern blacks he studied had settled outside of these neighborhoods.

29. Edith Whitney, "Three Decades of Employment in Flint's 'Black Belt' and its Effects on the Socio-Economic Condition of the Blacks" (unpublished paper dated November 10, 1972), FPL.

30. Lawrence Gustin, *The Flint Journal Centennial Picture History of Flint* (Flint, 1976), 173; and Donna Cunningham, "Americanization in Flint in the 1920s" (unpublished paper dated November 10, 1972), FPL.

31. Gustin, *Centennial Picture History*, 172. See chapter 5 for more details on the role of religion in the political culture of normalcy in Flint.

32. Files: "Local History: Ethnic Groups" and "Statistics: Population," Michigan Room Information Catalog, FPL.

33. For a brief biographical sketch of Niedzielski, see Williams "The Rise and Fall of Piano Box City," unpublished paper, Alfred P. Sloan Museum Collection, Flint.

34. Tamara Hareven, "The Laborers of Manchester, New Hampshire, 1912–1922: The Role of Family and Ethnicity in Adjustment to Industrial Life," *Labor History* 16 (Spring 1975):260.

35. Meister, "Two Industrial Cities," 10. Census figures reveal that the number of native-born whites in Flint never fell below 82 percent of the population during this era.

36. Flint's first Irish settlers arrived before the Civil War, establishing Saint Michael's Church and school in 1856. Their numbers swelled during the lumber boom of the 1870s, but then dropped off as many of the loggers moved on. By the early 1900s, Irish-Americans in small businesses saw their fortunes grow with the town. William McKeighan was one of the most successful of these entrepreneurs.

37. Ihdler, "When Men Make Automobiles":553.

38. "Exhibit 19: Preliminary Report on the Study of Regularization of Employment and Improvement of Conditions in the Automobile Industry," U.S. National Recovery Administration, Research and Planning Divi-

sion, Leon Henderson, director, January 23, 1935, 4–5. (Hereafter cited as NRA Report). Also see NRA Hearings for evidence of individual earnings in various job categories, upon which this report is based. The ratio of skilled workers in the labor force comes from interviews done with plant managers by William Chalmers for "Labor in the Automobile Industry: A Study of Personnel Policies, Workers' Attitudes, and Attempts at Unionism" Ph.D. diss., University of Wisconsin, 1932), 65.

39. Andrew Dawson, "The Paradox of Dynamic Technological Change and the Labor Aristocracy in the United States, 1880–1914," *Labor History* 20 (1979):335.

40. HOLC City Survey File, "Flint, Michigan Master File."

41. Like the other generalizations that follow, these points were elaborated on in the testimony given by 105 automobile workers to the National Recovery Administration investigators in Flint on December 17–18, 1934. Transcripts of these hearings (which were also held in Detroit, Pontiac, and other automotive production centers) are a remarkable source of information on the material lifestyles of auto workers in the 1920s. Hearings were held day and night to accommodate both shifts. All participants were volunteers, who responded to posted notices asking them to discuss their working conditions with government officials. The questioning was very informal; in fact, most workers were simply asked to tell how the depression had changed their work and living standards. For Flint, the transcripts of these interviews in the National Archives fill two volumes, with more than six hundred typed pages of testimony.

42. In 1923, Flint workers first enrolled in the new plan. By 1928, a year in which General Motors reported 89 percent of the eligible workers participating, over four thousand Flint workers contributed to the program. That year a worker who had put $300 into the plan in 1923 received $2,680 back when the investment reached maturity. See *Annual Report of the General Motors Corporation 1928*, 21–22; and Meister, "Two Industrial Cities," 15.

43. In 1925, a survey of 867 homes in the "more crowded, less prosperous" sections of Flint found more than 40 percent were owner occupied. A Civil Works Administration survey of Flint housing conducted in early 1934, after many auto workers had lost their homes, found 46 percent of the city's units owner-occupied. Based on these data, it seems reasonable to assume that roughly half of the city's homes were owner-occupied at the height of the boom in the late 1920's. See Ethel Best, ed., *Women Workers in Flint, Michigan*, Bulletin of the Women's Bureau No. 67, U. S. Department of Labor (GPO, 1929), 12–3 and 49; and A. C. Findlay, "The Housing Situation in Flint, Michigan" (Flint Institute of Research and Planning, February 1938), FPL.

44. NRA Hearings, 1:142–151.

45. Pound, "General Motors Old Home Town," 89–90.
46. For instance, see the biography of Harry Clyde Parkhurst, a Flint area farm boy who rose from carriage assembler at the Flint Wagon Works and Durant-Dort to superintendent of Chevrolet's No. 1 assembly plant, in the *Accelerator: For Our Mutual Benefit*, June 14, 1919. Copies of the *Accelerator* and other company newspapers may be found in the Sloan Museum.
47. Membership lists, Knights of the Loyal Guard, clipped from the *Flint Daily News*, March 2, 1895, Michigan Room, microfiche collection, FPL. At the time, carriage and wagon workers made up the largest occupational groups in the Masons.
48. Front-page examples of this kind of boosterism may be found in the May 11, 1923; August 31, 1923; May 14, 1926; and September 2, 1927 editions of the newspaper.
49. See letters from J. D. Dort to John Jay Carton, May 22, 1918; and from Daniel Reed, secretary of the Board of Commerce, to Carton, June 19, 1918, in Box 14 of the John Jay Carton Papers, MHC, for details on the organization of the war bond drive. Carton was a prominent attorney who served many of Flint's leading business figures during the automobile boom years.
50. The role Flint's nominal labor organizations and newspaper played in shaping the city's political culture is discussed in the next chapter.
51. Warren Susman, *Culture as History: The Transformation of American Society in the Twentieth Century* (New York, 1984), xxiv.
52. NRA Hearings, 2:307.
53. This point is elaborated on in chapter 5.
54. NRA Hearing, 2:508.
55. UAW Oral History Project interview with Lester Johnson, June 3, 1959, 16. The failures of the Auto Workers Union in Flint are discussed in chapter 5.
56. This estimate is taken from Best, *Women Workers in Flint, Michigan*, 12.
57. For general figures see Bernstein, *Lean Years*, 67. The stability of basic prices in Flint is indicated by an Industrial Conference Board survey of local rents, which showed absolutely no change between 1923 and 1929. See memorandum report, "Current Housing Situation Flint, Michigan as of March 31, 1941," Division of Research and Statistics, Federal Housing Administration, RG 207, Box 6, National Archives.
58. This discussion uses definitions and figures drawn from Irving Bernstein, *The Lean Years: A History of the American Worker 1920–1933* (Baltimore, 1966), 63–65. Income levels for Flint auto workers are taken from NRA data previously cited.
59. Best, *Women Workers in Flint, Michigan*, 21–22 and 41–46. Fragmentary evidence from the NRA Hearings confirms the hypothesis that even

female auto workers experienced higher, steadier earnings in the late 1920s.

60. For example, Luther Cain told NRA investigators that he and six other Buick janitors averaged $1,500 per year from 1927 to 1930. See NRA Hearings, 2:244–247.

61. For examples see the wage records of Everett Francis, a Fisher Body trimmer, in the Everett Francis Papers, WSU; and testimony in the NRA Hearings, 1:133 and 1:143.

62. In 1920, Flint had just 3.7 persons per factory worker, far below the usual 6–7 persons the Department of Labor found in most manufacturing centers. See Best, *Women Workers in Flint, Michigan*, 40.

63. Best, *Women Workers in Flint*, 46. A recent study (Winifred D. Wandersee Bolin, "Economics of Middle Income Family Life in the Great Depression," *Journal of American History* 66 (June 1978). reveals that the percentage of all women who were gainfully employed and the number of married women who worked in Flint were almost exactly in line with the national averages in the 1920s. The fact that many young women (and some young men) lived at home with their families during their first years in the labor force helped raise some household incomes.

64. Best, *Women Workers in Flint, Michigan*, 49.

65. Best, *Women Workers in Flint, Michigan*, 1.

66. Schnore, "The Separation of Home and Work," 5 and 46.

67. Schnore, "The Separation of Home and Work," 16.

68. Several auto workers complained in the 1934 NRA Hearings of the hardships imposed on themselves and others by the loss of their automobiles. See NRA Hearings, 1:60, 95, and 150.

69. Ihdler, "When Men Make Automobiles," 555; and Debbie Narde, "Culture in Flint, 1915–1930," (unpublished paper dated November 30, 1971), FPL.

70. *Flint Daily Journal*, March 1, 1925; and Narde, "Culture in Flint."

71. Best, *Women Workers in Flint*, 46–47.

72. Best, *Women Workers in Flint*, 18ff.

73. The *Flint Daily Journal* began running regular fashion features in the 1920s.

74. By the late 1920s, the General Motors Institute had become the corporation's central training center. It offered practical courses in automobile service and the technical trades, in addition to its four-year management training program. In 1927–1928, when enrollment in the management program topped five hundred, enrollment in other courses neared seven thousand. Of course, the Great Depression forced drastic cutbacks in all of these programs. See *The Reflector* for 1928 (the first yearbook of the graduating class of the GMI), FPL; and Young and Tuttle, *The Years 1919–1969*, 61–64.

75. See UAW Oral History Project Interviews with Everett Francis, Ted LaDuke, Bud Simons, and Carl Swanson for personal histories and motivations.
76. UAW Oral History Project interview, August 4, 1960, 1.

5. The Political Culture of Normalcy in Flint

1. Pound, "General Motors Old Home Town," 85–86.
2. This welfare-capitalist policy was widespread. See Sumner Slichter, "The Current Labor Policies of American Industry," *Quarterly Journal of Economics* 43 (May 1929) 393–435; and Stuart Brandes, *American Welfare Capitalism* (Chicago, 1970), 140.
3. Frank Rodolph, "An Industrial History of Flint," unpublished ms. in Automotive History Collection, FPL, 508–509; and Franklin V. V. Swan, "Industrial Welfare Work in Flint, Michigan," *The Survey* 32 (July 1914):411.
4. Swan, "Industrial Welfare Work," 412; and John Ihdler, "Flint: When Men Build Automobiles Who Builds Their City," *The Survey*, September 2, 1916, 553–554. Weekly dues were checked off and scaled from five to fifteen cents. On that scale, weekly benefits ranged from three to nine dollars, while death benefits were graduated from twenty-five to seventy-five dollars per family.
5. Approval for these extended benefits required the assent of a management-dominated review board, not the worker-controlled board of the Mutual Benefit Association.
6. Although the amounts offered were not large, they did have public relations value. For instance, in 1920, Chevy management made a big story out of its aid for worker-victims of the flu, even though sick workers got only $319. See *Chevrolet Accelerator*, February 21, 1920.
7. During the boom years, the YMCA served as a vehicle for the implementation of many social programs desired by the automotive business class. D. D. Aitken and William Ballenger both had enormous influence on the YMCA board in the 1920s. This is not surprising. Elsewhere, the "Y" had been used as a welfare-capitalist organization since the 1870s. See Brandes, *American Welfare Capitalism*, 15.
8. All the major companies and GM divisions published newspapers for their employees. They explained management policies, urged workers to cooperate with their supervisors, and spread information about welfare and recreational activities. *The I.M.A. News* was aimed at all industrial workers. In the later 1920s, the widely circulated *Flint Weekly Review* began to feature I.M.A. news and advertisements right along with its regular stories on the local Federation of Labor and various fraternal organizations.
9. It is hard to judge workers' responses to welfare capitalism. General

participation in the programs before they were made mandatory and heavy use of the I.M.A. facilities would seem to indicate widespread worker acceptance of them.

10. Brandes, *American Welfare Capitalism*, 33.

11. The issue probably worked to the Socialist's favor that year, but there is no evidence that it divided the candidates who ran for office in April.

12. John Steby, "Prohibition in Flint, 1909–1934" (unpublished paper dated November 11, 1971), FPL. Between 1914 and 1918, McKeighan was arrested, tried, and acquitted three times on a variety of charges. In 1917, a local court permanently enjoined him from storing, selling (or permitting to be sold) any liquor on premises he owned.

13. Ihdler, "Flint."

14. Dort to John Carton, May 16, 1918, Box 14, Carton Papers, MHC.

15. The choral union was permanently organized as the Community Music Association after the War. In 1919–1920, it was still able to attract 166,000 people to its events; by 1926–1927 attendance had fallen to less than 12,000 persons (see Debbie Narde, "Culture in Flint 1915–1930," (unpublished paper dated November 30, 1971), FPL. The "Unconditional Surrender Club" is discussed in a letter from John Carton to Bradley, August 8, 1918, Box 14, Carton Papers, MHC.

16. George Kellar, a leading realtor who had preceded Mott as mayor in 1917, followed him in office in 1919. E. W. Atwood, a woolen mill and hardware store owner and past president of the old Board of Commerce, was elected in 1920 and 1921. Mott, who had obvious political ambitions, ran for governor in the GOP primary of 1920. He finished third out of nine candidates, and he never ran for public office again.

17. This point is explained in Clarence Young and William Quinn, *Foundation for Living: The Story of Charles Stewart Mott and Flint* (New York, 1963), 97–99.

18. Banner headline, *Flint Weekly Review*, August 31, 1923, 1. The article that followed praised local industrialists for their accomplishments and urged all workers to cooperate with their efforts at the factory and in the community.

19. David Brody, "The Rise and Decline of Welfare Capitalism," in *Change and Continuity in the Twentieth Century: the 1920s*, ed. John Braeman, Robert Bremner, and David Brody (Columbus, Ohio, 1968), 148.

20. For example, in this era, the public library was expanded from one branch with 25,000 volumes to eleven branches holding 140,000 volumes, partly through private funding. William Ballenger founded the Community Chest in 1922 and contributed heavily to the construction and running of the city's women's hospital. J. Dallas Dort helped plan the city's park system and donated some of his own lands to it. Among the charities C. S. Mott supported, the Rotary's Crippled Childrens Pro-

gram and the Lion's Sight Saving Fund, extended invaluable assistance to people in real need.

21. Welch also established a day care center in the same neighborhood for working mothers. See Ihdler, "Flint," 553.

22. "A Close-up on Bolshevism" *Flint Daily Journal* December 5, 1919. The same editorial page also featured another tirade entitled, "A Notice to Parlor Reds."

23. See *Flint Daily Journal*, January 23 and January 30, 1920. Publisher Bradley was his own chief editor at this time.

24. Interview with *Business* magazine, quoted in *The Auto Worker: The Official Journal of the United Automobile, Aircraft, and Vehicle Workers of America*, March 1920.

25. *Flint City Directory 1922*, quoted in Donna Cunningham, "Americanization in Flint in the 1920s" (unpublished paper dated December 5, 1972), FPL.

26. Special Labor Day edition, *Flint Weekly Review* August 31, 1923.

27. Quoted in "Third City in Michigan Owes Growth to Sterling Citizenry," *The Christian Science Monitor*, May 14, 1926.

28. In 1920, McKeighan was back in court, successfully defending himself against vote fraud charges. All totaled, the durable McKeighan went to trial and was acquitted seven times during his political career.

29. This summary is based on newspaper accounts in the *Flint Daily Journal* and the *Flint Weekly Review*.

30. *Flint Daily Journal*, April 3, 1923.

31. *Flint Daily Journal*, April 4, 1923.

32. *Flint Daily Journal*, April 3, 1923.

33. See Norman Weaver, "The Knights of the Ku Klux Klan in Wisconsin, Indiana, Ohio, and Michigan" Ph.D. dissertation, University of Wisconsin, 1954).

34. Official recall petition as described on the ballot, reprinted in the *Flint Daily Journal*, June 11, 1924.

35. The recall vote went 8,259 to 6,037 against the mayor.

36. *Flint Daily Journal*, July 8, 1924.

37. *Flint Daily Journal*, July 10, 1924.

38. Though each major candidate carried nineteen precincts, Transue polled 53 percent of the votes to Cuthbertson's 45 percent.

39. Less than two weeks after the election, the *Flint Daily Journal* agreed editorially with the dismissal of married women workers.

40. Given the Klan's ability to influence the outcomes of elections in Flint (and Lansing) at this time, Kenneth Jackson's claim that "Detroit became the unquestioned center of Klan strength in Michigan" seems mistaken. See Kenneth Jackson, *The Ku Klux Klan in the City 1915–1930* (New York,1967), 129.

41. *Flint Daily Journal*, April 3, 1925. Also see William McKeighan scrapbook, Michigan Room, FPL.
42. Final vote totals showed Transue with 12,055; McKeighan with 10,454; and Cuthbertson with 1,535.
43. Klan-backed candidate Lester Mott got just 1,900 votes, 14 percent of the total.
44. The final tally gave McKeighan a 1,377 vote margin over Adair. In the First Ward, McKeighan's edge was 2,344 votes.
45. *Flint Daily Journal*, February 22, 1928.
46. Harold Sylvester, "City Management: The Flint Experiment, 1930–1937" (Ph.D. diss. Johns Hopkins University, 1938), 9–10.
47. William McKeighan reappeared in 1936 as a supporter of Dr. Townsend and again in the mid-1940s, when he was once again indicted for liquor-related bribery charges. He spent his last years in Florida, avoiding extradition to Michigan.
48. Weaver, "Knights of the KKK," 301ff. Unfortunately there seems to be no way accurately to estimate the size or precise membership of Flint's KKK.
49. Fred W. Green, governor, Records of the Executive Office 1927–1930, Box 33, File 4—"Ku Klux Klan," Michigan State Archives, Lansing, Michigan; and *Flint Weekly Review*, September 2, 1927.
50. A handful of Klansmen appeared in Flint in September 1967 to protest racial desegregation. See Clippings Collection, "Ku Klux Klan," in Michigan Collections, State Library, Lansing, Michigan. At its peak in 1924–1925, Weaver estimated total Klan membership in Michigan may have reached eighty thousand persons.
51. In the 1920s, for example, Republican candidates held on to the traditionally Republican 6th District seat (which represented Flint, Lansing, and the farm areas in between), winning an average of 73 percent of the vote. By comparison, in the period 1896–1916, the GOP averaged just 54 percent of the total vote.
52. Gabriel Kolko, "The Decline of American Radicalism in the Twentieth Century," in *For a New America: Essays in History and Politics from Studies on the Left* (New York, 1970), 208.
53. Sidney Fine, *Sit Down: The General Motors Strike of 1936–1937* (Ann Arbor, 1969), 27.
54. Roger Keeran, "Communist Influence in the Automobile Industry, 1920–1933: Paving the Way for an Industrial Union," *Labor History* 20 (Spring 1979):190.
55. Jack Skeels, "Early Carriage and Auto Unions: The Impact of Industrialization and Rival Unionism," *Industrial and Labor Relations Review* 17 (July, 1964):576ff.
56. Keeran, "Communist Influence," 225.

57. See chapter 4, and William Chalmers, "Labor in the Automobile Industry: A Study of Personnel Policies, Workers' Attitudes, and Attempts at Unionism" (Ph.D. diss., University of Wisconsin, 1932), 99–100.

58. Best, *Women Workers in Flint*, 21.

59. NRA interview with John Tischler, 1:6.

60. See NRA interviews with Edwin Meyers, Erwin Kiser, Rheinhold Draheim (NRA Hearings, 1); and with Frank Davidson, George Langley, Lauri Niemimen, Carl Michael, Jasper Matthews (NRA Hearings, 2) for variations on this theme.

61. Best, *Women Workers in Flint*, 17. In the auto plants, women workers put in slightly fewer hours than the men. The 48–50 hour week was most common. See "Women's Bureau Survey Material," RG 86, Bulletin 67 in the National Archives.

62. Though layoffs were not quite predictable, workers learned to expect them. Disgruntled workers often used layoffs to search for different jobs. See Chalmers, "Labor in the Automobile Industry," 140–143.

63. Fine, *Sit Down*, 54; and B. J. Widick, "Work in the Auto Plants: Then and Now" in B. J. Widick, ed., *Auto Work and its Discontents*, ed. (Baltimore, 1976), 6–17.

64. "The Effects of Technological Changes Upon Occupations in the Motor Vehicle Industry," *Monthly Labor Review* 34 (February 1932):248–52; and Charles Reitell, "Machinery and its Effects Upon Workers in the Automotive Industry," *Annals of the American Academy of Political and Social Science* 116 (November 1924):40.

65. UAW Oral History Project Interview with Everett Francis, October 13, 1961, 4. Also see Joyce Shaw Peterson, "Auto Workers and their Work, 1920–1933," *Labor History* 22 (Spring 1981):213–236.

66. Mortimer LaFever, "Workers, Machinery, and Production in the Automobile Industry," *Monthly Labor Review* 19 (October 1924):26.

67. Chalmers found that a general policy of hiring only young workers for production lines had emerged by the late 1920s (Chalmers, "Labor in the Automobile Industry," 144). He also reported that monotomy was not a serious grievance among such workers (85–92); and that he was unable to uncover any strikes "by the really skilled men" in the years immediately preceding the Great Depression (227).

68. UAW Oral History Project interview with Herbert Richardson, July 10, 1960, 1–4.

69. In fact, when the UAW was recognized in 1937, twenty-two of these workers asked for and got reinstatement at Fisher Body 1. See UAW Oral History Project interview with Herbert Richardson:4–6.

70. Chalmers, "Labor in the Automobile Industry," 160.

71. Turnover remained a significant problem in Flint as late as 1928. For figures see: O. W. Blackett, "Factory Labor Turnover in Michigan," *Michigan Business Studies* 2 (November 1928):13, 30.

72. F. W. Hohensee, "Our Men and Our Methods," *Chevrolet Review* 1 (June 1917):7 (to be found in the Sloan Museum).
73. *Buick News*, October 19, 1924.
74. Chalmers, "Labor in the Automobile Industry," 140ff.
75. The U.S. Department of Labor's study, Ethel Best, ed., *Women Workers in Flint Michigan*, Bulletin of The Women's Bureau No. 67, which was based on research completed in 1925, clearly shows that longer service resulted in increased earnings. At the time, a sample of workers with less than one year experience earned just over half the weekly wage of workers in the same job category who had more than five years on the job (22). The base rate figures are taken from an interview with Fisher Body trimmer Everett Francis, UAW Oral History Project, 4. Francis' recollection is supported by evidence from NRA Hearings, which are summarized in "Exhibit 19: Preliminary Report on The Study of Regularization of Employment and Improvement of Conditions in The Automobile Industry," U.S. National Recovery Administration, Research and Planning Division, January 23, 1935. (Hereafter cited as NRA Report or as "Exhibit 19").
76. Alfred P. Sloan, *Adventures of a White Collar Man* (New York, 1941), 144.
77. Working conditions were never a major grievance, even among Auto Workers Union organizers. When Department of Labor investigators surveyed conditions in all of Flint's major factories in late 1925, they found the lighting, heat, and first aid facilities generally satisfactory. Their biggest complaint concerned dirty washrooms and unsanitary drinking fountains (Best, *Women Workers in Flint*, 35–39). Other data indicate that while auto work was undeniably dangerous, it was less so than in most manufacturing industries, and that its dangers were being significantly reduced in Flint during the 1920s. See *Flint Weekly Review*, Labor Day Edition 1923, section 3, 7.
78. Information reported to the Auto Workers Union shows ten of the twenty-six strikes in the industry between 1926 and 1928 occurred in body plants. Henry Klaus Collection, Box I "Pre AFL Period," WSU; and Richard Whiting, "Strikes in the Motor Industry: a General Introduction" (Paper read at Nuffield College, Oxford, January 8, 1975).
79. National War Labor Board Case File 406, Washington National Records Center, Suitland, Maryland (hereafter cited as NRC).
80. *The Auto Worker: Official Journal of the United Automobile, Aircraft, and Vehicle Workers of America* 1 (June 1919):4. The UAAVWA had been formed out of the old Carriage and Wagon Workers Union after that organization was expelled from the A.F. of L. for insisting on its right to set up an industrial auto workers union.
81. *The Auto Worker* 1 (July 1919):14; and 1:13. Police harrassment reported in "Notes from the *Auto Workers News*," Box 1, Edward Levinson Collection, WSU.

82. The *Auto Worker* 2:14. President W. A. Logan told delegates to the union's Cleveland convention in September 1920 that "practically ninety percent" of the strikers had left Flint. See "Convention Proceedings of the Sixth Biennial Convention," 16–24, WSU.

83. UAW Oral History Project interview with Al Cook, August 31, 1960, 1, emphasis added.

84. *Flint Daily Journal*, November 11, 1925; and UAW Oral History Project interview with Ted LaDuke, 2.

85. Clippings from the *Auto Workers News*, Box 1, Henry Klaus Collection; and Box 1, Robert Dunn Collection, WSU. Also see James J. Flink, *The Car Culture*, (Cambridge, 1975), 161–168.

86. B. M. Marshman to Hugh L. Kerwin, Director of Conciliation, July 23, 1928, National Conciliation Service, Case File No. 170–4544, NRC.

87. Marshman to Kerwin.

88. *Auto Workers News*, August 1928, (WSU); and National Conciliation Service Case File No. 170–4544.

89. "Report of the General Executive Secretary, UAAVWA, (1928)" in Box 2, Dunn Collection, WSU.

90. *Auto Workers News*, June 1929.

91. Warren Susman, *Culture as History: The Transformation of American Society in the Twentieth Century* (New York, 1984), 202.

6. The Great Depression in Flint

1. UAW Oral History Project interview with Everett Francis, October 13–27, 1961, 5.

2. By 1929, Buick sales were off 29 percent from the 1926 peak of 268,000 units. One year later, they had fallen to just 122,000 vehicles, a decline of 56 percent from the pre–Depression peak. See Alfred P. Sloan, *My Years with General Motors* (Garden City, 1964), 446–47.

3. All totaled more than seven thousand Flint workers were officially counted as unemployed in 1930. See *Fifteenth Census of the United States: 1930: Unemployment Volume 1* (GPO, 1931), 500 and 518.

4. *Investigation of Communist Propaganda: Hearings before a Special Committee to Investigate Communist Activity in the United States*—Pursuant to H. Res. 220 4, 1, 71st Cong., 2nd Sess., (July 25 and 26, 1930):1–3. Also see Roger Keeran, *The Communist Party and the Auto Workers Unions* (Bloomington, 1980), 67–69.

5. Testimony of Police Chief Scarvarda, *Investigation of Communist Propaganda*, 3. Federation of Labor leader Starkweather praised the police intervention in the first hunger march, editorializing, "Why, if they are not allowed to hold protest meetings in Russia are they sent over here to stir us up?" *Flint Weekly Review*, March 14, 1930.

6. *New York Times*, July 4, 1930.

7. Raymond had been elected president in May, after the AWU was once again reorganized and affiliated with the Trade Union Unity League.

8. As the last major plant to open in the city before the Great Depression, Fisher Body 1's workforce best reflected GM's increasing emphasis on recruiting youthful workers. Police Chief Scarvarda testified that the strikers "forced everyone to cease working." He also claimed workers deliberately scratched car bodies and threw tools at the unsympathetic. (*Investigation of Communist Propaganda*, 4–5). No other contemporary account corroborates the Police Chief's testimony on this point. It seems likely that Chief Scarvarda embellished his recollections of the strike to appeal to the obvious anti-radical prejudices of the representatives.

9. Whiting admitted to 3,600 strikers in "Federated Press Central Bureau," Sheet 2, 0707, Box 1, William Ellison Chalmers Collection, WSU; Cecil Comstock claimed 4,500 in the *New York Times*, July 4, 1930.

10. Testimony of Police Chief Scarvarda, *Investigation of Communist Propaganda*, 6; and *Flint Daily Journal*, July 2, 1930.

11. UAW Oral History Project interview with F. R. "Jack" Palmer, July 23, 1960, 4. The creation of a large strike committee in which their members were a minority was the favored tactic of AWU leaders. See James R. Prickett, "Communists and the Automobile Industry in Detroit before 1935," *Michigan History* 57 (Fall, 1973):193.

12. Strike demands are listed in "Federated Press Central Bureau." Sheet 2, 0708. The AWU platform is described in "Application for Membership," *Investigation of Communist Propaganda*, 8.

13. UAW Oral History interview with Alexander Cook, August 31, 1960, 7.

14. Front-page editorial, *Flint Weekly Review*, July 4, 1930.

15. *Flint Daily Journal*, July 2, 1930.

16. Testimony of Chief Scarvarda, *Investigation of Communist Propaganda*, 9; *Flint Daily Journal*, July 3; *New York Times*, July 4, 1930.

17. *Flint Daily Journal*, July 3, 1930. Contemporary accounts vary on the number of those arrested. The *New York Times* reported a total of twenty-five; the *Flint Daily Journal* claimed that were just nineteen.

18. *Flint Daily Journal*, July 7, 1930; Testimony of Chief Scarvarda, *Investigation of Communist Propaganda*, 9–12.

19. UAW Oral History Project interview with F. R. Palmer, 4.

20. On July 3, F.F.L. officials also took it upon themselves to advise National Conciliation Officer Marshman that he need not come to Flint, because the strike was Communist-led and was under control. These matters are revealed in National Conciliation Service Case File No. 170–5721, NRC.

21. *Flint Daily Journal*, July 5, 1930. On July 5, Flint police were holding twenty-three organizers and strikers without charges.

22. Jack Stachel, "Coming Struggles and Strike Strategy," *The Communist* 10 (March 1931): 211–212. UAW Oral History Project interview with Philip

Raymond, January 14, 1960, is flawed by factual confusions and Raymond's obvious bitterness towards Chief Scarvarda.

23. Statement of the executive committee, *Flint Daily Journal*, July 5, 1930.

24. These particulars are recorded in the July 6, 1930 *Flint Daily Journal* under the banner headline "Strike Leaders Oppose Peace Plan." In his UAW Oral History Project interview, Al Cook described brief additional meetings between strike representatives and Governor Green and Edward and Laurence Fisher (3–4). These meetings are not mentioned in other accounts of the strike.

25. Testimony of Chief Scarvarda *Investigation of Communist Propaganda*, 11; and *Flint Daily Journal*, July 7, 1930.

26. *Flint Daily Journal*, July 7, 1930. All totaled, at least forty-nine people were arrested and held during the strike without being formally charged.

27. *Flint Daily Journal*, July 8, 1930.

28. UAW Oral History Project interviews with Herbert Richardson: July 10, 1960, 4, and with Al Cook, 5; and *Flint Daily Journal*, July 9, 1930.

29. Sworn and notarized deposition of N. Olds, dated July 11, 1930, attached to "Caroline Parker (chairman, executive board of the Detroit branch of the American Civil Liberties Union) to Hon. Edward Black, July 15, 1930," Edward Black Papers, MHC. Judge Black had owned a considerable block of General Motors stock since 1912. During the big General Motors sit-down strike of 1936–1937, the UAW publicized Judge Black's interest in the company to discredit an injunction he issued against the union.

30. The Big Three share of the domestic car market jumped from 75 percent to 90 percent in the 1930s. See John B. Rae, *American Automobile Manufacturers: The First Forty Years* (Philadelphia, 1959), 191–192.

31. Sloan, *My Years With General Motors*, 447.

32. The speed-up and wage cuts are discussed in detail in chapter 7.

33. These measures are described by Alfred Sloan in the *Annual Report of the General Motors Corporation 1932*, 15–19.

34. Net profits after taxes fell from $296 million to $8 million in 1932. They then climbed steadily to $240 million in 1936. GM's total American vehicle production topped the 1929 record in 1936 and 1937. See Alfred D. Chandler, Jr. *Giant Enterprise: Ford, General Motors, and the Automobile Industry* (New York, 1964), 6–7; and Sloan, *My Years*, 446–447.

35. Quoted in A. C. Findlay, "The Housing Situation in Flint, Michigan," Flint Institute of Research and Planning, February 1938, FPL. Statistics from "Confidential Report of a Survey," HOLC Division of Research and Statistics (July 27, 1937) in "File: Flint, Michigan, File #1," Home Owners Loan Corporation City Survey File, RG 195, Box 24, National Archives.

36. Just over one hundred units were built in 1939 and 1940. See memorandum report: "Current Housing Situation in Flint, Michigan as of March 31, 1941," Division of Research and Statistics, Federal Housing Administration in Housing and Home Finance Agency, RG 207, Box 6, National Archives.
37. This summary is based on a brief filed by the city and the state for emergency RFC funds. See 1932 Records Relating to Emergency Relief to the States, Reconstruction Finance Corporation, RG 234, Box 47, National Archives.
38. 1932 Records Relating to Emergency Relief to the States, National Archives.
39. This generalization is based on "Exhibit 19: Preliminary Report of Individual Conferences With Workers," in U.S. National Recovery Administration, Research and Planning Division's *Preliminary Report*, January 23, 1935; and on the actual testimonies of affected workers, given in Flint in December 1934. Figures released by Buick in March 1935 reveal the priority its supervisors placed on the retention of experienced workers. In that month, 80 percent of its workers had been with that company at least five years, 44 percent at least ten years. See General Motors Scrapbook, Buick Motor Division: Volume 1, FPL.
40. "Exhibit 19" NRA Report, 4–5.
41. Specific data on local price deflation are hard to come by. My own calculations indicate food prices probably fell as much as 40 percent from 1929 to 1933. The National Industrial Conference Board index of local rents indicates a decline of roughly 20 percent in the same period, after a decade of near stability. See the FHA memorandum, "Current Housing Situation in Flint," National Archives, 12.
42. Irving Bernstein, *The Lean Years: A History of the American Worker 1920–1933* (Baltimore, 1966), 255.
43. "Current Housing Situation in Flint," FHA, National Archives 4. Unfortunately FHA data do not cover the early 1930s. However, testimony given to NRA investigators in 1934 indicates that the foreclosure problem peaked in those years. Of the 105 auto workers who testified in Flint, twenty-nine voluntarily described problems with house payments and back taxes as a major concern.
44. UAW Oral History Project interview with F. R. Palmer, 4.
45. This generalization is based on the NRA Hearings; the NRA Research and Planning Division's "Exhibit 19" *Preliminary Report*, 51–53; and State of Michigan, State Emergency Relief Commission, *Michigan Census of Population and Unemployment*, First Series (hereafter cited as Michigan Census), No. 9, "Age and Industry of Gainful Workers" (Lansing, 1937) 6 and 12.
46. Sidney Fine, *Sit-Down: The General Motors Strike of 1936–37* (Ann Arbor,

1969) 104–105; and Frank Rodolph, "An Industrial History of Flint" unpublished ms, Automotive History Collection, FPL, 275–276.

47. Fine, *Sit Down*, 104.

48. Beynon, "The Southern White Laborer Migrates to Michigan" *The American Sociological Review*, 3 (June 1938), 337. Beynon reported that Flint's southern black population dropped 19 percent and its southern white population declined 35 percent in this period.

49. Schnore, "The Separation of Home and Work in Flint," Institute for Human Advancement, University of Michigan (Ann Arbor, 1954), 24. Michigan's farm labor supply jumped from 85 to 118 percent of "normal" between 1929 and 1930. See Blanche Bernstein's report, "The Labor Market in the Automobile Industry" (January 1937), Box 2, William E. Chalmers Collection, WSU.

50. The increase in the fringe area topped 15,000 persons in the 1930s. In 1940 more than half the fringe area homes had no running water; three-quarters had no flush toilets. In addition, virtually all the land remained farmer-owned. For details see I. Harding Hughes, "Local Government in the Fringe Area," Institute for Human Adjustment, University of Michigan (Ann Arbor, 1954), 1–11.

51. Recent studies of the industrial labor forces in not-yet-fully industrialized societies like Italy have identified similar groups of "marginal" or "peasant" workers (Charles Sabel, "Marginal Work and Marginal Workers in Industrial Society," paper in my possession).

52. According to a Civil Works Administration census conducted in early 1934, fifty-five thousand Flint residents (over one-third of the total population) had lived in the same place for at least five years. See Beynon, 340.

53. Interview with Keleman Sajko, NRA Hearings, 1:160.

54. Beynon reported, "From 1930 through 1933, the total number of migrants both *entering and leaving* Flint was 49,135, a number equal to 34.0 percent of the total population in 1934" (337, emphasis added). These figures, taken from the Civil Works Administration census done between January and March 1934 do not reflect the impact of General Motors' recovery on the city's demography. Rather, they illustrate the unsettling impact of economic collapse and mass unemployment. The *Michigan Census*, No. 8, "Geographic and Occupational Mobility of Gainful Workers," Lansing, April 1937, 5); and 1940 U.S. census figures illustrate the stabilization that occurred in the later 1930s.

55. NRA Hearings, 2:452. Pipes' use of the boom period as a standard for making comparisons with depression conditions was typical, and extremely important. See chapter 7 for a complete discussion of this point.

56. These family problems are examined fully in Minna Faust, "Juvenile Delinquency in Flint in Light of Social, Economic, and Cultural Factors," an

unpublished report done for the Michigan Juvenile Delinquency Information Service, University of Michigan, (Ann Arbor 1935, FPL.

57. "Exhibit 19," NRA Report, 4.

58. In recognition for its services in the winter of 1930–1931, the city council exempted IMA stores from the tax rolls. The stores were restored to the rolls in 1935, after merchant protests were heard by the state tax commission. See Rodolph, "An Industrial History of Flint," 516. A description of IMA benefits may be found in the testimony of Wilbert Hill, NRA Hearings, 1:32–35.

59. It is interesting to note that Alfred Sloan later claimed that the savings and investment plan was suspended in 1935, after the passage of the Social Security Act had rendered it obsolete. (Sloan, *My Years With General Motors*, 391) *The Annual Report of the General Motors Corporation 1932* very clearly states that the plan was suspended in that year for financial reasons.

60. Rodolph, "An Industrial History of Flint," 517. For examples of worker complaints about the IMA see the NRA Hearings, the testimonies of William Conners (1:15–20), Vera Hobson (1:86–87), Ervin Latluck (2:297–300), Dow Kehler (2:399–400), Arnold Seyfarth (2:494–500), and Walter Nugent (2:579–582).

61. Manley's initial programs received help from the Federal Emergency Relief Administration, Works Progress Administration, and the National Youth Administration. See Clarence Young and William Quinn, *Foundation for Living: The Story of Charles Stewart Mott and Flint* (New York, 1963), 115–150. Considering the assistance his foundation got from the New Deal, Mott's later recollection of Franklin Roosevelt as "the great destroyer" seems particularly unbalanced. See Studs Terkel, *Hard Times* (New York, 1970), 163.

62. Michigan Council on Governmental Expenditures, "Relief Expenditures in Michigan Cities in 1931 and 1932: Material for Independent Study and Application," a pamphlet in the Michigan State University Research Library, Lansing, Michigan.

63. In late 1931, Flint established a citywide relief commission to comply with a request from the president's organization on unemployment relief. A few months later, following guidelines set by the state's unemployment commission, a Genessee County Emergency Relief Committee was formed. Each of these quasi-public bodies was composed of prominent citizens, especially businessmen and clergy. They were charged with coordinating local welfare efforts, promoting work-spreading, and creating work relief by starting public works and neighborhood clean-up and repair campaigns. In two years, they supervised the spending of nearly two million dollars.

64. In fiscal year 1931–1932, Flint collected just 56 percent of the taxes owed it, while relief expenditures rose from $3.9 to $7.3 per capita.

65. This summary is based on Harold Sylvester, "City Management: The Flint Experiment, 1930–1937" (Ph.D. diss., Johns Hopkins University, 1938), 70–99; and William H. Chafe, "Flint and the Great Depression," *Michigan History* 53 (Fall 1969):228–30.

66. For details see Chafe, "Flint and the Great Depression," 230–237.

67. Bernstein details the nationwide voting shift in *The Lean Years*, 508–512. Frances Fox Piven and Richard A. Cloward clearly identify Roosevelt's strong stand on federal responsibility for relief as essential to the Democratic victory in 1932. See Francis Fox Piven and Richard A. Cloward, *Regulating the Poor: The Functions of Public Welfare* (New York, 1972), 69–72. Walter Dean Burnham put the realignment in a long-term perspective in "The Changing Shape of the American Political Universe," *American Political Science Review* 59 (March 1965), 7–28.

68. UAW Oral History Project interview with Al Cook, 6.

69. This summary is based on the University of Michigan-Flint's Labor History Project oral interviews with William Weinstone, head of the Michigan Communist Party in the mid-1930s, and with Dr. Nan Pendrell, both on March 15, 1979; and with Bob Travis and Charlies Kramer, both on December 13, 1978. Also see Keeran, *The Communist Party and the Auto Workers Unions*, 150–151.

70. The recruiting efforts of Flint's Communists are highlighted by a collection of handbills signed variously by "the Buick unit of the Communist Party" and "the Communist Party, Flint section." These handbills date from 1934 and are located in the Garman Collection, Box 4, Reuther Library, Wayne State University, Detroit, Michigan. Also see the *Flint Weekly Review*, July 5, 12, and 26, 1935.

71. Victor G. Reuther, *The Brothers Reuther and the Story of the UAW: A Memoir* (Boston, 1976), 125. See also the *Flint Weekly Review*, October 26, 1934, and University of Michigan-Flint Labor History Project oral history interview with Genora Dollinger, September 22, 1978, University of Michigan-Flint Labor History Project.

72. Minutes of the Flint Trade Unionists Progressive Club, Homer Martin Collection, Box 2, WSU.

73. The connections between the automobile companies and the Civic League were explicit. Six of the league's first seven commissioners were either active or retired automotive officials. See Sylvester, "City Management," 49.

74. For details see Peirce F. Lewis, "Geography in the Politics of Flint" (Ph.D. diss., University of Michigan, 1958).

75. Sylvester, "City Management," 72–77. Also see Carol Ernst, "Newspaper Coverage of the Major Local Political Issues in the Thirties" (unpublished paper dated November 30, 1971), FPL.

76. Sylvester, "City Management," 82–83.

77. The most prominent "Green Slate" commissioners were recalled by a two-to-one margin in November, while the Citizens League members were retained by nearly the same margin. For details see Sylvester, "City Management," 90–108.

78. There were just 33,000 registered voters in 1927, and at least 60,000 by 1932. Voter participation in the general elections climbed from 37 percent in 1928 to 85 percent in 1932. Given the overwhelmingly blue-collar character of the city (86 percent wage earners, two-thirds industrial workers in the labor force in 1934), and the socio-economic characteristics of the precincts where the biggest voting increases occurred, it seems fair to assume that most of the new voters were working people. See *Flint Daily Journal*, March 8, 1927; Max Heavenrich, Jr., "The Participation of Flint Citizens in Elections," in *Studies Prepared by the Governmental Research Division of the Flint Institute of Research and Planning* (1938–1940), FPL; Chafe, "Flint and the Great Depression," 227; *Michigan Census*, No. 4, "Social-Economic Occupational Classification of Workers in Selected Industries," 12; and Lewis, "Geography in the Politics of Flint," 84ff.

79. See Heavenrich, "Participation of Flint Citizens," 3. Local issues and the clear differences between the national candidates on prohibition also contributed to the heavy turnout.

80. Chafe found "the order of federal bureaucracy replaced the confusion of local voluntarism" as soon as a County Emergency Relief Administration was set up in 1933. See Chafe, "Flint and the Great Depression," 231.

81. Local General Motors employment reached 47,000 by December 1937. See Fine, *Sit-Down*, 105.

82. Chafe, "Flint and the Great Depression," 232–233. Under the Civil Works Administration and the Works Progress Administration, Flint workers built the city's three-runway Bishop Airport, paved and repaired hundreds of streets, laid much needed sewers and drains, and conducted traffic, land use, and zoning surveys. For additional details see "Appraisal File Report—Michigan," Records of the Works Progress Administration, RG 69, Box 195, National Archives.

83. *Flint Weekly Review*, October 26, 1934.

84. *Flint Weekly Review*, January 25, 1935.

85. Mimeographed flyer dated October 15, 1936, one of several dealing with the election in the Kraus Collection, Box 8, WSU.

86. See Heavenrich, "Participation of Flint Citizens," 3ff.

87. Lewis, "Geography in the Politics of Flint," 70.

88. "Announcement," dated March 13, 1935, Kraus Collection, Box 8, WSU.

89. Passage was driven from office in 1936 by older F.F.L. members, who charged him with having diverted central labor union funds into his

Teamsters' organizing drive. See Wilbur S. Dean (Recording Secretary of the F.F.L.) to Frank Morrison (Secretary of the A.F. of L.) November 21, 1935, in "AFL Executive Correspondence to Flint Federation of Labor, October–December 1935," A.F.L.–C.I.O. Archives, Washington, D.C.

90. Participation bottomed out in 1935, when just 9 percent of the eligible voters went to the polls.

91. Sylvester, "City Management," 124ff. The Black Legion is discussed in note 76, chapter 7.

92. Questions included such items as "Has the client expressed to you an interest in or indicated that he was informed about the A.F. of L.? the Unemployed Workers' Council? other proletarian groups?" See William Haber to Henry Kraus, December 1, 1936; and Victor S. Woodward (former relief administrator) to Kraus, December 16, 1936, in the Kraus Collection, Box 8, WSU.

93. The *Flint Auto Worker* 1 (July 1937):1; also see the *Flint Weekly Review*, July 23, 1937.

94. *The Chevrolet Worker* 2 (September–October 1938) discusses the P.A.C. strategy. This Communist Party newsletter and other documents relating to the activity of Flint's small radical political groups may be found in the Kraus Collection, Box 16, WSU.

95. Flint politics in the 1940s are discussed in detail in chapter 8.

7. From Company Town to Union Town

1. UAW Oral History Project interview with Norman Bully, October 12, 1961, 3.

2. UAW Oral History Project interview with Carl Swanson, August 8, 1960, 3.

3. UAW Oral History Project interview with Arthur Case, August 4, 1960, 2.

4. UAW Oral History Project interview with Everett Francis, October 13, 1961, 7. The backgrounds of the rank-and-file organizers are revealed in the UAW Oral History Project.

5. Flint's MESA executive committee actually scaled down their wage demands to $1.00 per hour in meetings with Chevrolet Division Head William Knudsen on September 21. See "Stenographic Report of Hearing in the matter of Tool and Die Makers Strike in the Detroit Area, National Labor Board of the National Recovery Administration, October 18, 1933," Sidney Fine Papers, MHC.

6. A. J. Muste's argument that the MESA strike stopped wage cutting and improved conditions in the industry is unconvincing. See A. J. Muste, *The Automobile Industry and Organized Labor* (Baltimore, 1936), 29–31. For more balanced accounts see Sidney Fine, *The Automobile Under the Blue Eagle* (Ann Arbor, 1963), 163ff; and Harry Dalheimer, *A History of the Me-*

chanics Educational Society of America in Detroit from Its Inception in 1933 to 1937 (Detroit, 1951), 3–5.

7. Chalmers to Perlman, November 9, 1933, in the Philips S. Garman Collection, Box 3, WSU. At the time, Chalmers was reporting on labor activities in the automobile industry. Professor Perlman had directed his dissertation, "Labor in the Automobile Industry," at the University of Wisconsin.

8. UAW Oral History interview with Jack Palmer, July 23, 1960, 5.

9. "Hearings on Regularizing Employment and Otherwise Improving the Conditions of Labor in the Automobile Industry," December 1934, 1, 163 (hereafter cited as NRA Hearings).

10. UAW Oral History Project interview with Ted LaDuke, August 5, 1960, 3.

11. UAW Oral History Project interview with Al Cook (the president of this local council), August 31, 1960, 13. Cook's claim was obviously inflated. Official paid-up membership for Flint in March totaled just fourteen thousand persons. See AFL Membership Lists, Garman Collection, Box 1, WSU. The Federal Labor Unions were essentially locals set up at each major factory. According to national A. F. of L. strategy, auto workers would be temporarily organized into FLUs before being sorted out among the various established craft unions.

12. AFL Membership Lists, Garman Collection, WSU. Roosevelt is quoted in Fine, *The Automobile Under the Blue Eagle*, 223.

13. Fine, *Automobile Under the Blue Eagle*, 148.

14. NRA Hearings, 2:536.

15. UAW Oral History Project interview with Herbert Richardson, July 10, 1960, 9. Other remembrances of this demoralizing period confirm the notion that the A.F. of L. was deserted because it had failed to act. In particular, see the interview with Carl Swanson, a rank-and-file leader at Buick, UAW Oral History Project interview, 9–10.

16. AFL Membership Lists, Garman Collection, WSU. Also see Fine, *Sit-Down: The General Motors Strike of 1936–1937* (Ann Arbor, 1969, 108–14.

17. A plant-by-plant breakdown on the Automobile Labor Board elections in Flint can be found in the Garman Collection, Box 2, WSU.

18. UAW Oral History Project interview with Al Cook, 14; Fine, *Automobile Under the Blue Eagle*, 159ff; and Records of the United States Senate, 75th Cong. 1st Sess. (La Follette Civil Liberties Committee), RG 46, Box 123, Files N1 and N2, National Archives.

19. UAW Oral History Project interview with Ted LaDuke: 11–12. Also see UAW Oral History Project interview with Al Cook, 15; and Fine, *Sit-Down*, 37ff.

20. The evidence (which runs more than seven hundred pages) is located in

Violations of Free Speech and the Rights of Labor: Hearings before a Subcommittee of the Committee on Education and Labor, U.S. Senate, 75th Cong. 1st sess., pursuant to S. Res. 266, Parts 6 and 7 (GPO 1937).

21. Interoffice memorandum from Arnold Lenz, "To all Superintendents, General Foremen, and Foremen," dated May 8, 1936, in National Conciliation Case File 176–1034, NRC. Also see general statement on company personnel policy in memoranda, "To all General Managers, Car Group," dated April 13, 1934 and August 13, 1935 in Records of the La Follette Civil Liberties Committee, RG 46, Box 123, File N1, U.S. Senate, 75th Cong. 1st sess. Additional information is located in material from GM's executive training program dated 1933 and 1935 in Henry Kraus Collection, Box 16, WSU.

22. National Conciliation Service Case File 176–1034, NRC.

23. *Violations of Free Speech and Labor*, Part 7:2320, U.S. Senate.

24. Ward Lindsay to Senator La Follette (January 10, 1937), Records of the La Follette Civil Liberties Committee, RG 46, Box 123, File N4.

25. UAW Oral History Project interview with Clayton Johnson, June 1, 1961, 5–6.

26. NRA Hearings, 1:95 (emphasis added).

27. NRA Hearings, 2:474 and 479–80 (emphasis added).

28. Minzey to Kimmerling, March 18, 1934, Kraus Collection, Box 8, WSU, (emphasis added).

29. Laurence Goodrich, chairman A.C. Employees Association, to all A.C. Employees, April 20, 1934, Kraus Collection, Box 8, WSU.

30. Mortimer to International Executive Officers, September 27, 1936, Homer Martin Collection, Box 1, WSU.

31. The agreement announced on May 16 simply allowed all workers on the payroll before the strike started to return to their jobs without discrimination. The company further agreed to hear workers' grievances and send them on to the Automobile Labor Board if they could not be settled. See Scrapbook, volume 1, Francis Dillion Collection, WSU.

32. "Minutes 1935–37," Local 599 Collection, Box 1, Series 3, WSU; AFL Membership Lists, Garman Collection, WSU; UAW Oral History Project interview with Carl Swanson, 6; *Flint Weekly Review*, May 3, 10, and 17, 1935; and Fine, *The Automobile Under the Blue Eagle*, 393–94.

33. Militant auto workers in Flint had been in contact with the C.I.O. since December 1935. These people were among the first contacted by the U.A.W. in 1936. See "Minutes of the Flint Trade Unionists Progressive Club" for November–December 1935, Box 2, Homer Martin Collection, WSU.

34. Homer Martin, a politically conservative ex-preacher from Kansas City, was the union's compromise president, but the Executive Board was dominated by political radicals. All eleven board members, including

Vice-President Mortimer, had worked in auto plants. Mortimer and Travis both had experience leading rank-and-file strikes in Cleveland and Toledo respectively. See Fine, *Sit-Down*, 89–93.

35. UAW Oral History Project interview with Arthur Case, 5.
36. University of Michigan-Flint Labor History Project oral history interviews with Bob Travis and Charlie Kramer, December 13, 1978, 108.
37. Travis to Pieper, October 19, 1936 is one of Travis' many very descriptive letters, located in Box 8, Kraus Collection, WSU.
38. Telegram: Travis to Kraus, December 16, 1936; and Travis to Adolph Germer (of the C.I.O.), October 28, 1936; in Box 8, Kraus Collection, WSU. Also see Keeran, *The Communist Party and the Auto Workers Unions*, 150–51.
39. See correspondence between Ed Geiger, recording secretary of Local 156, and H. H. Curtice, dated October 29 and November 3, 1936, in the Kraus Collection, Box 8, WSU. Also see Fine, *Sit-Down*, 117; and *Flint Auto Worker* 1, (November 1936):3.
40. The figure remains in dispute. Sidney Fine estimated 10 percent (Fine *Sit-Down*, 146), but Roger Keeran quotes Michigan Communist Party leader William Weinstone as claiming just 2,500 members, or roughly 5 percent. (Keeran, *The Communist Party and the Auto Workers Union*, 159). In his UAW Oral History Project interview in 1960, Bud Simons stated there were only six hundred union members at the key Fisher Body 1 plant (out of eight thousand workers) when the big sit-down strike began.
41. Sidney Fine's *Sit-Down* is the standard "biography" of the strike. Henry Kraus' *The Many and the Few: A Chronicle of the Dynamic Auto Workers* (Los Angeles, 1947) is a far more dramatic, insider's account. Roger Keeran's version in his *The Communist Party and the Auto Workers Union* (159–185) clarifies the role of the Communist Party by drawing on material that was unavailable to Sidney Fine.
42. Mary Heaton Vorse, "The Emergency Brigade in Flint," *New Republic* 90 (February 1937):38. The recent documentary film, "With Babies and Banners" *New Day Films*, Women's Labor History Project, 1978, details the work of the Emergency Brigade.
43. UAW Oral History Project interview with Bud Simons, September 6, 1960, 28.
44. University of Michigan-Flint Labor History Project interviews with Bob Travis and Charlie Kramer, 11.
45. UAW Oral History Project interview with George Addes, June 25, 1960, 15–16.
46. Records of the La Follette Civil Liberties Committee, RG 46, Box 123, Files N1, N2, N4 and N7, U.S. Senate, National Archives. The Judge reportedly owned $200,000 worth of GM stock. Later in the strike, the

union used news that Genesee County Prosecuting Attorney J. R. Joseph owned GM stock to undercut his effort to serve three hundred "John Doe" warrants against strike leaders.

47. Evidence of the kind of pressure applied may be found in files "Flint Sit-Down—Flint Alliance" and "Flint Sit-Down—Employee Groups Against the Strike," Kraus Collection, Box 9, WSU.

48. Interview with Larry Huber, director UAW region 1–C, February 22, 1977, notes in my possession.

49. The attack on Fisher Body 2 is described in greater detail in Irving Bernstein, *Turbulent Years: A History of the American Worker 1933–1941* (Boston 1971), 529–531.

50. Kraus, *The Many and the Few*, 138.

51. Reuther, *The Brothers Reuther*, 157.

52. Terkel, *Hard Times*, 162–63 (emphasis added).

53. See "Brief Resume of My Trip through the Strike Area," Frank Murphy Papers, Box 56, MHC. Also see UAW Oral History Project interview with Clayton Johnson, 7–13; and Fine, *Sit-Down*, chapter 6, "The Sit-Down Community."

54. For example, in July 1937, a mass meeting of more than five thousand auto workers heard representatives of the Youngstown, Ohio, steel strikers request food for their people. Flint workers responded by sending two truckloads of food, including 1,500 pounds of sugar, 650 pounds of coffee, 700 pounds of rice, 500 pounds of navy beans, and hundreds of cases of assorted canned goods. Flint workers also picketed in Monroe, Michigan, that month during its very violent steel strike. In April 1941, Flint workers drove to Dearborn in hundred-car squads (five men to a car/one squad per shift) to provide assistance to striking Ford workers. See the *Flint Auto Workers* 1 (July 1937); see also Ted Silvey (C.I.O. Relief director in Youngstown) to Bob Travis, July 27, 1937, Kraus Collection, Box 1, WSU.

55. General Motors was able to produce just 151 automobiles in the first ten days of February. One of the lessons it learned from the strike involved the decentralization of production facilities to decrease its vulnerability to strikes like the great sit-down.

56. *The Flint Auto Worker* 1 (February 1937):1. Also see Sylvester, "City Management," 124ff. Barringer was rebuked by the City Council on February 8, after the two worker members of that body raised questions about his conduct of police affairs. On February 23, after the strike was settled, Barringer was removed from office by a five-to-three council vote.

57. Homer Martin to Alfred P. Sloan and William Knudsen, January 4, 1937 in the John Brophy Papers, Catholic University Archives. Copies of the first U.A.W.–General Motors contract are located in the Frank Murphy Papers, Box 17, MHC.

58. Quoted in Victor Reuther, *The Brothers Reuther*, 171.

59. UAW Oral History Project interview with John McGill, July 27, 1960, 6.
60. Travis to Lester Boyd, UAW organizer in Philadelphia, March 16, 1937, Kraus Collection, Box 10, WSU.
61. UAW Oral History Project interview with Jack Palmer, 15.
62. For examples see UAW Oral History Project interviews with Bud Simons (49ff) and Everett Francis (37ff) for Fisher Body 1; Carl Swanson (12ff) and Norman Bully (6ff) for Buick; Ted La Duke (24ff) for Chevrolet; and Clayton Johnson (14ff) for Fisher Body 2.
63. UAW Oral History Project interview with Bud Simons, 49.
64. Information on these strikes is compiled in the scrapbooks entitled, "Strikes: Auto: Feb. 15–28, 1937," "Strikes: Auto: March 1–31, 1937," "Strikes: Auto: April 1–30, 1937," and "Strikes: Auto: May 1–June 2, 1937" in FPL. Additional information is located in the Joe Brown Collection, vol. 8, WSU.
65. Travis to Kraus, March 8, 1937, Kraus Collection, Box 10, WSU. In these early shop steward systems, each department had many stewards, who in turn elected chief stewards as their representatives to the shop (plant) committee.
66. The interim agreement of March 13 established a grievance procedure governed by committeemen (between five and nine per plant). It also set up seniority rules that restricted seniority by occupational classification and department. Under this contract, the eight-hour day/forty-hour week was standardized, and the union agreed to allow time-study men to set the speed of production. Copies of this contract are located in the Frank Murphy Papers, Box 56, MHC.
67. Travis to Governor Frank Murphy, April 6, 1937, Kraus Collection, Box 10, WSU.
68. Interviews with William Genske (Fisher Body 1) and Larry Jones (Chevrolet), March 29, 1983, notes in my possession.
69. Travis to Germer, May 17, 1937, Kraus Collection, Box 11, WSU.
70. This dispute would plague the union until 1941. A detailed discussion of its origins is beyond the scope of this study, but it is an obsession of every autobiography or personal memoir of the union's leadership. For a balanced discussion of this volatile subject see Jack Skeels, "The Development of Political Stability within the United Auto Workers Union" Ph.D. diss., University of Wisconsin, 1957).
71. Martin's earliest visits to Flint were reported on by George Starkweather in the *Flint Weekly Review* for March 1935. Starkweather became a friend of Martin's at that time.
72. Election results may be found in the Kraus Collection, Box 11 WSU. Also see Blackwood, *The United Automobile Workers of America, 1935–1951.* (Chicago, 1951), 85ff; and Roger P. Keeran, "The Communists and UAW Factionalism 1937–39," *Michigan History* 60 (Summer 1976) 117–135.
73. The Buick plant remained strongly loyal to the radical, or "Unity," cau-

cus. For this reason, Martin opposed a separate charter for Buick in the spring of 1937. See UAW Oral History Project interview with Arthur Case, 8–18; and the UAW Oral History Project interview with Tom Klasey, September 10, 1960, 34–36 for the clearest recollections of this period.

74. Affidavit on the meeting of the Independent Automobile Employees Association, held April 24, 1937, signed by Wilbert Hill, Kraus Collection, Box 10, WSU.

75. *Flint Auto Worker* 1 (May 1937):1; and "Flint Enemies of UAW Organize for Battle" by Martin Hayden, article clipped from the *Detroit News*, May 2, 1937, in the Joe Brown Collection, vol. 8, 76, WSU.

76. Rumors of Black Legion activity had circulated freely in Flint since mid-1936. By that time, its members had been implicated in the murders of four union organizers in southern Michigan. It was also involved in many bombings and beatings of union activists. Estimates of its membership ran as high as thirty thousand statewide. By 1939, thirteen Black Legionaires had been sentenced to life in prison for their activities; thirty-nine had received lesser sentences.

77. Quoted by Hayden in "Flint Enemies of the UAW," *Detroit News*, May 2, 1937.

78. Interview with Larry Huber, notes in my possession.

79. "List of units in Local 156, June 15, 1937," Kraus Collection, WSU. Of the thirty firms whose workers were listed as being enrolled in the local, only ten were automobile shops.

80. The best source of information on these many long-forgotten strikes is the file "Strikes: Flint: Miscellaneous," FPL.

81. For details see *Auto Women in Advance*, the official monthly magazine of the Women's Auxiliary in Flint, No. 10, April 1937, Kraus Collection, Box 10, WSU. Also see "Strikes: Flint: Miscellaneous," FPL.

82. "Review of Year's Federation Work," *Flint Weekly Review*, December 31, 1937.

83. This incident occurred during a strike against the Mary Lee Candy Company on June 25th. Repeated violence between pickets and the police in the downtown shopping district during this strike led local merchants to form an anti-union Law and Order League, which successfully pressured the City Council into dismissing the city manager for failing to preserve order.

84. Copies of this contract signed by Wyndham Mortimer and John L. Lewis for the C.I.O. and Wendell L. Wilkie, chairman of Commonwealth and Southern (Consumers Power parent company) may be found in the Murphy Papers, Box 56, MHC.

85. A meeting of more than five thousand local members overwhelmingly endorsed a resolution in support of the purged leaders in the second

week of July. Buick unionists were particularly adamant in their protests against the transfers of Travis and Dale. Ed Geiger, a rank-and-file leader, told the *Flint Journal*, July 6, 1937, "if Ralph hadn't been there, there would have been sit-downs too numerous to mention." Protest letters, petitions, and other related materials are located in the Kraus Collection, Box 10, WSU.

86. All these actions are described and criticized in detail in a letter from Wyndham Mortimer to John Brophy dated September 29, 1937, Brophy Papers, Catholic University Library, Washington, D.C. Mortimer charged that one of the special committee members, Bert Harris, was a Black Legionaire who was "thoroughly discredited up there." This charge was often made by "Unity" caucus supporters, but it cannot be verified.

87. In particular, see the page-one articles in the *Flint Weekly Review*, April 23, June 18, and October 1, 1937.

88. Quoted in the *Flint Weekly Review*, August 20, 1937.

89. Chafe, "Flint and the Great Depression," *Michigan History*, 53 (Fall 1969): 234; and Joe Brown Collection, Vol. 12, 10–11 and 75, WSU.

90. Chafe, "Flint and The Great Depression," 236; and clippings from the Detroit Free Press, April 16–19, 1938 in Civil Rights Congress of Michigan Collection, Box 51, WSU.

91. William H. McPherson, *Labor Relations in the Automobile Industry* (Washington, 1940), 21–30; and UAW Oral History Project interview with Tom Klasey, 40–43.

92. Company managers closed the plant hoping to weaken the union by encouraging factionalism and adverse publicity for the already much-criticized UAW. The national news media did respond as General Motors hoped; for example see "Strikes at Flint: A New Epidemic," *Newsweek* May 2, 1938, 32–34. Also see the clippings in the Joe Brown Collection, 12, 71–74, WSU.

93. UAW Oral History Project interview with Arthur Case, 25.

94. Joe Brown Collection 12, 43–49, WSU.

95. William Genske, "Dual Unionism: Group Formation in the United Auto Workers" (a term paper prepared for professor Thomas Smith's Sociology 469, University of Michigan-Flint December 3, 1970), 4, in my possession.

96. "Confidential Report of the Socialist Party on the Inner Situation in the Auto Union," June 7, 1938, Kraus Collection, Box 16 WSU. Also see Skeels, "The Development of Political Stability," 69–70; and Keeran, "The Communists and UAw Factionalism" 129.

97. Joe Brown Collection, 12, 74–76 and 82, WSU.

98. UAW Oral History Project interview with Norman Bully, October 12, 1961, 10.

99. Reuther, *The Brothers Reuther*, 192.
100. Martin did retain a core of supporters at Fisher Body 1, but not enough to win the NLRB elections in 1940. During the war years, most Martin supporters joined the U.A.W.–C.I.O. See the *Flint Daily Journal*, June 15, 1939; and UAW Oral History Project interview with William Genske, July 23, 1960 (one of the Local 581 stewards caught in the union hall) for an account of this "strike."
101. Howell John Harris, *The Right to Manage: Industrial Relations Policies of American Business in the 1940s* (Madison, 1982), 28–29. Harris goes on to explain this shift made GM a model for other large companies to follow in the 1940s.
102. Little, Palmer, and another worker, "Pop" Warner, were elected by a majority of Chevy No. 3 workers to lead a sit-in in the plant manager's offices until he reestablished negotiations. After this demonstration, Jack Little returned to work in No. 3 and never ran for a leadership spot again. UAW Oral History Project interview with F.R. Palmer, 23.
103. UAW Oral History Project interviews with John McGill, July 27, 1960, 9–10; and Tom Klasey: 46.
104. Reuther, *The Brothers Reuther*, 171.

8. The Decline of Class Conflict in Mid-Twentieth-Century Flint

1. William Serrin, *The Company and the Union: The Civilized Relationship of the General Motors Corporation and the United Automobile Workers* (New York, 1973).
2. These points are discussed at length in Frederick Harbison and Robert Dubin, *Patterns of Union-Management Relations: United Automobile Workers (CIO), General Motors, and Studebaker* (Chicago, 1947), especially 17–46; and Howell John Harris, *The Right to Manage: Industrial Relations Policies of American Business in the 1940s* (Madison, 1982), 26ff.
3. Harbison and Dubin, *Patterns of Union-Management Relations*, 46–50.
4. UAW Oral History Project interview with Ted La Duke, August 5, 1960, 30.
5. See UAW Oral History Project interview with Everett Francis, October 13, 1961, 46–47, for a clear explanation of this activity.
6. National Conciliation Service Case File No. 199–5863, NRC.
7. National Conciliation Service Case File No. 199–5883, NRC.
8. UAW Oral History Project interview with William Genske, July 23, 1960, 22.
9. See UAW Oral History Project interviews with Everett Francis, 47–48 and William Genske, 37–39 for the impact of this event.
10. Nelson Lichtenstein, *Labor's War at Home: The CIO in World War I* (Cambridge, 1982) 55–56; and Blackwood, *The United Automobile Workers of*

America, 1935–1951 (Chicago, 1951), 170ff. Later in May, Buick's day-shift workers voted two-to-one to renew the strike over local issues, but second and third-shift workers voted the walkout down. See "Membership Minutes–1941," Local 599 Collection, Box 1, WSU.

11. "Survey of the Employment Situation in Flint, Michigan" dated January 3, 1941, marked "Confidential" and other variously titled Flint labor market reports 1941–1942, in Records of the Bureau of Employment Security, RG 183, Box 185, National Archives, Washington, D.C.

12. Alan Clive, *State of War: Michigan in World War I* (Ann Arbor, 1979), 25.

13. "Labor Supply and Demand for War Production in Flint, Michigan," U.S. Employment Service, March 5, 1942, in Records of the Bureau of Employment Security, National Archives.

14. See correspondence between H. W. Anderson (of Chevrolet) and Walter Reuther (July 3 and 13, 1942), UAW–General Motors Department Collection, Box 1, WSU. The *Searchlight's* warning was published on page six of the June 24 issue, under the banner "To all Plant #9 Workers."

15. The effectiveness of GM's loan plan depended on "the interest of the personnel manager" in each plant. See "Survey of Employment Situation in Flint, Michigan, " January 3, 1941, Records of the Bureau of Employment Security for details.

16. UAW Oral History Project interview with John McGill, July 27, 1960, 22.

17. UAW Oral History Project interview with Arthur Case, August 4, 1960, 36.

18. The fight against the no-strike pledge has received considerable attention in recent years. See Nelson Lichtenstein, *Labor's War at Home: The C.I.O. in World War II* (Cambridge, 1982), 194ff; also Ed Jennings, "Wildcat: The War-time Strike Wave in Auto," *Radical America* 9 (July–August 1975), 77–105; and Alan Clive, *State of War: Michigan in World War II* (Ann Arbor, 1979), 79–87.

19. For reasons that are still unclear to me, Fisher Body 2 workers did not display the same upsurge of discontent in 1944–1945. In fact, its dues-paying membership declined rapidly in 1944–1945. See "Correspondence with Local 598," George Addes Collection, Box 69E, WSU.

20. This pattern conforms to the industrywide trend. See Lichtenstein, *Labor's War at Home*, 121–123. Generalizations are based on an examination of the relevant National Conciliation Service Case Files, and the strike scrapbooks in the Automotive History Collection, FPL.

21. "Report to Local (581)," in the Everett Francis Collection, Box 7, File: "War Years," WSU; various reports dated July 15, July 18, July 20, and July 22, 1942 in the Records of the Emergency Protection Defense Board, Box 4, File 3033, State of Michigan Archives; and Lichtenstein, *Labor's War at Home*, 194–197.

22. Jennings, "Wildcat!": 97.

23. UAW Oral History Project interview with John McGill: 23.

24. National Conciliation Case File No. 453–1180, NRC.

25. See the George Addes Collection, Box 69E, WSU, for the various resolutions.

26. This point is emphasized in Barton Bernstein's fine article "Walter Reuther and the General Motors Strike of 1945–46," *Michigan History* 49 (September, 1965), 263–277; and Lichtenstein, *Labor's War at Home*, 221–30.

27. Thomas' correspondence with GM president Charles Wilson on this question may be found in the R. J. Thomas Collection I, Box 9, WSU.

28. See UAW Oral History Project interview with F. R. Palmer for the best recollection of the end of the strike in Flint. Also see Flint CityWide Strike Committee to R. J. Thomas, February, 1946, Thomas Collection, Box 9, WSU. Harris, *Right to Manage*, 139–43, presents the best analysis of management's strategy in the long strike.

29. UAW Oral History Project interview with Jack Palmer, 40.

30. UAW Oral History Project interview with John McGill, 22–23.

31. UAW Oral History Project interview with Arthur Case, 47. Also see the UAW Oral History Project interview with former regional director Carl Swanson, August 8, 1960, 32, for similar recollections.

32. For details, see Roger Keeran, *The Communist Party and the Auto Workers Unions* (Bloomington, 1980), 254–57.

33. UAW Oral History Project interview with John McGill, 24.

34. Keeran, *The Communist Party and the Auto Workers Unions*, 257.

35. UAW Oral History Project interview with Jack Palmer, July 23, 1960, 38–40.

36. UAW Oral History Project interview with Stanley Brams, November 23, 1959, 28–29.

37. This last point was made especially clear to me in my interviews with former rank-and-file workers William Genske and Larry Jones on March 29, 1983, notes in my possession. Also see UAW Oral History Project interview with Everett Francis, 58–60, for a summary of the fate of other Flint activists.

38. This incident is discussed in Kathy Groehn El-Messidi, *The Bargain: The Story Behind the Thirty-Year Honeymoon of General Motors and the UAW* (New York, 1980), 46–48; and the UAW Oral History Project interview with Jack Palmer, 41–43.

39. Quoted in El-Messidi, *The Bargain*, 48.

40. El-Messidi, *The Bargain*, 49.

41. Reuther was hit by shotgun blasts fired through his kitchen window by an unknown assailant after returning home from a late night Executive Board meeting. The shooting made Reuther a martyr in the eyes of many UAW members, making it harder to criticize him, even after he fully recovered.

42. UAW Oral History Project interview with Norman Bully, October 12, 1961, 30.

43. See James Green, "Fighting on Two Fronts: Working-Class Militancy in the 1940s," *Radical America* 9 (July-August 1975), 7–47, for a review of this literature.

44. David Brody, "The Uses of Industrial Power I: Industrial Battleground," in David Brody, *Workers in Industrial America: Essays on the Twentieth-Century Struggle* (New York, 1980), 205.

45. Green, "Fighting on Two Fronts," 40.

46. These generalizations are based on the materials gathered on Flint in the Records of the Committee on Fair Employment Practices, RG 228, Box 669, Regional File, Region V, National Archives; and on a very clear discussion of the local race problem in the UAW Oral History Project interview with Arthur Case (who was twice regional director in these years), 30–32.

47. Report on Complaint against Management, January 9, 1942, in file "Chevrolet Motor Company—Flint, Michigan"; and To Colonel Strong from J. Duncan of the Fair Employment Practices Committee, July 15, 1942, both in the Records of the Committee on Fair Employment Practices, National Archives, Washington, D.C. Generally, it seems that rank-and-file movement leaders at Buick, Chevrolet, and at the AC Sparkplug fought hardest to remedy black workers' discrimination complaints.

48. The U.S. Employment Service's "Labor Market Report for Flint Michigan, March 1943" (Records of Bureau of Employment Security) showed AC's Sparkplug's workforce was 42 percent female, while the rest of the local GM facilities were less than 5 percent female.

49. These generalizations are based on special employment surveys conducted by the National Conciliation Service in Flint on May 31, 1945 (Case Files No. 453–2188, 2190, 2191); and on the quarterly "Labor Market Development Reports" for 1944–1947 found in the Records of the Bureau of Employment Security, National Archives, Washington, D.C.

50. U.A.W. Oral History Project interview with Carl Swanson, 45.

51. The role of the UAW in postwar Flint politics is examined at length in George D. Blackwood, *The United Automobile Workers of America: 1935–51* (Chicago, 1951), 395ff. Blackwood surveyed voter behavior in three heavily working-class wards for the period 1940 to 1950. He found that UAW-backed candidates were successful in approximately half of all the decade's elections. However, this figure disguises labor's real influence, since union-backed candidates won nearly all the "important" (national and state) contests. Apparently, just 13 percent of the union families in these wards never voted with the union. Significantly, George Blackwood discovered that nearly 40 percent of the union wives he surveyed voted against the UAW's candidates (and thus, against their husbands).

He speculated that this opposition stemmed from resentment against the union as a force that took the men out of the home.

52. John Higham, *Strangers in the Land: Patterns of American Nativism 1860–1925* (New York, 1981), 330.
53. Green, "Fighting on Two Fronts," 41.
54. The estimate of local Communist Party membership is drawn from the combined testimony of witnesses who appeared before a subcommittee of the House Committee on Un-American Activities, which held hearings in the city on April 30 and May 12–14, 1954. See "Investigation of Communist Activities in the State of Michigan–Parts 8–1" Hearings before the Committee on Un-American Activities, House of Representatives, 83rd Cong, 2nd Sess, (GPO, 1954).
55. Lichtenstein, *Labor's War at Home*, 237.
56. James A. Maxwell, "What's Bad for General Motors is Bad for Flint," *The Reporter*, March 20, 1958.
57. The black population of Flint doubled in the 1940s, but still stood at less than 14,000 persons (8.5 percent of the total population) in 1950. However, in the 1950s, Flint's black population soared to nearly 45,000 people. By 1970, more than 54,000 blacks lived in the city of Flint (or more than a quarter of its total population). It was this rapid growth of the city's black population *after* 1950, and the failure fully to integrate black people into the local prosperity that caused severe racial tensions in the mid-to-late 1960s. Among other things, these tensions led to some rioting and appearance of a tiny, but violent Ku Klux Klan group. More positively, in the late 1960s, Flint's city council selected a black mayor, and city voters narrowly passed the nation's first major open housing referendum. Even so, racial tensions remained strong in Flint in the 1970s.
58. Quoted in Maxwell, "What's Bad for General Motors is Bad for Flint."
59. UAW Oral History Project interview with Norman Bully, 20–21.
60. UAW Oral History Project interview with William Genske, 42.

9. Conclusions

1. For an excellent example of this kind of innovative business class, see Ronald W. Schatz's discussion of the men who led the electrical industry in this period, in *The Electrical Workers: A History of Labor at General Electric and Westinghouse* (Urbana, 1983), especially 11–24.
2. Erich Fromm, "Individual and Social Origins of Neurosis," quoted in David M. Potter, *People of Plenty: Economic Abundance and the American Character* (Chicago, 1954), 11.
3. Warren I. Susman, *Culture as History: The Transformation of American Society in the Twentieth Century* (New York, 1984), xxix.
4. Flint's recent economic troubles have been examined in numerous

newspaper and magazine articles. For examples see "A Tale of Two Auto Towns," *Newsweek*, April 1, 1974; "Flint—A City Fighting Back," *U.S. News and World Report*, July 7, 1975; "Hard Times in the Heartland," *Time*, December 7, 1981; and "The Uneven Burden of Today's Recession," *U.S. News and World Report*, March 1, 1982.

5. McDonald is quoted at length in "GM Centralizing, Decentralizing," *Automotive News*, February 14, 1983. Jack Liztenberg's plans for Flint, including the construction of a $60 million AutoWorld amusement park, are discussed in Daniel Zwerdling's "And Then There's the Disneyland Solution," *The Progressive* (July 1982) 34–35. Since Daniel Zwerdling wrote his critical article, the Six Flags AutoWorld amusement park has been opened (in May 1984), and then closed (in January 1985) for lack of attendance. Current plans call for it to be run on a limited May-September schedule.

6. Herbert Marcuse, *One-Dimensional Man: Studies in the Ideology of Advanced Industrial Society* (Boston, 1968), 12.

7. Interview with Al Christner, March 29, 1983 (notes in my possession). Also the *New York Times*, July 5, 1981:III, 4.

8. Lichtenstein, *Labor's War at Home: The C.I.O. in World War II* (Cambridge, 1982), 248.

SELECTED BIBLIOGRAPHY

Manuscript and Special Collections

A. F. of L.–C.I.O. Archives, Washington D.C.
    A. F. of L. Executive Correspondence.
Archives of Labor History and Urban Affairs, Walter P. Reuther Library, Wayne State University, Detroit, Michigan.
    George Addes Collection.
    Joe Brown Collection.
    William E. Chalmers Collection.
    Civil Rights Congress of Michigan Collection.
    Francis Dillion Collection.
    Robert Dunn Collection.
    Everett Francis Collection.
    Philips L. Garman Collection.
    William Genske Collection.
    Henry Kraus Collection.
    Edward Levinson Collection.
    Local 599 Collection.
    Homer Martin Collection.
    H. G. Mezerick Collection.
    Walter Reuther Collection.
    Bud and Hazel Simons Collection.
    R. J. Thomas Collection.
    U.A.W.–General Motors Department Collection (Series 1, 2, and 6).
    U.A.W. Oral History Project
Catholic University Library, Washington, D.C.
    John Brophy Papers
Flint Public Library, Flint, Michigan.
    Automotive History Collection.
    Genessee County Biography File.
    Michigan Room Collection.

Bibliography

Michigan Historical Collections, Bentley Historical Library, University of Michigan, Ann Arbor, Michigan.
   Edward D. Black Papers.
   John Jay Carton Papers.
   Sidney Fine Papers.
   Frank Murphy Papers.
   William Henry Phelps Papers.
   U.A.W. Oral History Project.
Michigan State Archives, Lansing, Michigan.
   Records of the Executive Office.
   Records of the Michigan State Police Intelligence and Security Bureau.
Michigan State Library, Lansing, Michigan.
   Michigan Collections.
National Archives, Washington, D.C.
   Records of the Bureau of Employment Security.
   Records of the Fair Employment Practices Committee.
   Records of the Federal Housing Administration.
   Records of the Home Owners Loan Corporation.
   Records of the National Recovery Administration.
   Records of the National Youth Administration.
   Records Relating to Emergency Relief to the States, Reconstruction Finance
      Corporation.
   Records of the U.S. Senate, 78th Congress (LaFollette Civil Liberties Com-
      mittee).
   Records of the Works Progress Administration.
   Women's Bureau Survey Material (U.S. Department of Labor).
University of Michigan-Flint: Labor History Project, Flint, Michigan.
   Oral History Collection.
Washington National Records Center, Suitland, Maryland.
   Records of the National Conciliation Service.
   Records of the National War Labor Board.

Newspapers

The Auto Worker
The Auto Worker News
Flint Auto Worker
Flint Daily Journal
Flint Flashes
Flint Journal
Flint Labor News
Flint Weekly Review
New York Times

Books and Articles

Allen, Frederick Lewis. *Only Yesterday*. New York, 1931.

Aronowitz, Stanley. *False Promises: The Shaping of American Working Class Consciousness*. New York, 1973.

Auerbach, Jerold. *Labor and Liberty: The LaFollette Committee and the New Deal*. New York, 1966.

Baran, Paul, and Sweezy, Paul. *Monopoly Capital: An Essay on the American Economic and Social Order*. New York, 1968.

Barnouw, Erik. *The Sponsor: Notes on a Modern Potentate*. New York, 1978.

Barraclough, Geoffrey. *Introduction to Contemporary History*. London, 1967.

Belasco, Warren James. *Americans on the Road: From Autocamp to Motel, 1910–1945*. Cambridge, 1979.

Berle, Adolf A., and Means, Gardiner C. *The Modern Corporation and Private Property*. New York, 1932.

Bernstein, Barton. "The Automobile Industry and the Coming of the Second World War." *The Southwestern Social Science Quarterly*, 41, no. 1 (June 1966).

———. "Walter Reuther and the General Motors Strike of 1945–46." *Michigan History* 49 no. 3 (September 1965).

Bernstein, Irving. *The Lean Years: A History of the American Worker 1920–1933*. Baltimore, 1966.

———. *The New Deal Collective Bargaining Policy*. Berkeley, 1950.

———. *The Turbulent Years: A History of the American Worker 1933–1941*. Boston, 1971.

Beynon, Erdman. "The Southern White Laborer Migrates to Michigan." *The American Sociological Review* 3 no. 3 (June 1938).

Blachett, O. W. "Factory Labor Turnover in Michigan." *Michigan Business Studies* 2 no. 1 (November 1928).

Blackwood, George D. *The United Automobile Workers of America, 1935–1951*. Chicago, 1951.

Bolin, Winifred D. Wandersee. "The Economics of Middle Income Family Life in the Great Depression." *Journal of American History* 66 (June 1978).

Bottomore, T. B. *Classes in Modern Society*. New York, 1966.

Brady, Robert A. *Business as a System of Power*. New York, 1943.

Braeman, John; Bremner, Robert; and Brody, David, eds. *Change and Continuity in the Twentieth Century: the 1920s*. Columbus, 1968.

Brandes, Stuart. *American Welfare Capitalism*. Chicago, 1970.

Braverman, Harry. *Labor and Monopoly Capital*. New York, 1974.

Brody, David. *Steelworkers in America: The Non-Union Era*. New York, 1960.

———. "The Old Labor History and the New: In Search of an American Working Class." *Labor History* 20, no. 1 (Winter 1979).

———. *Workers in Industrial America: Essays on the Twentieth-Century Struggle*. New York, 1980.

Burnham, Walter Dean. "The Changing of the American Political Universe." *American Political Science Review* 59, no. 1 (March 1965).

Cantor, Milton, ed. *American Working-Class Culture: Explorations in American Labor and Social History.* Wesport and London, 1979.

Chafe, William H. "Flint and the Great Depression." *Michigan History* 53 no. 3 (Fall 1969).

Chalmers, William Ellison. "Labor in the Automobile Industry: A Study of Personnel Policies, Workers' Attitudes and Attempts at Unionism." Ph.D. diss., University of Wisconsin, 1932.

Chandler, Alfred D., Jr. *Giant Enterprise: Ford, General Motors, and the Automobile Industry.* New York, 1964.

––––––. *The Visible Hand: The Managerial Revolution in American Business.* Cambridge, 1977.

Chandler, Alfred D., and Salsbury, Stephan. *Pierre S. DuPont and the Making of the Modern Corporation.* Cambridge, 1971.

Chinoy, Eli. *Automobile Workers and the American Dream.* Garden City, 1955.

Chrysler, Walter P. *Life of an American Workman.* New York, 1950.

Clive, Alan. *State of War: Michigan in World War II.* Ann Arbor, 1979.

Cochran, Thomas C. *200 Years of American Business.* New York, 1977.

Cohen, Jon. "The Achievements of Economic History: The Marxist School." *Journal of Economic History* 38, no. 1 (March 1978).

Cray, Ed. *Chrome Colossus: General Motors and Its Times.* New York, 1980.

Dalheimer, Harry. *A History of the Mechanics Educational Society of America in Detroit from Its Inception in 1933 to 1937.* Detroit, 1951.

Dawson, Andrew. "The Paradox of Dynamic Technological Change and the Labor Aristocracy in the United States, 1880–1914." *Labor History* 20, no. 3 (Summer 1979).

Derber, Milton, and Young, Edwin, eds. *Labor and the New Deal.* Madison, 1957.

Dunham, Walter. *Banking and Industry in Michigan.* Detroit, 1929.

Edsforth, Ronald. "Divergent Traditions: Union Organization in the Automobile Industries in Flint, Michigan and Coventry, England." *Detroit in Perspective: A Journal of Regional History* 5, no. 3 (Spring 1981).

Edwards, Richard. *Contested Terrain: The Transformation of the Workplace in the Twentieth Century.* New York, 1979.

El-Messidi, Kathy, *The Bargain: The Story Behind the Thirty Year Honeymoon of GM and the UAW.* New York, 1980.

Ewen, Stuart. *Captains of Consciousness: Advertising and the Social Roots of Consumer Culture.* New York, 1976.

Fine, Sidney. *The Automobile Under the Blue Eagle.* Ann Arbor, 1963.

––––––. *Sit-Down: The General Motors Strike of 1936–37.* Ann Arbor, 1969.

Flink, James J. *The Car Culture.* Cambridge, 1975.

Ford, Harold. "The Year of Living Dangerously," *Michigan Voice* 7, no. 6 (September 1983).

Friedlander, Peter. *The Emergence of a UAW Local; 1936–1939: A Study in Class and Culture*. Pittsburgh, 1975.

Goldstein, Robert Justin. *Political Repression in Modern American from 1870 to the Present*. Cambridge, 1978.

Gordon, David; Edwards, Richard; and Reich, Michael. *Segmented Work, Divided Workers: The Historical Transformation of Labor in the United States*. Cambridge, 1982.

Green, James. "Fighting on Two Fronts: Working Class Militancy in the 1940s." *Radical America* 9 nos. 4–5 (July–August 1975).

———. *The World of the Worker: Labor in Twentieth Century America*. New York, 1980.

Green, James, and Kraditor, Aileen. "Debate: American Radical Historians on Their Heritage." *Past and Present* 60 (August 1973).

Griffin, C. E. "The Life History of Automobiles." *Michigan Business Studies* 1, no. 1 (1926).

Gustin, Lawrence. *Billy Durant: Creator of General Motors*. Grand Rapids, 1973.

———. *The Flint Journal Centennial Picture History of Flint*. Flint, 1976.

Gutman, Herbert. *Work, Culture and Society in Industrializing America*. New York, 1977.

Haber, William, ed. *Labor in Changing America*. New York, 1966.

Harbison, Frederick and Dubin, Robert. *Patterns of Union-Management Relations: United Automobile Workers (CIO), General Motors, and Studebaker*. Chicago, 1947.

Hareven, Tamara. "The Laborers of Manchester, New Hampshire 1912–1922: The Role of Family and Ethnicity in Adjustment to Industrial Life." *Labor History* 16, no. 2 (Spring 1975).

Harris, Howell John. *The Right to Manage: Industrial Relations Policies of American Business in the 1940s*. Madison, 1982.

Heilbroner, Robert. *Business Civilization in Decline*. New York, 1976.

Henretta, James A. "The Study of Social Mobility: Ideological Assumptions and Conceptual Bias." *Labor History* 18, no. 2 (Spring 1977).

Hobsbawm, Eric. *Industry and Empire: The Pelican Economic History of Britain Volume 3: From 1750 to the Present Day*. London, 1969.

Holt, James. "Trade Unionism in the British and U.S. Steel Industries 1888–1912: A Comparative Study." *Labor History* 18, no. 1 (Winter 1977).

Hugins, Walter. "American History in Comparative Perspective," *Journal of American Studies* 2, 1 (April 1977).

Ihdler, John. "Flint: When Men Build Automobiles Who Builds Their City?" *The Survey*, September 2, 1916.

Isserman, Maurice. "'God Bless Our American Institutions': The Labor History of John R. Commons." *Labor History* 18, no. 3 (Summer 1976).

Jackson, Kenneth. *The Ku Klux Klan in the City 1915–1930*. New York, 1967.

Jennings, Ed. "Wildcat! The Wartime Strike Wave in Auto." *Radical America* 9, nos. 4–5 (July–August 1975).

Keeran, Roger. "Communist Influence in the Automobile Industry 1920–1933: Paving the Way for an Industrial Union." *Labor History* 20, no. 20 (Spring 1979).

———. *The Communist Party and the Auto Workers Unions*. Bloomington, 1980.

———. "The Communists and UAW Factionalism 1937–39." *Michigan History* 60, no. 2 (Summer 1976).

Kindleberger, Charles. *Economic Growth in France and Britain*. Cambridge, 1964.

Kolko, Gabriel. *Main Currents in American History*. New York, 1976.

———. *The Triumph of Conservatism: A Reinterpretation of American History, 1908–16*. Chicago, 1967.

———. *Wealth and Power in America: An Analysis of Social Class and Income Distribution*. New York, 1962.

Kraditor, Aileen. "American Radical Historians on Their Heritage." *Past and Present* 56 (August 1972).

Kraus, Henry. *The Many and the Few: A Chronicle of the Dynamic Auto Workers*. Los Angeles, 1947.

LaFever, Mortimer. "Workers, Machinery, and Production in the Automobile Industry." *Monthly Labor Review* 19, no. 4 (October 1929).

Laslett, J. H. M., and Lipset, Seymour Morton, eds. *Failure of a Dream? Essays in the History of American Socialism*. Garden City, 1974.

LeFevbre, Henri. *Everyday Life in the Modern World*. London, 1971.

Levinson, Harold. *Unionsim, Wage Trends, and Income Distribution 1914–1947*. Ann Arbor, 1951.

Lewis, Peirce. "Geography in the Politics of Flint." Ph.D. diss., University of Michigan, 1958.

Lichtenstein, Nelson. "Defending the No-Strike Pledge: CIO Politics During World War II." *Radical America* 9, nos. 4–5 (July–August 1975).

———. *Labor's War at Home: The CIO in World War II* Cambridge, 1982.

Lockwood, William W. *The Economic Development of Japan: Growth and Structural Change*. Princeton, 1968.

Lynd, Robert S. and Lynd, Helen Merrell. *Middletown: A Study in Modern American Culture*. New York, 1929.

———. *Middletown Revisited: A Study in Cultural Conflicts*. New York, 1937.

Mandel, Ernest and Novack, George. *The Revolutionary Potential of the Working Class*. New York, 1974.

Marcuse, Herbert. *One Dimensional Man: Studies in the Ideology of Advanced Industrial Society*. Boston, 1968.

Marquart, Frank. *An Auto Worker's Journal: The UAW from Crusade to One Party Union*. State College, Pennsylvania, 1975.

Marwick, Arthur. *Class: Image and Reality (In Britain, France and the United States Since 1930*. New York, 1980.

May, George S. *A Most Unique Machine: The Michigan Origins of the American Automobile Industry.* Grand Rapids, Michigan, 1975.

Meier, August and Rudwick, Elliott. *Black Detroit and the Rise of the UAW.* New York, 1979.

Meister, Richard. "The Rise of Two Industrial Cities: A Comparative Study of Gary, Indiana, and Flint, Michigan." Paper presented at The Duquesne University History Forum, October 28, 1971. Michigan History Collections, Ann Arbor, Michigan.

McPherson, William H. *Labor Relations in the Automobile Industry.* Washington, 1940.

Miliband, Ralph. *The State in Capitalist Society.* New York, 1969.

Montgomery, David. "To Study the People: The American Working Class." *Labor History* 21 no. 4 (Fall, 1980).

―――. *Workers' Control in America: Studies in the History of Work, Technology, and Labor Struggles.* Cambridge, 1979.

Meyer, Stephen. *The Five Dollar Day: Labor Management and Social Control in the Ford Motor Company 1908–1921.* Albany, 1980.

Muste, A. J. *The Automobile Industry and Organized Labor.* Baltimore, 1936.

Noble, David. *America by Design: Science, Technology, and the Rise of Corporate Capitalism.* Oxford, 1971.

Ortquist, Richard T. "Depression Politics in Michigan." Ph.D. diss., University of Michigan, 1968.

Pelling, Henry. *American Labor.* Chicago, 1960.

Perlman, Selig. *A Theory of Labor Movement.* New York, 1928.

Peterson, Joyce Shaw. "Auto Workers and Their Work, 1920–1933." *Labor History* 22, 2 (Spring 1981).

Piven, Frances Fox, and Cloward, Richard A. *Regulating the Poor: The Functions of Public Welfare.* New York, 1972.

Polenberg, Richard. *War and Society: The United States, 1941–1945.* Philadelphia, 1972.

Potter, David M. *People of Plenty: Economic Abundance and the American Character.* Chicago, 1954.

Pound, Arthur. "General Motors' Old Home Town." *Michigan History* 40 (March 1956).

―――. *The Iron Man in Industry.* Boston, 1922.

―――. *The Turning Wheel: The Story of General Motors Through Twenty-Five Years.* Garden City, 1934.

Preis, Art. *Labor's Giant Step: Twenty Years of the CIO.* New York, 1964.

Prickett, James R. "Communists in the Automobile Industry Before 1935." *Michigan History* 62, no. 3 (Fall 1973).

Rae, John B. *American Automobile Manufacturers: The First Forty Years.* Philadelphia, 1959.

―――. *The Road and Car in American Life.* Cambridge, 1971.

Bibliography

Reitell, Charles. "Machinery and Its Effect Upon Workers in the Automobile Industry." *Annals of the American Academy of Political and Social Science* 116 (November 1924).

Reuther, Victor. *The Brothers Reuther and the Story of the UAW*. Boston, 1976.

Rodolph, Frank. "An Industrial History of Flint." Manuscript dated 1940. Flint Public Library.

Rothschild, Emma. *Paradise Lost: The Decline of the Auto Industrial Age*. New York, 1973.

Rosenblum, Gerald. *Immigrant Workers: Their Impact on American Labor and Radicalism*. New York, 1973.

Saville, John. "The Radical Left Expects the Past to Do Its Duty." *Labor History* 18, no. 2 (Spring 1977).

Schatz, Ronald W. *The Electrical Workers: A History of Labor at General Electric and Westinghouse*. Urbana, 1983.

Schumpeter, Joseph. *Business Cycles: A Theoretical, Historical, and Statistical Analysis of the Capitalist Process*. New York, 1964.

Serrin, William. *The Company and the Union: The Civilized Relationship of the General Motors Corporation and the United Automobile Workers*. New York, 1973.

Shergold, Peter R. *Working Class Life: The American Standard in Comparative Perspective 1899–1913*. Pittsburgh, 1982.

Skeels, Jack. "The Development of Political Stability Within the United Auto Workers Union." Ph.D. diss., University of Wisconsin, 1957.

―――. "Early Carriage and Auto Unions: The Impact of Industrialization and Rival Unionism." *Industrial and Labor Relations Review* 17, no. 4 (July 1964).

Slichter, Sumner. "The Current Labor Policies of American Industry." *Quarterly Journal of Economics* 43 (May 1929).

Sloan, Alfred. *Adventures of a White Collar Man*. New York, 1941.

―――. *My Years With General Motors*. Garden City, 1964.

Sobey, Albert. "General Motors Institute." *Foreman's Magazine* 3, no. 3 (March 1923).

State of Michigan, State Emergency Welfare Relief Commission. *Michigan Census of Population and Unemployment, First Series*, No. 1–10 (Lansing, July 1936–April 1937).

Steindl, J. *Maturity and Stagnation in American Capitalism*. Oxford, 1952.

Susman, Warren I. *Culture as History: The Transformation of American Society in the Twentieth Century*. New York, 1984.

Svennilson, Ingvar. *Growth and Stagnation in the European Economy*. United Nations Economic Commission for Europe, New York: 1954.

Swan, Franklin V. V. "Industrial Welfare Work in Flint, Michigan." *The Survey* 32, no. 16 (July 1914).

Sweezy, Paul. *Modern Capitalism*. New York, 1972.

Sylvester, Harold. "City Management: The Flint Experiment 1930–37." Ph.D. diss., Johns Hopkins University, 1938.

Taylor, A. J. P. "Accident Prone or What Happened Next?" *Journal of Modern History* 49, 1 (March 1977).

Terkel, Studs. *Hard Times: An Oral History of the Great Depression.* New York, 1970.

Thernstrom, Stephan. *Poverty and Progress: Social Mobility in a Nineteenth Century City.* New York, 1972.

Thompson, E. P. *The Making of the English Working Class.* New York, 1963.

———. *The Poverty of Theory and Other Essays.* New York, 1978.

———. "Time, Work-Discipline, and Industrial Capitalism." *Past and Present* 38 (December 1967).

U.S. Congress, House. *Investigation of Communist Propaganda: Hearings before a Special Committee to Investigate Communist Activity in the United States—Pursuant to H. Res. 220, iv, 1, July 25 and 26, 1930* (GPO, 1931).

U.S. Congress, House. *Investigation of Communist Activities in the State of Michigan—Parts 8–10: Hearings before the Committee on Un-American Activities, Eighty-Third Congress, Second Session, April 30 and May 12–14, 1954* (GPO, 1954).

U.S. Department of Labor. *Women Workers in Flint, Michigan,* Bulletin of the Women's Bureau Box 67, prepared by Ethel Best (GPO, 1929).

U.S. Senate. (75th Congress, 1st Session) *Violations of the Free Speech and the Rights of Labor, pursuant to S. Res. 226* (GPO, 1937).

Veblen, Thorsten. *The Theory of the Leisure Class: An Economic Study of Institutions.* New York, 1953.

Vorse, Mary Heaton. "The Emergency Brigade in Flint." *New Republic* 40 (February 1937).

Wallerstein, Immanuel. "The Rise and Future Demise of the World Capitalist System: Concepts for Comparative Analysis." *Comparative Studies in Society and History* 16 (September 1974).

Weaver, Norman. "The Knights of The Ku Klux Klan in Wisconsin, Indiana, Ohio, and Michigan," Ph.D. diss., University of Wisconsin, 1954.

Weinstein, James. *The Decline of Socialism in America, 1912–1925.* New York, 1967.

Weinstein, James, and Eakins, David, eds. *For a New America: Essays in History and Politics from Studies on the Left.* New York, 1970.

Widick, B. J., ed. *Auto Work and Its Discontents.* Baltimore, 1976.

Young, Clarence and Tuttle, Robert. *The Years 1919–1969 . . . a History of the General Motors Institute.* Flint, 1969.

Young, Clarence and Quinn, William. *Foundation for Living: The Story of Charles Stewart Mott and Flint.* New York, 1963.

Zieger, Robert. "Which Side Are You On?—Workers, Unions, and Critics." *Labor History* 17, no. 2 (Spring 1976).

INDEX